Touching Lives

Memoirs of an
Alexander Technique Teacher
working with the
RSC and National Theatre

For Sheila with love
& thanks for your care &
invaluable help over many
years,

By Sue Laurie

from
Sue. x

First published in 2016 by HITE
HITE Limited, 10 Harley Street, London W1G 9PF
Email: info@hiteltd.co.uk
Website: www.hiteltd.co.uk

A CIP catalogue for this book is available from
the British Library.

Cover design: N Thapen
Printed in the UK by Imprint Digital

hite
Healthcare Integrated
Training & Education

ISBN: 978-0-9568997-7-4

This book is dedicated,

with greatest love, to my children

Daniel, Sophie and Thomas

Contents

List of Photographs and Illustrations

Acknowledgements

I don't know really how to begin to thank all of the people who have been instrumental, at key points of my career, in helping me along the way.

However, starting from the beginning, I am immensely grateful to Julian Bream CBE for introducing me to the Alexander Technique in the first place, Anne Battye for giving me my first lessons, the late Marjory Barlow for my life changing Alexander training and the late Lady Eila Mallinson who paid for that training.

My introduction to the world of theatre was facilitated by the late Joe O'Conor who paved my way to the Royal Shakespeare Company. The lovely Lindsay Duncan later insisted that I apply to teach at the National Theatre Studio. Then, when I started there, it was Sue Higginson who gave me confidence in my work. She included me in all activities at the Studio and enabled me to travel and teach abroad with the company.

There is a long list of pupils, wonderful actors, directors, stage managers and members of both theatre companies, whose names are in the book, but are too numerous to mention individually here. I have to thank them all for their enormous encouragement and for what I learned through working with them. Many of these courageous people have remained friends and have given me endless pleasure, love and support over many unforgettable years of teaching.

A special thanks as well to all those who have taken the time from their busy schedules to write feedback about my teaching and the technique.

Heartfelt thanks to Dame Judi Dench, whose generosity in allowing her photograph to be on the cover of both my CD and this book, I am eternally grateful.

I must also thank Jerome Bullard, as without his expertise in computer technology, I simply would not have been able to start to write this book.

Finally, my editors and publishers, Claire Rennie, Kamal Thapen and Ian Rennie at HITE who have propped me up when I have felt down and encouraged me when I often felt like giving up. But with their support we have made it together. Thank you so much.

Sue Laurie

Foreword

Sue Laurie supports a wide range of British Theatre practitioners with a subtle and empowering system to allow each of them to thrive.

Speaking as a director she is invaluable during rehearsal. Her sessions centre me so I can be fully authentic in the room. If I am standing and sitting without tension, I exude a confidence towards the actors which is infectious. If my neck is free my thoughts and ideas are crucially oxygenated. If I am centred and open I can do what my job primarily is: being in the present, concentrated and calm.

When an actor comes back into my rehearsal room after an appointment with Sue they seem wider, to be breathing deeper, perhaps even more receptive.

If everyone had a Sue Laurie in their process, we would all be very lucky.

Alexander feels to me beautifully paradoxical: gentle, yet deep, almost imperceptible yet with palpable results.

Ian Rickson
Theatre Director

Preface

Over the last eighteeen months I have been privileged to speak frequently with Sue Laurie as she has been writing her memoirs. She has written this book while continuing to teach at the National Theatre and has an unrelenting passion to share her knowledge with actors, puppeteers and directors. Sue, who celebrated her 80th birthday in July 2016, full of verve and the consummate professional, juggles her work at the National and at home in Barnes with her roles as mother, grandmother and friend to many. This has become quite simply her way of being. So much so, that perhaps even Sue has not realised quite how remarkable her commitment to the fields of acting and the Alexander Technique has been over the last forty years. The impact she has had, touching the lives of those with whom she has worked and indirectly on so many avid theatre goers and film aficionados, has been immense. Most of these have probably been unaware of the unseen influence of the technique in the actors and actresses they watch.

And so for some context. Sue is a delightful, humorous story teller and the story goes back to Alexander himself.

FM Alexander (1869-1955), the founder of the work, did not set out to discover something. As Sue says, rather he was a young man passionate about being an actor, when he ran into breathing and vocal difficulties which put his career in jeopardy. Seeking a remedy for this when doctors and vocal coaches had been unable to help, he decided to help himself. Over a ten-year period of observing and experimenting he discovered principles which enabled him to stop 'getting in his own way' through what had become subconscious habit.

The basis for the 'poise and presence' of the best actors that we so enjoy on stage comes from the absence of that which is unnecessary. The absence of idiosyncratic habits that are the tell-tale signs of most of us in the expression of who we are. The foundation for the multitude of choices that an actor can make is a certain neutrality. A blank canvas on which to paint the nuances of the character he or she is to portray. Not a dulled, senseless being, but someone who embodies the optimum, natural state of psycho-physical readiness for action. When an actor takes unnecessary habits into their role, the character is muddied from an audience perspective, though they may not be able to explain why.

The application of the principles Alexander discovered became the Alexander Technique. Alexander began to teach other actors in Australia and his work became known to senior medical professionals who recommended that he travel to England to ensure that the knowledge and skills became established. It had become apparent that the work of Alexander had a fundamental influence on health and wellbeing as a whole, not only on breathing, voice and presence on stage, significant as those aspects are.

So, on the recommendation of doctors, and fortuitously financed by a win on the horses, Alexander came to England in 1904 and taught near Victoria, London, until his death aged 86 – apart from several visits working in the USA.

Alexander played his own 'part' as an Edwardian gentleman within the higher echelons of society and taught, amongst others, Sir Stafford Cripps the Chancellor of the Exchequer, Professor John Dewey the philosopher and pragmatist, William Temple, the Archbishop of Canterbury and the writers Aldous Huxley and George Bernard Shaw, who then left money in his will to support the Alexander work at the Royal Academy of Dramatic Arts (RADA)[1].

But theatre was always Alexander's first love, much to the despair of his first teacher trainees whom he demanded perform *The Merchant of Venice* and then *Hamlet* at the Old Vic as part of their training. Alexander enjoyed the London theatre scene and was part of it – working with all of the leading actors and actresses of the day.

Just as the audiences of that time knew of Sir Henry Irving

---

[1] McEvenue, K., (2016) *The Alexander Technique For Actors*, EPUB eBook, Edition: 1st Extent: 176, Bloomsbury Methuen Drama Series

and George Bernard Shaw as household names, far fewer had heard of FM Alexander. So it is with the name of Sue Laurie, who has continued the legacy, behind the scenes, for so many of the finest actors in our generation including Sir Ian McKellen, Dame Judi Dench, Vanessa Redgrave, Sir Lenny Henry, the late Alan Rickman and Benedict Cumberbatch.

Whilst Sue's own story of learning and teaching the Alexander Technique is both remarkable and inspirational in its own right, Sue is not seeking the limelight. Nor is she only interested in teaching household names. Indeed, the fuel that has fired Sue to write these memoirs is her desire to share her experience and passion. To ensure that those entering the profession, those involved currently and in time to come, know about, and have access to learning the 'simple and stupendous truth' that is the Alexander Technique.

And for the actors themselves, an initial course of Alexander lessons becomes, for so many, far more than preparing for a specific role, but a way of being. It becomes emotionally, mentally and physically a bedrock to work from and return to through the multifaceted challenges of acting careers and personal lives. Like a loyal friend.

And as I have spoken to Sue and read her words over the previous months I have been struck by how Sue has been such a loyal Alexander teacher and friend to the theatre and so many others. Sue epitomises what the late Kitty Wielopolska, who trained with FM Alexander on his first training course in the early-1930s, said about teaching: '*You must love the* ***person*** *you're teaching,* **what** *you're teaching, and the* **art** *of teaching – and like any art, teaching the Alexander Work is love*'[2].

Claire Rennie
Alexander Teacher

---

[2] *Never Ask Why*, The Life-Adventure of Kitty Wielopolska – as told to Joe Armstrong, 2001, Novis Publications: Denmark

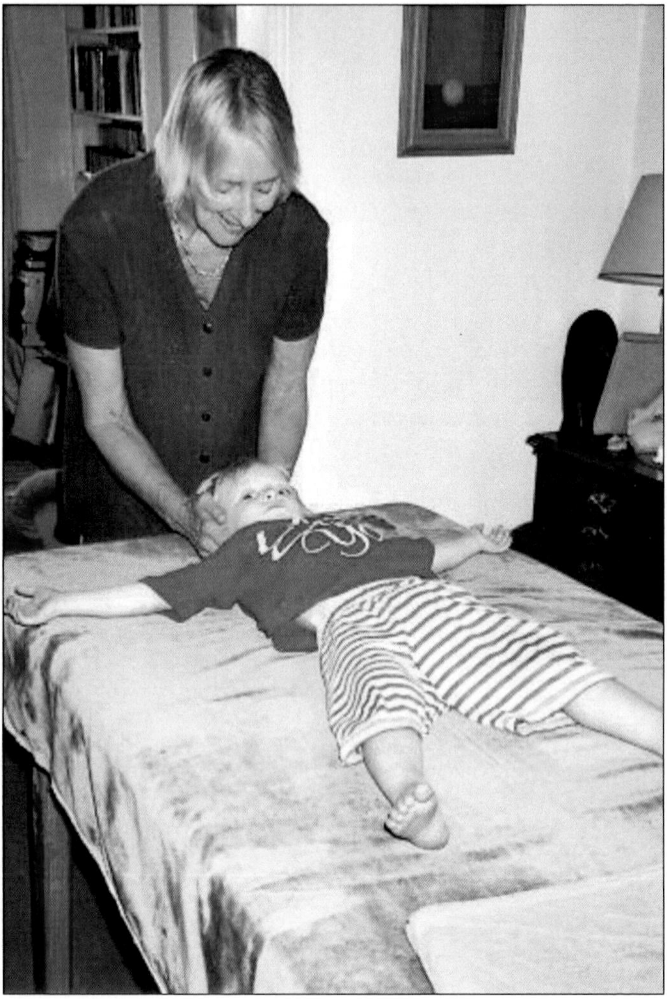

Joe Laurie, Sue's grandson, has an Alexander lesson

1. Dramatic Ambitions and Early Life

For some time, I have been trying to galvanise myself into writing my memories of a very exciting journey lasting over thirty years working with the Royal Shakespeare Company and the National Theatre. It is a journey that is still evolving.

Above all I want this book to be fun as I often feel that the Alexander Technique is thought of as rather hard work, that it means being very disciplined, a bit of an austerity, and just about acquiring 'good posture' or curing back pain. But it does in fact open the door to so much more than that. Using the technique is immensely practical and can be used with everything one does. With a teacher, the pupil can learn to become much more aware of how they are using and misusing their bodies, very often causing unnecessary pain and discomfort. After the pupil starts noticing these habitual patterns, they will be learning how to change their habits, which in some cases have been going on for many years, and so transform their life.

My own Alexander lessons – and ultimately training to teach – certainly transformed my life, which is another reason why I want to share these experiences. I am personally a very grateful student of the Alexander Technique.

From the age of seven I was in love with the theatre, music and ballet and went through the whole gamut of ballet and tap lessons. There was also lots of singing in the evenings after supper with my mother and my aunt, both of whom had lovely voices and played the piano. 'Sing Songs' around the piano were a regular occurrence and, as there was no television, we made our own entertainment.

One of my very first memories was when, at the age of seven, I was taken to the pantomime at the Theatre Royal Norwich where we had stall seats as a great treat. 'Hey Little Hen' was the song of the moment and the words were scrolled down so that the audience could all sing along. As far as I can remember, the Panto was *Cinderella* and an ugly sister came on and asked if any little girl would like to come up onto the stage and sing 'Hey Little Hen'. To my parents' amazement I pushed past everyone, marched up and climbed onto the stage so quickly that the girl who had been planted to sing didn't have a chance to get there before me and had to be invited up after I had done my bit.

I went to boarding school and when I reached the sixth form I was made head girl. I always directed plays and the end of year musical. This was a major occasion that was always enjoyed tremendously as exams were over and it was such a relief from studying. In the holidays I was also an enthusiastic member of the local amateur dramatic group. One of the highlights of my involvement with the acting profession at that stage was having my photograph in the Eastern Daily Press. I had also been highly commended for my part as the Mock Turtle in *Alice* and my rendition of 'Beautiful Soup' at the Assembly Rooms in Norwich.

My father had dreams of me being a ballet dancer and took me to every ballet that came on at the Theatre Royal Norwich, but those dreams were shattered when I just grew and grew until I was much too tall to be considered by any company. In those days the height limit for dancers was something like five feet six inches (168cm) or maybe even smaller.

Alas, my career as an actress was also not to be. My parents could not cope with the idea and anyway there were no drama schools nearby. University was also out of the question as the priority was my brother Simon's education. Boys went to university and in those days it was not considered important for girls – it was much more important for the boy of the family to be properly educated. This was something that I have always regretted – especially as my brother then ran away from school at seventeen and went off around the world without finishing his education.

I passionately wanted to go to drama school but my parents were dead against it and I didn't know how to set about it. I was sent instead to art school as I was thought to be quite good at drawing and painting. At Norwich Art school I did a foundation course and chose dress design as my craft.

I then had the most wonderful offer from my cousin Elizabeth to go to live in America for six months. I went on the ocean liner Queen Elizabeth in tourist class with my hero Noel Coward in first class – but I did not manage to meet him. Elizabeth lived in Princeton, New Jersey and I was there to help with the two children while she was having another baby. She arranged for me to do a dress design course at the Traphagen School of Fashion in New York right next door to Birdland.

New York in the late fifties was an exciting place. I was at the fashion school three days a week and spent the rest of the time enjoying living in Princeton amongst the university life. My cousin was an academic and knew many of the tutors, professors and their children, all of whom seemed to enjoy entertaining me. I was taken to the United Nations to listen to debates, spent a day in a High school, went to a Junior prom in Princeton (with a chaperone), and went for the weekend to Bryn Mawr College in Pennsylvania to see what life was like in a very select girls' university.

I came back to England and, because in the late fifties it was impossible to get started as a young fashion designer, (Norman Hartnell offered me two shillings a day to pick up pins and be a general dogsbody), I regretfully gave up the idea and did a secretarial course instead whilst living with a family as a nanny in Roehampton. I hated secretarial work and so then ended up waitressing in a restaurant, the Knightsbridge Soup Kitchen, where I eventually became manageress. It was the 'Swinging Sixties' so what could have been better, I loved it. The owner of the Soup Kitchen also started a nightclub, The Satire Club in St James' and for a really short time I ran that, which was exhausting but quite an experience. Shortly after, I became pregnant, married and had three children one after the other.

I have hurried through my early life as it had very little to do with teaching the Alexander Technique – and there is probably another book there. As the three children were all very close together in age (three under five) it meant that I had very little opportunity to go to the theatre, which was a great sadness and for a long time I completely lost touch with that world.

I suffered a great deal from neck and back pain especially after my pregnancies and could trace this back to when I had sustained a riding accident, aged fourteen, whilst out hunting.

I did not like hunting at all and was pushed into it as all of my peers did it. I was always on a borrowed pony and feeling wretched in rather strange clothes as they were handed down to me by my cousins and never seemed to fit properly. On one occasion I was trying to hold my pony back as he was desperate to get up with the hounds and he had quite a hard mouth. My hat had slipped over one eye and two very elegant women in bottle green habits riding side saddle drew up beside me and one said to the other 'My dear, who on earth is this?'

The occasion of my riding accident is etched as clearly in my mind as if it was yesterday. I was riding Malta, a retired polo pony of whom I was extremely fond, as she was very safe and placid in temperament. The air was fresh as it had been raining during the night and the early morning mist made visibility poor. But the fox had been spotted and we were suddenly chasing the poor creature in full gallop. Just ahead through the mist a very high hedge loomed up in front of us which was higher than I was accustomed to. It had a very large ditch in front. Malta took it easily, but I didn't.

I landed heavily in the ditch with my bottom in a pile of muddy water and with horses flying over my head. Luckily it was very deep. I was terrified. I waited until I could no longer hear the sound of the hunt and then climbed out with a soaking wet bottom, aching all over but thinking thank goodness I had no broken bones. I found my pony waiting patiently for me chewing a bit of grass. She looked completely unconcerned and I realised that she was waiting for me to pull myself together because she wouldn't go on without me. She lifted her head and looked at me and I could almost hear her say 'Up you get, we're going home now'. Even though the last thing I wanted to do was to ride again, I trusted her completely and climbed back up. When I was safely back in the saddle, she took me straight back home where I gave her a hug and spoilt her rotten with sugar lumps and carrots.

I am convinced that the fall upset the balance of my pelvis as I was still growing and from then on I always had an aching back and any form of exercise seemed to be painful. In those days, no one seemed to have any solutions, and so I accepted it. Back pain just became a part of life.

Years later, we were spending a weekend with guitarist Julian Bream at his beautiful home in Wiltshire and my back was really troubling me. Julian who had been having Alexander lessons with Marjory Barlow for a long time insisted I went to see her. He still had his Battersea accent before the BBC tried to get him to change it and I can hear him saying:

'What you must do, Sue, is have a taste of the Alexander Ragtime Band, because its great stuff.'

So that was the beginning, at a time when I had little faith in anything helping having tried doctors who had sent me to the physiotherapy department at the Middlesex. Here I had been made to strip down into bra and pants and throw balls over high wires whilst my bewildered children watched. X-rays had discovered nothing amiss, a chiropractor made the situation worse by over manipulating me. He so loosened the ligaments such that my back was always slipping in and out of alignment. The chiropractor was also a neighbour and friend, which was one of the reasons why I was 'over manipulated'. Whenever my back seized up I only had to go down the road and it would be clicked back into place in a few minutes – being a friend he did not charge me – so it became the easiest solution.

Of course, I had never heard of the Alexander Technique as it had not been very widely publicised. Also, although FM Alexander had earlier been supported by some doctors, now, when brought to the attention of the medics, it was frowned upon – as indeed were so many alternative therapies at that time. It was in 1973 that Dr Wilfred Barlow, a rheumatologist who had been trained in the technique by

FM Alexander himself, wrote his book *The Alexander Principle*[3]. At this point the technique began to be recognised as a very valuable tool to be taught to those suffering from excessive stresses and tensions, which often cause a great deal of pain and discomfort.

[3] Barlow, W. (1990) *The Alexander Principle*, London: Victor Gollancz

2. Finding Alexander

Anne Battye was my first Alexander teacher and was at that time working with Dr Wilfred (Bill) and Marjory Barlow at Albert Court in Kensington. Marjory, who led the Alexander Teacher Training course at Albert Court, was the niece of FM Alexander and she had worked with her uncle from the age of seventeen.

I had wanted to go to Marjory as Julian had suggested, but she was busy training young teachers and had very little time to give new pupils individual lessons. However, I soon discovered that Anne was a very good teacher whose life had been transformed by her Alexander lessons after her car accident.

I went for lessons with Anne twice a week, which were cut back to once a week later on. It is said that FM insisted that pupils who were beginning lessons with him had fifteen lessons, one every day, and then went down to two or three lessons a week after that. These days, that intensity would be completely impractical for most working people. With my pupils, I aim to make it twice a week for about a month and then once weekly after that. As you will see later on, it has to be a very different arrangement with the actors.

I was very fortunate to have Anne as my teacher. She was one of the most experienced in the UK and had had to work her way through the aftermath of a car accident using the technique every step of the way. My whole body was really out of balance after years of misuse following the riding accident and then the birth of my three children. This had taken its toll on my back as well as my nervous system. Because of the constant pain, I had become depressed. Very often, however, after the lessons, I felt a very different pain. Anne explained to me that this was because some parts of the body had been doing too much. Now, as a result of the lessons, muscles which had got away with doing very little, were being made to work.

One day I remember that I said to her that my legs seemed as if they would not work, all the tension had gone from them and I thought I was going to fall over. Anne simply asked me if I ever did actually fall over, to which I had to say 'No'. We both fell about laughing and I realised that it was essential that I keep a sense of humour.

To begin with, I found the Alexander Technique all very confusing as taking on board my strong urge to DO (more on this later), which was so much a part of my personality, meant that it was very difficult to accept that I DO nothing. I was a very hyperactive person and, bearing in mind I had three children very close together in age, life was always hectic. We had very little money and so no 'Nanny' or child-minders to call on. A saving grace was that two of them were at school all day and my youngest, Tom, was at nursery till lunchtime, which allowed me some time for the technique. I gradually became fascinated by the subtle changes that my lessons were making to me both physically and psychologically. I had been very interested in psychology ever since I had worked helping with the children of a family in Roehampton as their father was a very eminent psychiatrist. I began to read Jung and Freud and secretly nurtured dreams of training to be a psychotherapist.

Now however, I began to discuss with Anne the possibility of training to teach the technique. She was very encouraging and so I plucked up courage to speak to Marjory to see if she would consider me as a student.

I was then interviewed by Dr Barlow and Marjory to see whether they thought I would be a suitable candidate. However, Marjory still had to decide whether or not to start another training course as at that point she was not sure. A training course was a three-year commitment and it was such hard work. She would not have a class bigger than eight students and felt that if she did have another one, it would definitely be her last. I then spent a nerve wracking eighteen months waiting to see what she was going to decide and after a tense period of waiting for news, one morning Marjory came through to me while I was waiting for a lesson with Anne and said, 'Sue, you're on – we start in August.'

I was one of the eight students who were lucky enough to be in what indeed proved to be the very last complete training course that Marjory gave. (Her age was a dark secret.) I have always been so grateful for that as Marjory was an extraordinary woman who lived and breathed the teachings of FM Alexander. She instilled into all of her students the necessity, as teachers of Alexander Technique, of staying with the basic principles that Alexander had developed, the very essence of his work.

Over the years, I have realised how important that that drilling from Marjory has been for me. Some other training courses have sprung up where teachers have developed different methods of teaching the technique. Sometimes, when I take on the teaching of a pupil who has been taught in another way, I need to take them back to the beginning again.

The next hurdle for me was to get the funding as the fees were one thousand pounds per term, which in those days was a great deal of money. As a family we were, of course, struggling with three children to bring up – my husband was not earning a great deal. For a while, I worked in a restaurant in the evenings three times a week, but there was still no chance that we could afford it. Most of the students were receiving grants from their local councils, but the Borough of Richmond would do nothing to help. I was desperate as I had never wanted something as much as I wanted this training.

By chance though, I went to have lunch one day with my past employer, Lady Eila Mallinson, the wife of Sir William Paul Mallinson. They were the family I had been so closely connected with ever since I had lived with them in Roehampton and on the Isle of Wight, where they had a most idyllic home. They had become very close friends and Eila became godmother to my daughter Sophie.

In the conversation during lunch, I touched on the training I wanted to do so much and Eila seemed to be very interested and asked me questions about it. This was both surprising and refreshing as I took care not to mention the Alexander Technique to many people because they had never heard of it. It was extremely difficult to explain and, like my husband, people were inclined to think it was 'another of my crazes'.

We then went on to talk of other things and I thought no more about it until about a week later when Eila rang me up one evening. She said that she had discussed my training with Angela, her eldest daughter, and they thought it was very important that I did the training and that they were going to pay for it.

If I had been able to, I would have jumped over the moon. Never had anyone been so generous and caring about my ambition to have a career apart from the role of housewife and mother. I was absolutely thrilled. I went off to have my hair cut and done before going to have supper with some very old friends where I was meeting my husband who was coming straight from work.

They were all there when I arrived and I burst out with my fantastic news. The reception I received was one of complete lack of interest. There was a slight pause while they listened to what I had to say and then the conversation continued about whatever else that was going on in their lives. None of them had ever heard of the Alexander Technique and again they thought I was just going through some sort of phase. So I said nothing, but thought to myself, 'One day you will take me seriously'.

However, when I went into Albert Court to tell Marjory the following day, there was a very different and unexpected response to my news. Marjory was sitting up in bed as she had a bad cold and she looked at me for a few moments and then said that she was very pleased for me but she and Bill had decided that money or no money they would have trained me anyway. 'Sue', she said, 'You simply *have* to do the training'.

3. Alexander's Discoveries

Before I start on my own experience of the training, I will try to give an explanation of what drove Alexander to make his discoveries. Quite simply, he was passionate about being an actor.

He was born premature in January 1869 in Tasmania. A combination of being a sickly child with respiratory problems and what one might describe now as a precocious nature, he was largely home schooled. His teacher, Robert Robertson, visited Alexander at home and inspired him with a love of Shakespeare. This was then to develop into a love of the theatre and a desire to be an actor.

As a young man, he went to Melbourne in 1889 and had singing and voice lessons from some of the best teachers of the time and started to gain a reputation as an actor and as a reciter of Shakespeare. However, in the early 1890s, he began to have great difficulties with his voice, which would fail during performance. So much so, that he thought he might have to give up all thought of being an actor, which was devastating for him.

He sought advice from doctors and throat specialists and his medical diagnosis was 'irritation of the mucus membrane of the throat and nose and inflammation of the vocal cords'. It was recommended that he have an operation but he did not follow this advice. He was also advised to rest his voice before performing, but the benefit was distressingly short-lived – the hoarseness returned before he was half way through his performance. In discussion with his doctor afterwards, he reasoned that it was something he was doing when using his voice while reciting that was the cause of the problem because he did not have the problem in ordinary speaking.

Alexander was an extremely determined young man and set himself the challenge of solving the problem by arranging mirrors in which he watched himself in minute detail to try to see exactly what happened to him when he spoke. After experimenting for some time, he eventually noticed that when he began to recite, he tended to pull his head back, depress his larynx and suck in air through the mouth making a gasping sound.

He was initially unsure as to which of these observations was in fact the primary cause of the hoarseness. In time, after much experimentation, he deduced that it was the pulling back of the head that was the first in the sequence of misuse. When he could stop that happening, his voice improved.

To his amazement he then noticed that this habitual pattern seemed to have an effect on the whole of his body as it appeared to also lift the chest and shorten the back so throwing the whole body out of alignment. This included tightening of the legs, feet and toes. This all affected his breathing and voice.

Having made this discovery, he was thrilled and thought he had solved his speech problem as now he could prevent pulling back his head. However, he found that he could not stop pulling his head back in actual performance – in fact whenever he even thought about reciting, the old habit returned. The mental and the physical were inseparable.

He was also shocked to discover that what he was actually doing was different to what he thought he was doing. He could not feel that he was pulling his head back when he was actually performing, even when he was. His sensory system was giving him misleading information.

So he was now even more determined to change this pattern of reaction, which he realised must be a long established habit.

He thought about what actually happens when we react to a stimulus, whether that stimulus comes from within ourselves or externally, and realised that without the brain automatically sending messages to the body to move, to react, we simply would not be able to move a muscle, nothing would happen.

The rather unnerving realisation was that in fact he never knew what he was doing because he was never 'present' enough when the body received the message to act. He had limited control over his reactions and much of what he did was on auto-pilot.

This in turn led to the realisation was that he was never present enough to see or feel what he was doing because his mind, his thinking, was always either ahead or behind. He referred to it as 'end gaining'. Having our minds on the goal but not being with ourselves on the journey.

He thought that somehow or other he had to change this habit to a more appropriate response, in fact he had to get in the way of the automatic messages from the brain to the body, and to be in control of his responses to any stimulus whatever and wherever the stimulus came from. On observing others, he was fascinated to see that he was not alone as everyone seemed, to a greater or lesser extent, to have the same reaction. Marjory reported that he famously exclaimed, 'I see, they are all at it, it's a universal habit'.

What he eventually came up with was thought by many to be a stroke of genius. He learned to inhibit any response at all to the stimulus to speak by 'thinking' NO. By thinking NO there was a moment of nothing happening at all. He was creating a space that he usually never had as he was always rushing along into the next thing on the agenda.

Before he then went ahead, he consciously gave himself new messages – these were thoughts not actions. These messages, which he called 'directions', were in opposition to the way in which his habitual thoughts had been shortening and tightening his body.

The primary directions that he worked out were, 'to let the neck be free, to let the head go forward and up, to let the back lengthen and widen and to let the knees go forward and away.'

All of the thoughts we have affect the body in ways that we are not necessarily aware of and this new thought pattern with directions was successful because it overrode the auto-pilot. This is sometimes a difficult concept to take on board, but is nevertheless true. Alexander had changed his habitual response by saying NO to his habitual reaction and had given himself a choice that he had never had before.

After working like this for a considerable time, he freed himself of his habitual pattern whilst reciting and was thrilled to find that his voice was restored and became even clearer. He also became increasingly aware of other habits that he had never realised existed and this method gave him a freedom, a choice of how to react. He was now in the driving seat, not being driven on automatic with no control over his reactions and was able to take responsibility for the actions he chose to take.

Alexander became so convinced by these discoveries that he continued to work on himself and then he started teaching others. To start with, it was other actors who had noticed the improvements in his performance, but soon, members of the general public. Doctors started to recommend patients to him and then encouraged him to travel to London in 1904 to further spread his work. It was in London that he went on to share this work with many influential people and train teachers and thus began the long journey of bringing 'The Alexander Technique' to be more widely known throughout the world. He started his first teacher training course in 1931. Marjory Barlow, Alexander's niece, began teacher training with him in 1933 and remained dedicated to the essence of his work to the end.

It was my Alexander Technique teacher training with Marjory and Bill Barlow that began to change my life forever.

4. The Training Course

It was in 1973 that I started having lessons with Anne Battye two days a week and then about two years later started three years of training to become a teacher of the Alexander Technique. I had mixed feelings. The overriding emotion was fear, worry that I would not be able to cope with the course and running the home whilst the children were still very young. I needed to be there for them when they got back from school and I had to pick up my youngest boy from school – that was a rule I made for myself that I would not break.

However only a few weeks into the course, I developed an excruciating pain in my right hip and I was finding it extremely difficult to walk. I was panic stricken and went to Dr Pattinson, an osteopath and friend, who sent me for an x-ray, which revealed arthritis that was quite advanced.

I took the x-rays to Dr Barlow who, having studied them, said that it would probably mean I would have to have a hip replacement in five years' time.

I felt as though all my plans of the training course would have to be abandoned as there was no way I could commit myself to the training course and that I should go to Marjory and tell her that I had considered what was best and that I should end the course immediately.

Marjory listened to me until I had finished my explanation and then she just said very quietly 'Sue, shall we decide that you will never have that operation?'. She said it so firmly and kindly that I felt filled with a determination to carry on in spite of the fears.

And so I did and the pain subsided and, whilst the occasional x-rays over the years have confirmed that the arthritis is still there, using the technique must have stopped the situation getting worse, and so far, I have never had that operation.

I have related this story to many of my pupils, not only about hip pain, but any other threatened operation, and I think in many cases it has helped the pupil to have confidence and do the work on themselves that is necessary to make changes in the way they are 'using themselves' both emotionally and physically.

I am by no means saying that surgery is never necessary – we should always be checked out by the medics. But we can also look into ways of looking after ourselves – and possibly avoiding an operation.

I was devoted to Marjory. She showed such wisdom and understanding of my situation, the worry of paying for my course and the genuine terror I had of a hip replacement. I have a great deal to thank her for and sometimes wish that she was still around to see how the teachers that she trained have so faithfully carried on her work.

There were eight of us in the training course. For three years every morning we went to Albert Court in Kensington and so began what was to be for me, and all of us, a process of change which was so subtle that looking back I wish I had kept a diary. I could have recorded how I felt and the differences I began to notice in myself as my awareness sharpened and I began to change my perception of self, and so to know myself as never before.

The flat in Albert Court was in the basement and had a damp, musty smell about it. It was dark, and in fact had practically no daylight at all. It now seems the most unlikely place for a training course of any sort, let alone the Alexander Technique. I always remember there were very strange lights, standard lamps, which looked as though they were a kind of cheap Art Deco, and the kitchen was tiny and very impractical. There were net curtains at every window and never any sign of anyone coming in to clean – so the teachers who worked there kept their own rooms tidy and swept and dusted. The windows looked out onto grey, dank basement areas. The only rooms that were comfortable and well decorated were Dr Barlow's consulting and teaching room and Marjory Barlow's room, where the training course took place.

Marjory and Bill went to their boat at Mersea, in Essex, practically every weekend so one felt that the flat was not really their home. They always enjoyed the weekends more when they could relax and maybe have their children and grandchildren to stay on the boat.

During the first few weeks and months of the training, I seemed to always have some sort of pain. In fact, I can say that I never had a pain free day as my back, and my whole body, was in a way being re-educated and different muscles were being made to work when they had not been used before. They complained even more than when I was having lessons with Anne Battye two days a week.

When I told Marjory about the aches and pains, I was told to rejoice as my whole being was waking up and not to expect change to be a pain-free process. So not much sympathy there.

I was going through an extremely difficult time in my personal life and feeling very insecure about myself. I am sure that when Marjory first interviewed me, I did not realise just how much she understood about me as a person – certainly a great deal more than I knew myself. She had much wisdom.

The first eighteen months of training was spent almost entirely working on ourselves with the guidance of other teachers and Marjory. We had mirrors as did Alexander and learned to observe, to watch the changes as we inhibited and directed our movements. It was as if we were being taken back to square one and building up from that point, which is something very difficult to describe unless you are going through it yourself. I frequently felt on the brink of tears but it didn't seem appropriate as no one else seemed to talk about their emotional feelings. On looking back, this is something that I think would have been helpful to us all. So maybe, at the end of the week, a session amongst ourselves would have been useful. Just talking about where we were and to make connections with one another, to share what we were feeling and our problems. I often felt very isolated and alone because I had no one to speak to about the feelings and changes that were going on during this process.

Inhibiting, thinking 'No', as our first response to any stimulus, was the most important principle, and to begin with I felt this was a very negative message I was giving myself. Then I began to realise that without inhibiting, there was no chance of anything changing because my habitual responses would still be taking place. Even though I was then changing the message to something positive, 'Neck Free' etc. I would have been sending messages on top of the old reaction rather than stopping it. I also began to feel that with all this stopping, thinking No and giving directions, I would never get anything done. As I was such an inveterate 'doer', I found it extremely tricky.

My mind raced with minutiae – the children would never get to school, I would never have enough time to do the shopping, I would be late for collecting them back and travelling to the training course and so on and so on.

I remember Rosemary Nott, who was a teacher with a wealth of experience, describing how she had been able to stop a fit of sneezing by simply inhibiting and ordering her neck to be free. Rosemary was very inspiring to me as she talked gently while she was working with me and I found the movements she was making with my body corresponded with what she was saying and with the thoughts that she was encouraging me to have.

The moment when the training took on a completely new dimension was when we were told that we could begin to work on the teachers, so positions became reversed. It was eighteen months into the training course before we were allowed to lift anyone's head. The first time I did, it was very nerve wracking. Lifting the teacher's head very gently when she was lying on the table was an extraordinary feeling. 'Treat your pupils as if they are spun glass', Marjory said. It was then that I realised I was trying to encourage the pupil to DO what I thought or wanted them to do by the way my hands touched them. They would therefore respond by reacting, doing or in some way helping.

Much later on I discovered that I needed to show a pupil what happens when I myself am DOING, when I am not inhibiting. They then feel that they are just being moved around rather senselessly.

If, however, I think 'No' before I move an arm or a leg and at the same time remind them to think 'No' with me, then, as I say the directions that I want them to think, our minds and bodies experience working together.

As well as working with the teachers, we then began to work with each other, which was in a way much more difficult. I found that it was quite easy to say 'that was good – the way you took my head or lengthened my back' – but if I did not feel comfortable I said nothing as I didn't want to hurt the person's feelings. It was probably exactly the same for the other student but I think this dilemma was something that maybe was not made clear enough. Or perhaps one should have had time with Marjory alone, and take her advice, but that never seemed the right thing to do.

Emotionally as well as physically there were also many changes. I remember becoming very short tempered, which was not at all characteristic. In fact, I was angry, and had moments of thinking that I was being 'brainwashed', being made to think what someone else thought I should think, what I should feel and how I should behave. I gave up smoking during the training using inhibition a great deal and it was one of the most difficult things I have ever done. I was not even smoking a great deal but I was definitely an addict. That cigarette was my friend and when it was no longer there, my prop, my best friend, I was bereft and felt as though I was in mourning. Giving up smoking coincided with one of the most difficult periods in my life.

My husband left with another woman and I was going through a divorce and managing three teenagers who were all in various forms of disarray. I also had to cope with moving from the wonderful house that we had lived in for seventeen years, where the children had all been brought up, and moving to another much smaller one with all the dogs and cats, and everything that goes with it. Also my mother had died quite suddenly two years previously, which meant that my father needed a great deal of help. On top of all of this I realised I was going through a very early menopause.

If it had not been for my training I think I might have had a nervous breakdown. I am convinced that the Alexander Technique helped me more than anything else could have. At the same time, I had to cope with the horrors of drug and alcohol addiction in those close to me, and so, as well as ending my training and becoming qualified to teach the technique, I entered another phase of my life where I had to work on myself as never before.

5. Trainee Teacher

During the last year of training Dr Barlow occasionally designated pupils for us to teach. We had classes in between the lessons, but it was a beginning and we always knew that we could go to Dr B or Marjory if there were any problems – which was a great support.

My first challenge was a dancer with a back that was giving her great pain and problems. Her back had a very pronounced curve and was not supporting her in any way.

Dancers are the most difficult because they are often asked to use their bodies in a way that is so anti-Alexander and it can be very problematical. This pupil was shortly to be married to the grandson of the Duke of Richmond and she had virtually stopped dancing so her body was thrown into a state of insecurity, the familiar routine had ended and the daily programme of exercise had been halted.

When I laid her on the table and gently lengthened her back, she experienced for the first time a feeling of the whole of her back spreading and flattening, which she described as extraordinary. I suggested that, before and after dance practice, she should lie down and bring her knees up towards her chest, giving the directions at the same time, in order to get herself back into her body after the exertions of the dancing routine. I also gave her the wall exercise, which I later found to be a very useful tool for pupils working on themselves.

Later I received an invitation for myself and my husband to her wedding at Goodwood House and she requested that I should give her a lesson before the service. In retrospect, I have always wished I had gone but my husband refused to go, in fact he disappeared to the allotment, so I chickened out as the thought of going on my own was too formidable. I would not have known a soul. The Archbishop of Canterbury took the service and the couple went off for their honeymoon in a hot air balloon – so it was a great occasion. I sat gloomily in front of the television, on one of the hottest summers that we had experienced for years, watching it being reported in the news.

My very first actror pupil was the unforgettable Sue Fleetwood. Sue always made an entrance and, for her first lesson with me, she rose up from her seat in the waiting room wearing a large, wide brimmed hat and greeted me with a hand shake as if she were meeting the Queen.

It was she who made me buy my very first Filofax as on another occasion she floated in clutching what looked to me like a brown leather wallet. 'Sue, you simply must have one' she said, 'You can keep your whole life in here and there is only one place to get them in London'. She told me the name, which I have now forgotten, and I did as I was told and have never been without one since. I still have the original which, like hers, was in a soft, brown leather and I then used it until it was almost in pieces.

She was very tall and elegant but with a great deal of back pain and took to the technique as if it was the most natural thing in the world. How we did laugh. She was so talented and we seemed to have the same wicked sense of humour and became very good friends for several years.

During the last year as a trainee teacher, I had a large variety of pupils with differing problems. The majority of them seemed to come because of back pain. As I had started Alexander because of a bad back, I could identify with them and, it seemed, they then felt understood. I always think it is difficult to really empathise with a person if one has not been through the same pain and can share one's experiences.

Dr B was very canny about choosing which new pupil would suit each teacher. Because I was a young mother, he allocated me several young women in various stages of pregnancy. I realised how helpful the technique was with this condition and wished that I had been given that assistance and care throughout my pregnancies. It had been during those times that my back pain had sometimes been unbearable.

So many people came because they seemed to think that the Alexander Technique was all about getting 'Good Posture'. This still irritates me because there is a tendency to think that they will be told what to do to 'get it', that it will mean standing up straight or sitting bolt upright. I try to say that 'good posture' comes about indirectly through using the technique not by 'doing it'. Explaining this as a young teacher was very often difficult but it made me realise that this was because I did not really understand the process myself. However, explaining it to the pupils became a learning process for me.

There were many amusing moments too and one in particular I remember well. Pupils were always asked to take off their shoes at the start of the lesson. I often had drama students sent to me and one young man from Webber Douglas (Academy of Dramatic Art) suffered from having incredibly smelly feet. He was obviously totally unaware of this and I couldn't think what to do about it. I found myself not breathing through my nose so as not to smell so much, which affected my voice, and so I came up with what I thought would be a solution. I suggested that next lesson there would be no need to take off his shoes. He obediently complied, but it was summer, so the following time he came in with open toed sandals – so I still had to go on not breathing through my nose until he eventually left.

I also had a very tall pupil, a man who must have been all of six feet four inches. I myself am quite tall (five feet eight inches and still not shrinking.). I remember peeping over his shoulder and trying to explain the technique whilst feeling very inadequate. He had very bad back pain from working in the Walls Meat Company and had to carry very heavy boxes in the factory. I was showing him the wall exercise, which I thought might be helpful for him, and was about to show him monkey when his face turned a very strange colour, a sort of mixture of green and grey, and he sank to the floor in a dead faint. On this one occasion, there was absolutely no one in the building except the secretary, who was no help as she was a very nervous young girl – she panicked too.

I went into the bathroom and put cold water onto a towel and sponged his face until he came back to life. The incident taught me that, when doing this particular exercise, I need to make sure that the pupil is not very tense in the stomach, and is in fact not holding their breath, which can result in them feeling very faint and puts them off trying it again.

Another pupil Dr B sent me was a young man, whom I was told had a sexual problem – he was a premature ejaculator.

I was terrified and said to myself, 'Thanks a bunch, Bill'. However, my pupil never mentioned this problem to me and I thought the best way to tackle it was to get him inhibiting every possible stimulus that might be causing him stress. In fact, I taught him to recognise the emotions and use the 'No' before he reacted to them rather than working so much with the physical movements.

Then there was the case of the American journalist coming in with the same complaint repeatedly. She and her boyfriend always rowing about one thing or another. She was having an ongoing tempestuous affair and would report every time she came on their sex life and the quality of her orgasms.

First thing in the morning I found this very difficult to deal with until one day she came in looking radiant saying that she had been in the middle of one of their rows and had suddenly broken off saying that she was going to the bathroom. She then went to the wall and moved up and down slowly as I had taught her, inhibiting and directing until she had felt much calmer. On going back into the room the whole situation changed and they had then talked quietly and reasonably and had sorted out many of their differences.

Later, this same pupil had come in one morning looking completely different and I asked, 'What's happened, have you won the lottery?'

'No', she said, 'For some time I have felt uncomfortable, as if things were not right. Then suddenly everything changed. It was as if I had put on a new coat and it had felt strange and then, quite suddenly, it felt comfortable. I was alright in it.'

Dr Barlow gave lessons to a great many, well known men and women and one day he sent me a journalist called Martha

Gellhorn. I had absolutely no idea who she was, that she had been married to Ernest Hemingway, and I just treated her as a normal person, as I am sure she would have preferred anyway. Martha had a very bright character, was often hilarious and the lessons were filled with laughter. The main problem was her back, which had obviously been brought on during the writing she was doing all the time. No computers, just typewriters, which create much the same problem. She came for many lessons and I think it helped her a great deal.

Years later, in 1998, I listened to Martha doing a radio documentary about the plight of the pit villages in South Wales, about how they had suffered after the closing of the coal mines in 1985. It was an excellent programme, but Martha sounded much older, which of course she was, and I suddenly felt moved to ring her up and congratulate her.

I searched through all my old Filofaxes and to my delight found the number of her flat in Kensington. I just thought I would give it a try as she might have moved anywhere since the years when I knew her.

I dialled the number and it was answered almost immediately and the gruff voice said hello. I said, 'You may not remember me, Martha, but I gave you Alexander lessons to help your back, many years ago. I just wanted to congratulate you on your excellent radio documentary which I have just listened to on Radio 4.'

Gruffly, 'Oh, thank you, very much', then she cut off smartly – but I was so glad I was able to speak to her as the following week she died, aged 89.

What fascinated me and I learnt from these first pupils, was that so many of their problems were related to what was going on in their lives emotionally. Although they had come for back, or shoulder, or knee pain, it only seemed to be a cover for other problems in their lives. I would talk to them gently and find out what was going on, what stresses they were under, and two instances amongst the many stick in my memory as examples of how the mind is so connected to the body.

One pupil was a very unhappy woman who had three younger sisters and their mother had died when they were very young.

The elder sister, my pupil, who shall be called Mary, took over the role of mother and counsellor. Because she was a very strong woman and inclined to be a controller, I was always told about the youngest sister's problems and about how she would not take her advice and what a worry it was, and so on.

This worry and the wish to organise the others' lives made Mary very stressed and tense, and as I talked to her I was trying indirectly to encourage her to release the extreme tension in her stomach.

One day, Mary came in and burst into tears, tears of frustration. She had realised at last that she must let go of her sister. Mary had tried every which way to advise and control the poor sister, but even so it was having no effect and in her own words, 'I see that I think I am ready to cut the umbilical cord'.

As she said this, her stomach muscles released in exactly the same area as the scar for the cutting of the cord is located and she completely broke down and let go, which to me was quite revelatory. It showed me quite clearly how connected the mind, body and emotions are, and, when they are not in balance, how much trouble it can cause in so many different areas of the whole person.

Another pupil was a very unhappy woman who was slight in build and extremely nervy. She will be called Shirley. Shirley had very painful back pain and strangely a lot of discomfort in the fingers of the right hand, two of which were permanently crooked. This was not due to arthritis or trigger finger, but they would bend and get stuck in one position.

Shirley had two adopted children who were not brother and sister. The boy, who was only six years old, had not grown since he was four and seemed to have stopped growing whereas bizarrely, the girl just grew taller and taller, so much so that she appeared to be in her early teens even though she was only eight and still had the emotional maturity of an eight-year-old girl. Also she had been given medication to bring on her periods early and the poor child was in a very muddled state – physically and mentally. I gave the young girl some Alexander lessons as she was becoming very slouched.

One day Shirley came in for her lesson tight and stressed. Once I had laid her down and began to gently work on her tense body, she began to talk, which was a rare thing as she had generally bottled up all of her worries.

The final straw was that she had discovered that her husband had been having an affair with her 'best friend' and that it had been going on for many months. As she was telling me this, she began crying uncontrollably. Her hands, those crumpled up hands, now spread out, the fingers un-crooked and the whole body opened out, almost in an expression of relief that she had been able to show her feelings to someone who would listen to her confessions in a safe place.

It was examples like these, where pupils carried a considerable emotional load, that encouraged me, much later on, to take a counselling course. This then helped me to help the pupil let go of emotional baggage, which was nearly always coming out in some way as a physical pain.

At the end of the three years of the training course we were given a test, which was to give a first lesson to a pupil with Dr Barlow and Marjory sitting and silently watching. The pupil was one of the teachers who then asked me a great many questions. Although I had worked with Marjory in the class often enough, and she would give me feedback as did the other teachers, somehow this was much more stressful. I knew that sometimes, if Dr and Mrs B thought that the student teacher was not ready to be qualified, they suggested that they stayed on for one more year. This thought had been causing me a great deal of pressure. I did not know where on earth the money would come from to finance one more year of training and the feeling of failure would be more than I could bear. Even so, I had to wait for a couple of days to hear the result.

After their weekend in Mersea, they came back with their

answer, which to my enormous relief was an OK. They had decided that I was ready to leave the womb and I was now a qualified teacher of the Alexander Technique. I then discovered that I was one of the lucky ones because Dr B said I could stay on at Albert Court and he would continue to pass pupils on to me. This also meant that he and Marjory were on hand to discuss any problems we might have had. Also, usually on a Friday, the young teachers would get together and work with each other, which made us feel that we were taken care of and we could discuss the week's work without fear of recrimination.

I found that, to begin with, I couldn't manage more than four pupils a day as it was very tiring and some days I would stand there when the pupil came in and wondered what on earth I was doing, what was I saying, was it making any sense at all? I would then find sometimes that by explaining the basics to the pupil, it was as if I was explaining it all to myself again. Gradually my confidence built and then came a breakthrough, which led me to working with the Royal Shakespeare Company (RSC) and my life changed dramatically once more.

I had quite a tricky relationship with Bill Barlow as I had always felt, probably quite wrongly, that he didn't really like me. And I was hypersensitive about whom I felt were the teachers' favourites – and that I was never one of them.

After starting at the RSC, I continued to work at the school for two or three years until one day I asked Bill if I could have more time off every month. I wanted to spend more time at Stratford-upon-Avon to teach at the RSC. He threw a wobbly. This culminated in me being told that I was now on my own and that it would be best if I just worked from home and with the RSC.

I was terrified as I relied on the money and had hardly any pupils at home. However, I felt that it would be best to go for it. I was heavily cautioned about taking any of my pupils with me even though I'd been teaching some of them once a week for months. The next worry was that when I sent in my account, Bill delayed paying me for ages but eventually I received it, some seven hundred pounds, which was a great deal of money in those days. I felt sad, as it felt as though I had left under rather a cloud. However, I saw the other teachers quite often, and Marjory in particular, who kept well out of anything political like that.

6. The Stratford Years: RSC Beginnings

The opportunity to take my career as an Alexander teacher into a completely different area came as a result of giving lessons to a well known Shakespearean actor, Joseph O'Conor.

Joe was a neighbour of mine in Barnes, where I had been building up a private practice when I was not working at Albert Court.

He had never had lessons before but was very interested in Alexander, not only for his back problems, but for helping voice and movement as well. He had just married a very beautiful young actress who later came for lessons too.

My break came when Joe announced that he was going to play Caesar at the Royal Shakespeare Theatre in Stratford. He suggested that I should go up there to see the show and give him a lesson at the same time.

When Joe arrived at Stratford, he enquired as to whether there was a resident Alexander teacher. When he discovered that there wasn't, and had never had been one, he discussed it with the theatre manager. She put up a notice asking actors to sign if they would be interested in having a teacher come to the theatre to give lessons.

The response was very enthusiastic, so, when I went up to Stratford to see *Julius Caesar*, I sought out the theatre manager, Sonja Dosanjh, and spoke to her. After some discussion, it was arranged that I should go up for one week every month for trial period to see how lessons would fit with both the rehearsals and when the plays were running. The arrangement was that my travel, bed and breakfast and a per diem would be paid, but the actors would pay me for their lessons. At that time, I was charging £8 per lesson and often, if I felt it was a bit much for the actors who had very small parts, I did without – as I felt I was learning so much from teaching them.

So began my twenty-seven year association with the RSC.

I had been given an entry into a world that I had only dreamt of accessing – but I was here in a quite different capacity from that of my dreams. I would have never been able to take the stresses of being an actress, out of work and living on the breadline with maybe only occasional glimpses of success. This now meant that I was in the midst of one of the most famous theatre companies in the world, with all the excitement of watching the process from the inside, without the fear of standing on that wonderful stage in front of a vast audience and giving a performance…I could never have done it.

On my first day, Sonja Dosanjh had put a list up on the board at stage door for the actors to fill in the times when they could come for lessons. I was taken around the main areas where I would be able to go freely and introduced to the staff at Stage Door. Sonja finished up the tour with the green room, the customary waiting room and lounge for the performers. It was lunchtime so filled to capacity with actors and theatre staff.

'Get yourself some lunch, Sue', she said and, 'Treat the theatre as your home'. It was truly terrifying and as there was no sign of Joe – so I just had to get on with it, talk to anyone and introduce myself. I soon discovered this was surprisingly easy, as actors, almost without exception, are the most generous, likeable and courageous human beings. I love them.

After lunch, I was shown my teaching room, which to begin with was the children's dressing room. Here I had a table, a chair and a mirror. I had brought with me a sheet of foam and cushions and my blue velvet cover. I believed in a bit of comfort, although I knew some teachers made the pupil lie down on the table's hard surface with a pile of paperbacks under their heads.

I was welcomed and found that I was quite naturally accepted into the company. The green room became my refuge when there was a gap in lessons, for a coffee or tea, and there was always someone there to chat to. It was right on the river and sunny and light. I found that the food was uninspiring, very much depending on the chef's mood, and often in the evenings I went up to 'The Duck', where everyone gathered – especially after the show.

Right at the start I had to learn to be adaptable. There was no way that the quiet and privacy, that I had come to expect when teaching at home, was going to be possible here. I had to learn to be flexible – I sometimes ended up teaching in the most extraordinary places depending on which dressing rooms were in use or free. In the beginning, as I had no movable table, I had to secure a suitable surface in whatever room I ended up, which was often unexpected.

The most comical place turned out to be the top of Trevor Nunn's desk. Trevor was the much loved Artistic Director at the time, but was famously hardly ever there, and he had a beautiful office with a big window overlooking the Avon river on one side and Waterside (road) on the other. On one occasion Kenneth Branagh, who was playing Henry V, the part for which he became famous, came for a lesson on the 'desk'. I remember it clearly, he was so young, and I asked him how old he was. After a pause he said, 'Twenty-two'. I thought to myself – help – I am old enough to be his mother.

On another occasion, he came with an unusual problem. He had just received his very first fan letter and didn't know quite what to do about it. I said I thought that it was important to answer every one – so I hope he did. I told him that, for a short time, I worked on 'She' magazine as a trainee sub-editor, a very lowly position. Nevertheless, great fun. My first job was to answer every reader's letter and then go to the editor to get it criticised, or if I was lucky, passed. The editor was insistent that all letters should be answered – and this did give an enormous amount of pleasure to the writer.

I had many moments of panic as it could be very lonely. I had to steel myself to start talking to actors, directors, anyone – and introduce myself as the Alexander Technique teacher, start up a conversation about the show I had just seen and get to know my Shakespeare. I had had so little education of his plays at school or indeed any of the famous playwrights, so my knowledge of the theatre was sorely lacking.

However, I fell in love with Stratford immediately. The theatre area became my 'home'. I used to walk along the riverside to and from The Other Place and sometimes just wander on past the church. I rarely went up into Stratford itself, which could be very touristy, especially in the summer, when it really was to be avoided.

My favourite seasons were the spring and autumn. The winters could be absolutely freezing, and the summers crowded with tourists and, even in the days before 'global warming', very hot and uncomfortable. It was difficult to teach as there was no air conditioning and no cool place to be.

I feel I must talk about the different places that I stayed in Stratford. Although I spent most of my time at the Rotherham House bed and breakfast, sometimes, to save money, people invited me to stay. I would take them out for a meal to thank them, but it was fun to change around. When I first went up, I used to stay with Joe O'Conor and his wife as he was working at the RSC, even after *Caesar.* Then they had a baby and there was not enough room for me with them all in a very small rented cottage.

Then I met Ed Rose through Roger Michell, who had a flat in Ed's rather marvellous house just outside Stratford at Charlecote. Ed was a great character, who owned all the river boats on that bit of the Avon. The house, which he was 'doing up', was late Victorian and reminded me very much of my grandfather's farmhouse in Norfolk. It had a very homely atmosphere with a vast kitchen where everyone seemed to congregate. Roger's flat was above a garage. It looked out over the driveway, which swept up to the front door rather grandly. On the lawn, at the side of the drive, Ed was building a boat. This wasn't just a small dinghy, but a very large sailing boat with living quarters and cabins. It was surrounded by scaffolding and loomed up like something out of a film set. So, with the house being in a constant state of being renovated, one had the feeling that maybe it would never be finished.

When I was visiting I stayed in a spare bedroom with my futon and duvet on the floor. I remember one time when there was a family of four staying as well. Ed had generously offered them shelter. The husband was an artist, and I think Wendy, his wife, was too – or she had a craft – but cannot remember clearly.

Where I stayed became very important for me. It could be very lonely spending the day teaching and then going back to a bedroom with no one to talk to, or discuss the play, or generally chat about Stratford news and gossip. However, more often than not, I would be in Roger's flat. When he wasn't there I would sleep in his bed, but gave it up when I developed terrible backache. The mattress was like a hammock, with a great dip in the middle, so once again the futon was a godsend as an alternative. Another eccentricity were the peacocks. Ed had three, one cock and two hens. I would lie in the bath and watch them on the garage roof. The chap would flirt by opening up his magnificent tail, turn around with his bottom facing the girls and rattle his feathers to turn them on. They would look at him witheringly and march off in the opposite direction. I had never had such bath time entertainment – and probably never will again.

Jeremy Irons, with his wife Sinead Cusack and their two boys, lived in a farmhouse right next door to Ed's place. I became friendly with them and often went to supper, which was great fun.

One memorable time was staying with Frankie de la Tour when she was playing Cleopatra to Alan Bates' Antony. Frankie was staying on Waterside in a delightful row of cottages opposite the theatre. They were owned by the RSC and rented out to the actors during their run. Alan had the cottage next door and he would come in for tea – it was then laughing non-stop. They were very great friends and the gossip and jokes about the rehearsal time came thick and fast. One night, I had dinner at The Duck with them, the director and some of the cast and I don't think I have ever laughed so much. I went to bed with my jaw and whole body aching from the laughter and I was still sore the following morning. I treasure that time, as it wasn't very long after that Alan became very ill and tragically died. This was such a loss as he was a very fine actor and I felt very privileged to have met him. He had never had Alexander lessons, but Frankie had many.

She was barefoot all the way through the show and had great trouble with her feet. They became very sore and walking was extremely painful. We worked a great deal on using Alexander with walking, which helped her to survive the run.

Rotherham House, where I stayed most of the time, became almost home. It was mainly filled with people connected with the theatre who had come up for a few days to work. The house was owned and run by the wonderful Dominic Maury and his wife Olive. Dominic was a terrific character, very French, with an accent that he had never lost even though he had lived in the UK for many years.

Dominic believed in everyone having a really good breakfast to start the day. There was always a great choice of wonderful fruit, yoghurt, cereals and anything cooked as well. The coffee too, was of course superb and I found I could almost avoid lunch if I had done well at breakfast.

The beds were extremely uncomfortable though. I used to get backache nearly every time I went – until I brought my futon up in desperation. This I lumbered up to the bedroom and the back pain diminished considerably.

Dominic found this all very amusing. When I came down to breakfast he would announce me to every one with, 'Ere comes Zooo with her Foooton', which earned us both a round of applause. However, Dominic and Olive became great friends. I was always welcomed in the evening with a glass of wine or two, and sometimes supper, and much theatre gossip. They undertook a great re-furb of the whole house at one point and their living area became very French. The kitchen was large and friendly and Dominic was a great cook. I was frequently invited for a meal with them in the evening after work and, as they went to see all the shows, there was much to talk about. The kitchen extended around the corner and became a sitting area, quite a large part of which was taken up by a huge bed. This was where Olive was mostly to be found reading a book. She was a copious reader and we often exchanged books as I was never without something to read myself. I went through a time when I brought my border collie, Jessie, up to Stratford as I could not find anyone to look after her whilst I was away. Dominic did not mind a bit and Jessie was so well trained that she would sit under my table at the theatre and not utter a squeak.

In 1985, towards the start of my teaching at Stratford, I had the most wonderful luck when I was very involved with the cast of the now legendary production of *Les Liaisons Dangereuses.* The play, written by Christopher Hampton, was adapted from the 1782 novel of the same title by Pierre Choderlos de Laclos. The cast included Alan Rickman playing Vicomte de Valmont, Juliet Stevenson was Madame de Tourvel, Lindsay Duncan was the Marquise de Merteuil, Lesley Manville played Cécile de Volanges and Sean Baker was the Chevalier Danceny.

The play was an unimaginable success and then, in early 1986, the production transferred to The Pit at the Barbican with the same cast. Those actors I went on teaching in other productions throughout my time with the RSC.

In addition to *Les Liaisons Dangereuses* Alan was playing Jaques in *As You Like It* while Juliet played Rosalind. Alan remains for me the best Jaques ever. He played the part with a seductive languor and was renowned for the way that he caressed the language, never hurried, always savouring every syllable.

I taught all the cast and will never forget the first run through. This was somehow a better performance than any other that I saw later. It had a truth and a vulnerability which somehow could never be repeated.

In fact, I became quite worried about Alan because he seemed to take on the character off-stage as well. I remember I gave him vitamin B tablets for his nerves and a multi-vitamin to go with it as he seemed so low. I worked with the company when it came to London to the Ambassadors and right on up until they went on Broadway.

I had been told about Cicely Berry, who was the head of voice at the RSC, and knew I had to introduce myself. I had heard that, in the past, she had had lessons with Dr Barlow and knew the value of Alexander for the actors. I had also heard that she was rather formidable and might not tolerate any interference with 'her actors'.

Nothing could have been further from the truth. We talked in the green room over lunch and Cicely did come for lessons with me. This was very gratifying and also interesting because Dr Barlow had not approached lessons in the same way that I had been taught by Marjory. Whereas I found that helping the student to inhibit and direct was top priority, he approached things slightly differently. It all worked out in the end however.

There were times when Cicely talked about various difficulties that actors were encountering and we would collaborate – with me giving her feedback from my lessons. I found this so helpful, learning from her vast experience of teaching voice. I now appreciated that Alexander was an essential link to voice and to movement.

I have so many fond memories of Cicely. I would often find myself going to the show at the same time as her and we would go to The Duck afterwards and discuss the production. I would learn so much from her views on the performances and the direction – and more about Shakespeare.

On one occasion, much later on, we had lunch on the balcony outside the green room by the river when Cicely had just had her 80th birthday. I asked her how it felt, as I had just had my 70th. She thought for a moment and then said, 'For a while I was very depressed, and then I thought to myself, you are so lucky. You have your children, your grandchildren, and, most importantly, you have your job, which you love. You are so lucky. Sue, it is the same with you so, don't get depressed, just carry on with it all, we are very blessed'. That was a piece of advice I have never forgotten.

I have often wished there could be more collaboration between the voice and movement world and Alexander work as these three components in an actors' world, to my mind, form a bedrock for actors.

One day, I asked for help from Andrew Wade (a great voice teacher who worked closely with Cicely Berry) and a great supporter of the Alexander Technique who had come to me for several lessons. During the production of *Troilus and Cressida*, when Anton Lesser was Troilus and Juliet Stevenson played Cressida, all the warriors were enormous men – all well over six foot. One of them, called Clive Russell playing Ajax, signed up for lessons. I freaked out as I thought that maybe my folding table would not support him, so I asked Andrew if he would come and help me lift his legs. Andrew was busy and could not come and seemed surprised that I was worried, so I just had to battle on. As it happened, Clive was great fun and very receptive to the whole lesson. To my amazement he flew off the table, light as a feather. Although a big man he was very light on his feet – almost like a dancer – and he had many more lessons not only in that play but whenever he came up to Stratford.

In those days at Stratford, I managed to get into all performances without paying. I made friends with the front of house manager who would sneak me in at the last minute. If it was a very popular performance I sometimes went into the directors' box, which was great fun. At other times, when there was a preview, I would sit in the front row of the circle, aptly named 'Death Row' because it was where the press sat on press nights.

I often saw the same production twice in a week and was fascinated to see how it grew and changed. Also it was important to see what parts my pupils were playing and then how I could help them. I was told by the theatre manager that I was not meant to approach the actors and suggest they came for Alexander, but I am afraid I ignored that. The great thing about actors is that they welcome notes, are eager to take help and were thrilled that I was there to give constructive criticism, something which always surprised me with my lack of theatrical experience.

I occasionally gave lessons in one of the wooden rehearsal rooms attached to The Other Place, which I liked as it was much quieter. On the other hand, I often ended up going backwards and forwards to the main house to look at the list or call actors up from stage door. This was in the days of no mobiles or computers.

My room, wherever it was, very often became a sanctuary where the actors could confide in me – talking about their various problems with the part, the other actors, the director or their own personal difficulties. I always made it clear that it was a safe place and anything they told me was never discussed with anyone else. My counselling training was an invaluable tool in these circumstances.

I needed to devise the best possible way of getting Alexander across in the simplest form, a way that would be of most help to the actor. Lessons could be frequently disrupted. I had to get used to the loud speaker calling actors back on stage. This had to be announced into each dressing room regardless of what was going on. All actors were called by their surnames, so it was Mr or Miss as a prefix, which I found rather quaint and old fashioned. There were other things too, like testing the fire alarm, or actors rushing in to collect something, but after a while it just became part of life and the challenge of teaching and giving a lesson in the best possible way.

Actors were sometimes called back to rehearsals and at other times I had to get out of the room quickly as it was needed suddenly for something else. I was forbidden, by the theatre manager, to be in the theatre after the half. However, on several occasions leading actors said, 'Bollocks to that'. I would then haul my own table, which the RSC had bought for me, up to the actor's dressing room and give them a relaxing lesson just before they went on.

Sometimes I was allowed to go into rehearsals if the director didn't mind or the actors were anxious for me to see what they were up against. This would be very helpful when it came to their lessons with me. One hilarious incident comes to mind when it was summertime, searingly hot and I was again teaching in one of the dressing rooms. There was absolutely no fresh air in spite of all the windows being open. This was the same throughout the building. In came an actor named David Schofield in nothing but his very skimpy bathing trunks and sandals. I managed not to look at all surprised (especially as pupils often thought they had to strip off as with a physio or osteopath), but pointed out that no way could I give him a lesson when he was almost naked as I would probably stick to him and certainly could not make a good job of his shoulders. 'Well, I thought it was important for you to see what happened to me after playing eighteen months as the Elephant Man', he said, pointing to his chest where there was a marked curvature down the centre through the breastbone area and, when he turned around, this was repeated in his back down the spine.

David had been experiencing quite a lot of pain and very often when this is the case, many things can help for a short time, as, for example, physiotherapy, massage and osteopathy. However, the nitty gritty is that the condition will keep returning if the pupil does not begin to be aware of what they are doing to cause the problem in the first place and this is where Alexander is of enormous benefit. If David had been having help with Alexander all through that production, there would have been a strong possibility that his scoliosis would not have developed at all.

I learnt a great deal from that meeting because I realised just how important it was to help the actor to leave the part behind at the end of the day and to get back into balance. I say try not to take the day to bed with you. My recommendation is, if it's not possible to find somewhere to lie down, then do some wall exercise. I think that going slowly up and down the wall, with inhibiting and directing, can be a sort of quick fix to get back to yourself and see where you are in your body.

One occasion in 1986, there was more great hilarity as I had to creep in like a naughty schoolgirl to give a lesson to Jeremy Irons who was exhausted as he was doing three shows back to back. These were *Richard II*, *The Winter's Tale,* where he played Leontes, and *The Rover* where he played the lead. He wanted a session before the evening performance so I went up, in fear and trembling in case I was caught, and had to wade through bottles of champagne as it was a first night. Jeremy gave me the go ahead and a glass of bubbly, and insisted that he would stand up for me if there was any trouble. I then watched the show. It was my first *Richard II* and from then on one of my very favourite Shakespeare plays. The language in so many of the speeches was like a very beautiful poem that went on and on. *The Rover*, by Aphra Behn, eventually transferred to the Mermaid Theatre and I also went up to the theatre there to teach.

The legendary John Barton was directing and they were rehearsing next door to my workspace at The Other Place. The walls were very thin so that it was impossible not to hear John's very loud voice coming through to my lessons. The stage managers tried to persuade John to have Alexander as he was always suffering from back pain, but luckily for me, he never came. It could have been a bit of a challenge as he was renowned for being rather impatient. He might have found the technique lessons too much of a lengthy process with not enough instant relief. John was often described as a genius, and an eccentric, the two very often going together.

He is still working for the RSC and apparently used to chew razor blades in rehearsal. Another of the many stories about him was that at one time he was sharing a house with another young director who had brought back the script of a new play. He had been asked to read it and it had been left on the kitchen table. When he came back in the evening ready to read it through, it had disappeared. He asked John if he had seen it. Indeed he had, John had wrapped up some fish that had been bought in the market. The play had been used as the wrapping and the lot put in the fridge. It was now unreadable.

John was a great lover of fish, alive or dead. Possibly a theatre fable, but apparently one day he went home and left his pet fish in its tank in Stratford. He then paid for a hire car to bring it back home to him, which was several miles away – he just could not leave it behind.

During the years at Stratford, I worked with several

productions of *Othello*. The one that stands out for me was the 1985 production with Terry Hands directing. The cast included Ben Kingsley as Othello, David Suchet as Iago and Niamh Cusack as Ophelia.

I worked with many of them but not with David Suchet. However, we had many talks about his narrow boat, which was moored on the Avon not far from the theatre. It had a roof garden and central heating. I had always nurtured a dream of having one just outside the theatre, moored outside the green room, and using it to live and teach on whilst in Stratford – saving money by not being at the bed and breakfast. Although it might not have worked – with the boat rocking in the water – I may have just made everyone slip off to sleep! So just a dream…

Those I did teach included Ben and Niamh and many of the others from the play. Penny Ryder, Janet Dale, Joe O'Conor and Tom Mannion all took lessons.

In one *Othello* production, directed by Trevor Nunn in 1989, Willard White played the lead. With him were Ian McKellen as Iago, Imogen Stubbs as Desdemona and Zoë Wanamaker as Emelia. Willard made a very impressive Othello. He said that he had found the scene where he knocks Desdemona down and calls her a 'whore', a 'crushing experience'. He had afterwards gone into his dressing room and broken down in tears. Willard, of course, is a trained, bass singer. He had not had any voice training so had some difficulty speaking clearly on stage with his deep, rich voice. However, I found the spectacle of his imposing black figure against the slight figure of Imogen, with her gorgeous shower of golden hair falling down her back, absolutely mesmerising. I never managed to teach Willard, but worked with Imogen a great deal. At this stage, although I worked with some other members of the cast, Ian McKellen escaped me. I did teach him much later, however, when I was with the National Theatre.

The 1989 production of *Coriolanus,* directed by Terry Hands, with Charles Dance as Coriolanus and Barbara Jefford as Volumnia was a triumph for Charles in particular. It was certainly a very challenging part. Charles loved his Alexander sessions. One particular night he insisted that I went up to his dressing room with my table to relieve his back pain when I was just about to start off back to London. I didn't really feel like it, as there was just a short time before the evening show. However, up I went again, quite against the theatre manager rules, but I think helped Charles feel better about doing the next performance. I know that it was a very strenuous part, and he was exhausted.

When I left, I was exhausted too. It was pitch dark, there was a gale force wind blowing, and about halfway home the clutch went on my little Renault. I managed to coast into a roadside café, which was about to close, and rang the Automobile Association. They came ninety minutes later and took me and my car on board. I arrived home at two o'clock in the morning. I won't ever forget that day.

During my time with the RSC there were repeats of many of the productions, mainly the plays that were in the school syllabus' at the time – so *Julius Caesar*, *The Merchant of Venice*, *Romeo and Juliet*, *Macbeth*, *The Taming of the Shrew*, *Much Ado About Nothing*, *As You Like It*, *Love's Labour's Lost* and *A Midsummer Night's Dream* made regular appearances.

I worked with characters in them all – so will only mention the ones that stand out in my memory.

My favourite *The Merchant of Venice* was Trevor Nunn's production in 1999. This one was set in the fascist 1930s, with Henry Goodman as the Jew seeking to maintain his Jewish identity in a barbarically hostile world. The performance by Henry, who was so obviously Jewish, moved me to tears – I found it almost unbearable to watch.

There have been so many *Macbeth's* that I'm not sure which to choose. However, Michael Boyd started his term as Artistic Director of the RSC with *Macbeth,* directed by Associate Director Dominic Cook. I worked extensively with Greg Hicks, Sian Thomas, Richard Cordery and many others in the cast.

Steve Orme, the theatre critic, reported that, 'There is no need for gimmicks when you have class actors in your company', and, 'Hicks is particularly dazzling in the scene in which he sees Banquo's ghost, eventually sending crockery crashing from the banquet table as he teeters on the verge of insanity.'

I worked a great deal with these three actors, both in Stratford and then later in the Clapham rehearsal rooms.

In 1985, Bill Alexander's *Merry Wives of Windsor* was a fantastic success. It was a superb production set in the fifties and hilariously funny – I watched it four times. William Dudley was the designer, Peter Jeffrey played Falstaff, the Mistresses Page and Ford were played by Janet Dale and Lindsay Duncan.

There was a very steep rake to the stage and the poor girls were wearing stiletto heels – so consequently they had a great deal of back pain. My main job was to help them walk on this uneven surface in such a way that they did not damage their backs. We won through in the end. I first showed them how to walk from the wall, without their heels, while using the technique.

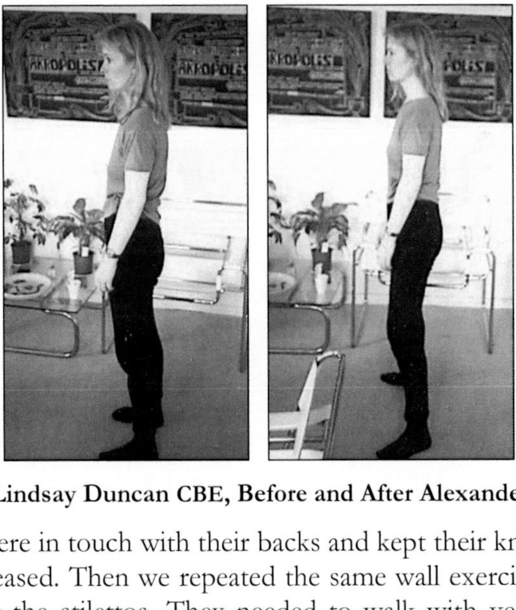

Lindsay Duncan CBE, Before and After Alexander

They were in touch with their backs and kept their knees soft and released. Then we repeated the same wall exercise while wearing the stilettos. They needed to walk with very small steps, which went with the parts, as they were teetering around trying to be ultra feminine and seductive.

For me it proved a great learning curve and much of my teaching was required when I needed to help actors deal with difficult situations.

I loved the production so much that I brought my children and friends. For the kids it was wonderful. They understood every word and roared with laughter, later admitting that they had had no idea that Shakespeare could be so funny.

A Midsummer Night's Dream was a particularly well loved Shakespeare by children. I remember one in particular when the actor who was playing Bottom was having a great deal of trouble with nerves and voice. Cicely and the girl who was at that time head of movement both collaborated with me to help the actor.

I have talked before about co-ordinating the support from the three functions – voice, movement and Alexander – but it was very difficult because I wasn't always in Stratford. Possibly my successor will find a way to address the problem.

It was at Stratford that I realised I needed to create a systematic way of getting Alexander across in a limited number of one-to-one lessons, which worked for me.

7. One-to-One Lessons

Lesson 1

In some ways this first lesson is the most important as in it I explain how FM Alexander evolved the technique.

I find that it is vitally important to explain Alexander's journey right at the start as otherwise the pupil has absolutely no idea what's going on and will have no idea how to work on themselves or to take responsibility for how they are leading their lives. I have met so many people, actors in particular, who have had Alexander where the teacher doesn't speak or explain what's going on. They are probably left feeling quite relaxed and pleasant but that's all there is to it.

So having explained how Alexander started using his technique, I will ask the pupil if they have any particular problems, emotional or physical. Or have had any accidents, because once we start work it will help to see how the body has been affected. This is also very important as it is extraordinary how even a small accident, or emotional upset from way back in childhood, will have affected the balance of the body and any habits that have developed around that.

I then will stand the pupil in front of the mirror and point out anything out of balance that I see. For instance, one shoulder may be higher than the other. Similarly with the pelvis, it may be twisted slightly or the head may tend to go to one side or the other.

They have probably never been aware of any of those things and they are usually quite taken aback and try to straighten the shoulders, pelvis or whatever they observe.

Then I ask them to just sit down perfectly naturally and get up again and ask them if they have any idea what they have done in that movement. Of course they haven't noticed if they stopped breathing, threw their head back or any other details. That is what we are up against.

For a new pupil it is quite a salutary thought to realise that in fact they have absolutely no idea of what they are doing. I very often get them to watch me from the side angle, getting in and out of the chair, imitating them, and, as I say, the rest of humanity making this movement, so they can see how the neck tightening and head going back and down throws the whole body off centre.

To give them the experience of how different the movement is when the technique is used, I guide them in and out of the chair using inhibition and direction. They can then feel the lightness, ease of the movement and a sense of being more in their body. And as this is all in front of the mirror they can also see the difference.

Table work is always included at the end of each session and I tell them that now you are going to have the best bit. Very often they will come in pleading exhaustion and head straight for the table, which I try not to allow as they must do some work first to earn it. I explain that if they do a bit of work first then the body releases much more and the mind quietens.

I always had an inch-thick sheet of foam on the surface of the table and covered it with blue velvet, blue being a restful healing colour. I would also cover three or four inch-thick cushions to put under the head, which could then raise or lower the head according to the needs of the pupil.

Once the pupil is lying on the table I move around the body lifting the head and rolling it gently from side to side. I move the legs to bend and point the knees to the ceiling and this lengthens and spreads the back onto the table each time I move them. I remind them to not help, to let go, and if they feel that they are helping then to go back to thinking No – noticing their neck muscles, telling the neck to be free, because, even though they are lying comparatively still, the neck always tightens first and sets up a subtle imbalance throughout the body. Having observed this, I explain that FM Alexander called the head-neck-back relationship the primary control as tensioning in the neck muscles triggers a response in the whole body and mind.

What I am importantly trying to help them with is to get the feeling of what it is like if the technique is working. The confusion is that very often everything feels slightly wrong when of course it isn't, they have simply become used to the misuse and they are entering a new place where the body and mind are being re-educated.

Apparently FM used to joke and say that the technique would probably attract every nutcase in the alternative health business. It sounded so unusual and was so difficult to explain without experiencing lessons.

To help the pupil understand the value of the directions or orders, as FM called the thought process, I give them a little exercise to demonstrate to themselves the use of thinking the new thoughts.

I suggest that they lie themselves down, with the appropriate number of books under their head, and go through the orders specifically in the order that FM worked out.

No; Neck Free; Head to go Forward and up; Back to Lengthen and widen; Knees to go Forward and Away. (I say Up to the ceiling when lying down.)

FM thought out not only the order of the directions but also the wording. When we react without stopping, the neck muscles are always the first to tighten. This sends the head back and down and shortens the whole body in a very subtle way. This is why, having inhibited with No, we then think Neck Free, as the neck tightening starts the whole misuse. In addition, to think of the back lengthening is very important. If the pupil thinks, 'neck to straighten', they tend to look like a very stiff robot.

Having quietened the body/mind, I suggest that the pupil then consciously thinks of something that will stress them – and notice where it makes them tense. It is very often in the stomach area or shoulders. The next stage is to return to giving directions, to quieten everything again and then to think about the stressful situation once more. This time, however, they inhibit the tensions that they have noticed.

I find it is like magic. When everything is quiet and peaceful, and you send a thought to the body, you can notice it landing like a butterfly and passing on the message. This will help the pupil trust that the directions work by just thinking them rather than doing them.

Later on I will share some of the remarkable discoveries that pupils have shared with me which have been very illuminating to both them and me as the teacher.

Lesson 2

Lesson 2 is more of Lesson 1, which means re-visiting the basics of the technique. I work on sitting and standing with an awareness of the necessity to keep checking that the pupil is sitting and standing with the legs hip width apart and feet very slightly turned outwards. Also noting that the weight is not more on one side than the other, which can often be a habit.

Most importantly, I will ask them if what they had been shown had been making sense to the them. I ask if there are any questions that need to be answered. There usually are, as the pupil has almost inevitably been going through exactly the same process as FM Alexander did. They have been trying to Do it in what they will think is the Right Way. This lesson, when I am guiding them in and out of the chair, I make them aware of their feet on the floor. They are allowed one message of thinking down, which is to send the heels down, at the same time as they think of sending their head forward and up, while they move in and out of the chair. I paint them an image of a concertina opening up – as the heels go down and the head goes up all of that which is in between has to open up and work to support the movement.

They often get a feeling of lightness of being, which before has escaped them, and this can be very exhilarating.

Lesson 3 – The Wall

Using the wall exercise can be the real beginning of pupils being able to use the technique for themselves. Working on their own is my prime objective when teaching. I am very aware that I am often going to have very little time to get the message across. This means that, unless they start practicing without me to guide them between the lessons, they will not learn. I remind them that having the lessons is about taking responsibility for themselves and beginning to bring the technique into their own lives. Unless they do this, it is as if they have been taking piano lessons and turn up each time for a lesson having done no practice. The result will be no changes at all, none of the new knowledge is being used.

Also the pupil is dying to DO something, and the experience of feeling and seeing what happens when they use the process will help them make their own discoveries.

I first of all get them to stand in front of, but away from, the wall with their feet slightly wider apart than their pelvis and their heels about five inches from the skirting. Toes turned out a bit, small second in dance terms.

I then ask them to point with their fingers to where their hip joint is on their body and practically everyone will point vaguely to the hip bone or even the waist. They just do not know or cannot make that connection. So I show them. I get them to actually dig into that slight dent where, at the side of the body, the head of the femur sinks into the socket, the very important ball and socket joint, which we are meant to use when bending, walking and sitting. I often show them a picture of the very same joint in a simple book of anatomy that I have to hand.

The next step is to take them back to the wall and ask them to be aware of how they land on the wall, for example which shoulder or buttock touches first. Next to inhibit doing anything at all and without wriggling around to make it feel right, noticing if there is a large gap between the back and the wall, whether the shoulders feel even or one higher than the other. Similarly with the buttocks and pelvis as to whether they are uneven too.

One thing that is vital is to watch that they do not press their heads back to the wall. If I then get them to positively do it, they see how this tightens the throat and better understand that throwing the head back and down has repercussions for the rest of the body.

I will then suggest that they make it feel 'right' by doing something, pushing the back to the wall or straightening the shoulders. They should then notice that, in fact, this action makes the whole body much more tense by their immediate reaction.

Then the pupil will need to stay with the balance point in the foot, the point that comes directly underneath the ankle bone, where all the leg bones end up in the foot. This reminds me of an actor who was playing the fool and in the performance was making the most amazing balanced movements. When I talked about the balance point, he said, 'Oh yes, when I trained with Le Coq in Paris he always said we must find 'point fixe', a fixed point in space'. This sounds like a dance term in French spoken in English, but I like it. Wherever you are, sitting, standing, lying down with legs bent, you can find 'point fixe' and know you have found equilibrium, which will have been achieved through using inhibition and direction.

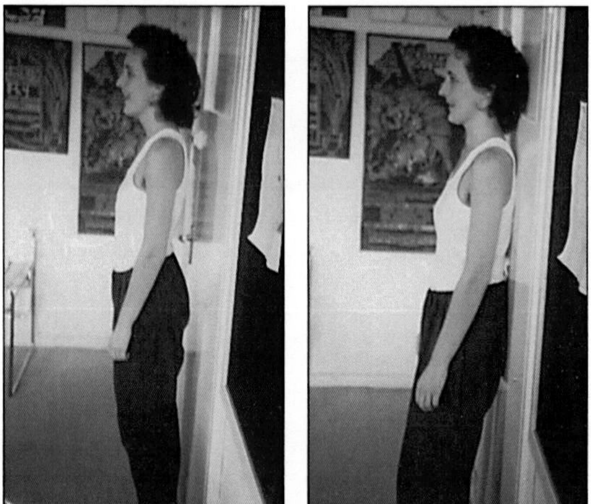

Fiona Shaw CBE working with the wall

After this, I ask them to think about bending the knees slowly just a little way, sending them forward and away from one another, out over the toes. Inhibiting the stimulus first and then, as this action takes place, to keep their minds on the directions. When they stop they will find that the whole situation in their back has changed. The back is flatter, shoulders have begun to level out and after slowly unbending the knees, still inhibiting and directing the movement, the back is flatter still and the shoulders are yet more level. This has been achieved without all the extra tension of striving to correct the curve in the back and the feeling of unevenness that was there at the beginning.

There are many uses for the wall exercise because once the back has opened up the breathing changes, sometimes quite dramatically, as the pupil is now not using the upper chest and shoulders to breathe with.

Following this, using the voice with some text is also very useful. It is encouraging for the pupil to hear and feel the difference as they go up and down the wall several times, checking that all the tension is not in the stomach and that the back is doing the supporting of both the movement and the voice.

Walking is another function that I talk about a great deal with the pupils as I often find that they are jogging as an exercise. In any event, walking takes up such a large part of our lives and it is a great time to focus on Alexander. I found it fascinating myself to watch other people walking and, of course, John Cleese, whose inspiration for his 'Silly Walks' was his Alexander lessons, often comes to mind. People do the most extraordinary things unconsciously when walking along with their minds elsewhere.

I start the pupil off with the wall exercise so that they have a very strong sense of having a back to support them and then, when they came away from the wall, almost taking the wall with them, I make them very aware of where their hip joints are by starting with walking on the spot using their ankle, knee and hip joints. Then, with the feet quite close together taking small steps forward, always thinking up as they lift the legs one at a time, and landing with the heel first and walking through the foot. I suggest that they think of taking a step backwards each time as they go forward, which is a wonderful way of keeping a central balance, rather than charging ahead with the weight forward onto the ball of the foot.

Lesson 4 – Monkey

This is about bending, and again really using the hip joints, knees and ankles. I will start pupils off by going up and down the wall a few times and one again building an awareness of the back, where the weight is felt just underneath the ankle bone, so finding the standing point, the point of balance. This is very important, as if the weight is too far forward or too far back, they will have lost the support of the back. At the beginning of monkey, I get them to lower a short way by bending the knees, with back in contact with the wall, and then I tip them forward from those hip joints – all the while thinking the back up out of the hip joints and imagining there is a hinge in the hip joint, keeping the thought of back and neck lengthening all the while.

It will be a completely new feeling, and often they will say it feels odd, but with that sensation it becomes obvious why the movement is called monkey.

We then go through the exercise again, but away from the wall. The tendency will usually be to lose the standing point and for the weight to go forward onto the balls of the feet instead of staying back.

This will be because as they bend forward from the hips they continue to bend the knees, instead of keeping them still and allowing the movement to be just from the hips.

Monkey is an extremely practical use of the body. The arms are wonderfully free to swing from the shoulder joints and do whatever they have to do without too much stress. The back is supporting the head, neck and shoulders and the legs are supporting the torso. It is a very balanced movement and great for the stomach muscles.

Later on I will get the pupil to bend forward in monkey and

lightly hold the back of a chair, with their wrists in and their elbows out imagining that they are lifting something very light. This is a situation when the whole of the body has been given directions. When cycling, as many of them do, if they employ this thinking, it means that they are not putting their weight on to the handle bars, but their lengthening and widening back is doing all the work.

With both the Walking and the Monkey exercises I always start from the wall so that the pupil will walk away from the wall having arranged his or her back to be opening out with an awareness of that support – otherwise all the strain will be back in the shoulders and neck.

Lesson 5 – The Whispered Ah…

This is something that I tend not to go through with non-performers until they have had many lessons as it would be too confusing. Actors and singers, however, have done voice work and have worked with their breathing all along, so they quickly find that the whispered ah is a beneficial exercise in so many ways.

Alexander was a great believer in the whispered ahs as a means of starting the day. It is reported that he went through twenty every morning and, of course, before a performance.

I stress that this is not a breathing exercise. Sometimes the very thought of 'doing' a breathing exercise can add tension rather than removing excess tension, which inhibits the flow of breath. It is more a way of monitoring the breath and going through the process only when the back is open and the neck is free.

To start, put the teeth together, the bottom teeth just meeting the top. The tongue rests just behind the bottom teeth and the pupil gently pushes the jaw forward as the mouth opens with a slight smile, releasing the cheek muscles. The backs of the hands are placed on the sides of the rib cage at the bottom and then the air is expelled out gently with a whispered aaaah sound. Then a pause before the mouth closes and, thinking the ribs to release and tummy to soften, the breath comes in through the nostrils and is directed into the back as if one has fish gills opening and closing. In this way the lungs are filled and any habitual upper chest breathing is avoided. There is a sense of a soft tyre of air surrounding the body. This is usually followed by finding the voice almost coming from another place and combined with that there is a sense of relaxation in the whole organism.

The whispered ah has been essential for all pupils', especially performers', voices. I very often get them to read some text both before and then after going through whispered ahs. The change is frequently quite remarkable.

Lesson 6

In this lesson I review those first sessions, elicit feedback and try to sort out any worries or confusions. I talk about walking and using the technique sitting at the computer where so much misuse occurs. Importantly, in the case of actors, we consider the part they are playing and I stress the need to leave the part behind at the end of the show. Lady Guinness is reputed to have said that she wished that Sir Alec, when playing Hamlet, would do just that, as it was extremely unsettling having breakfast with Hamlet every morning.

I think it's important to repeatedly come back to the criticality of inhibition, just to check that there is no confusion about what thinking 'no' means. So often the pupil finds that the 'no' thought is very negative when in fact it is actually the opposite. We are not thinking, 'No, I must not do that', but just wait, make a space, make room for thinking 'Neck Free'. It's 'no' to the old habit, it's a choice as to what we do and think. We don't normally have that choice as usually we are rushing ahead after a goal, which may or may not exist. As Alexander said, there is no reason not to have a goal, but it's the means whereby we get there that is all important.

Introducing the Alexander Technique to the actors in this extremely short time (only six lessons) was a challenge. But time pressure with these large theatre companies means that it is impossible to do otherwise and lesson content has to be thought out carefully.

What I have found is that in both companies the actors frequently return. Over the years they can carry on and this is very beneficial for both them and me. However, I felt that the greatest need was to help pupils work on themselves and to take the technique into every aspect of their lives. I therefore made a work audio tape, now a CD, which these pupils can put onto their iPod's to work with.

On the CD I describe Alexander's journey and then I talk through lying down using inhibition and direction. I also describe using the whispered ahs, the wall exercise, monkey and a bit about walking.

I encourage them to buy it so that pupils can work on themselves. The general feedback has been very encouraging. It gives them time with themselves, to be quiet and aware of what is going on in their minds and bodies. Time before the show or to start the day and then afterwards to wind down and leave the show, or the day, behind.

The Mirror

An essential part of my room is...the Mirror.

I always insisted that I had a mirror in the room where I was teaching. If this was a dressing room, which it frequently was, it would not be a problem. Otherwise one had to be pinched, and then returned to wardrobe or wherever it had come from. Alexander worked with a mirror to begin with and I like to do the same. I feel that it is important for the pupil to see what they are like physically, whether they have one shoulder higher than the other, pelvis is not balanced – one side of the pelvis lower or higher, head over to one side and so forth.

Actors were frequently surprised as, although they obviously had to look at themselves often, it was not with a very objective eye, more as to whether their make-up was okay or wig, costume and so on. I felt it was important that they began to see as FM Alexander saw. Even more exciting is to see the way things change, often quite dramatically, after just getting in and out of the chair using inhibition and direction and not trying to DO it correctly.

I found that sometimes after the first lesson or two the actor would realise what was involved, that it was not just like a massage, where I would make them feel better and I would be able to cure all ills. I always tried to get across that it was fifty fifty effort needed – that they were responsible for doing fifty percent of the work. So if nothing changes, nothing changes.

I found that using the mirror, facing the mirror and looking objectively at themselves, could sometimes be a tricky situation.

One or two instances spring to mind. One was of a now very famous actor whom, it turned out, really disliked his physical body, his appearance. He simply could not look at himself at all even though I said that we needn't work in front of a mirror if he didn't want to. After the first glimpse of his shoulders, I could see they were uneven with his head slightly on one side, something that is very common. He was a very intelligent man and when I had explained the process he just had that one lesson and never came back. He appeared to want to stay as he was and not embark on a journey of change. Nearly always when the pupil sees the change that occurs, even after one or two lessons, they are excited and want to go on. However, as far as I know, even now he still feels the same way in spite of being highly acclaimed and admired universally, he will never stand in front of a mirror.

Another instance was that of a director whom I was always nagging to come for lessons as he suffered a great deal of back pain. He was a very good looking man with the posture of a much older person. His back was bent over and his neck seemed to disappear into his shoulders.

He eventually came and after just the first lesson the change was dramatic. He was standing up to his full height and could look himself in the eye in the mirror. Here he saw a very good looking young man who was some four or five inches taller than his usual stance.

It turned out that he was going though a very difficult time in his marriage and his wife was having affairs. Even though he was a brilliant director, this did not make him feel confident about himself. So the outcome was that he would not continue. He could not face up to the change, the fear of being this very different human being was too great, and sadly that was the end of our time together.

Another mirror experience, which stays with me, was with a now very well known actor. I had taught him for some time through two Shakespeare plays where he had the lead part. I found it very difficult to get him to really look in the mirror. He didn't mind seeing himself, but I felt that it was only to admire himself, not to REALLY look and see and feel what was happening. In short no real awareness of himself on a deeper level. I was giving him his final lesson of the production and I found myself saying to him as we said goodbye, 'Well, maybe one day you will be able to look in the mirror.'

I said to myself, 'there you are Sue, you've done it this time. He will never speak to you again', which I was sad about, as we had had a very good relationship. However, several years later, when I had been teaching in a room at The Other Place and was just finishing for the day, there was a knock at the door and there he was back again in another lead role. I said, 'Hi, how are you?'. 'Alright-ish', he said, 'but I'm here this time to tell you that I'm now ready to look in the mirror.'

That moment started four years of working with this actor. I realised through this experience that sometimes there is a right time for the pupil to begin to work on themselves. It must be when they are ready to unlock the casket of goodies and to take a look at the possibilities that are within them and in all of us.

I feel that using the mirror, especially at the beginning of the lessons, is so important as right away we are going through exactly the same process as Alexander did. It teaches the pupil to have an all round awareness of how they are, without judging themselves. It is so easy to slip into thinking, 'the hair isn't right' or, 'I shouldn't wear that colour'. Rather, to quietly observe where they are, and then they can see the result of their work, guided by me, at the end of the lesson.

So the message is, 'Don't be afraid to look in the mirror', which is what was happening to the actor I was teaching. We are so full of fear about what we are doing, whether we are being quick enough, can get there fast enough, well enough. This is what society is pushing us towards on a daily basis – so that we tend to rush through life not enjoying the present moment – what is happening NOW.

8. Group Sessions

On the whole actors were extremely reliable about cancelling lessons they could not attend and there was a great sense of valuing their sessions. Last minute cancellations happened however. It might be due to rehearsal calls, a voice session, costume fittings, you name it – I would then phone others to fill the space, generally boxing and coxing.

This lack of time for the actors meant that I was asked to do group sessions. When a director suggested it, I went in before the rehearsal and explained Alexander to the cast. The first time was frightening, as I had never taken a group of pupils before and had to work out what would be most useful for them. I had not been taught how to cope with more than one pupil at a time in the training course. Marjory felt that hands on experience was the only way. I was very nervous speaking to so many people (another great learning curve) and I had to hide my lack of experience. First of all, I had them all sitting in a circle around me and then asked each individual his or her name and any problems they might have. To get their attention and hopefully their interest, I also asked them which part they were playing.

This was a format I continued to follow. After explaining Alexander's journey briefly I would get them all lying down with books under the heads, talk through putting their legs up and down, lifting their arms, rolling their heads gently from side to side, all the time inhibiting and directing. They experienced feeling their backs, their stomachs releasing, their breath flowing and beginning to release unnecessary tensions.

I then asked them to watch me from the side whilst I sat in and rose from a chair knowing that I was imitating them and, as I say, the rest of humanity. This showed them how the whole movement can be thrown out of balance. The neck tightens which then creates a general shortening of the whole body. This then constricts the lungs and reduces their effectiveness. The movement also uses much more energy than is necessary.

I point out that I do not look as if I am occupying my body as my mind will probably be elsewhere and also I would not have had a clue about what was actually going on. I then demonstrate the difference when I am thinking, giving myself my directions.

The danger of demonstrating in this way is that the pupils will then try to imitate me. I have always observed that pupils will try to 'do it' anyway, so when guiding them in and out of the chair my hands observe when they are 'doing' it and will go through it again. When they are just thinking the directions, they feel the lightness as they fly in and out of the chair.

For performers, it is rather important that they do 'look present' whenever they are on stage or in rehearsal, that they are 'in' the part they are playing and that their minds are not elsewhere – especially when they may have a very small part with only a couple of lines or even no lines at all – they still have to look as if they are part of the performance.

I remember one actor who had the very small part in The Histories Cycle, directed by Michael Boyd. He didn't even have one line to speak but was on stage a great deal of the time. Michael spent a great deal of time during rehearsal getting everyone to imagine what the life of this young soldier was so that he became a real person to be aware of. This gave the actor so much more confidence and a feeling that he was a very necessary part in the play.

Getting the pupil to work on themselves is, was and always will be of prime importance so I always try to find a room with a wall for them to work with. Often I would take everybody out in the passage and use the walls there. Here I learnt such a lot from their reactions and feedback. As we have seen earlier, it was necessary to make sure they were breathing normally and not tightening their stomach muscles as otherwise many of them would begin to feel faint. Another reaction was to throw their heads back so that they touched the wall, I found that I had to go to each pupil checking by putting my hands on them and talking to them all the while – explaining what I was doing.

9. Unforgettable Moments at the RSC

Right at the beginning of my time at Stratford, Sue Fleetwood, whom I mentioned earlier as the very first actor that I taught, came up to play Beatrix in *Much Ado About Nothing* and Rosamund in *As You Like It.* She was delighted that I was there so she could resume her lessons.

Sue became a close friend. She was such a wonderfully talented, funny actress, with a great sense of humour, that I would sometimes ache with laughter after our times together.

Dear, lovely Sue tragically died of cancer at the age of fifty and will be forever missed by her family, the many friends who loved her and the theatre and acting world to which she gave so much. My first visit up to Stratford was to see Sue in *As you Like It.* She invited me up to her dressing room. It was a heavenly day and she made me feel so special. She was in the leading ladies dressing room, which looked out over the river, and everything seemed so exciting. At the time I never dreamt that I would one day be up there amongst it all, but of course I was in for a great surprise and change in my life.

I went a great deal to The Other Place, which in those days, before the rejuvenation, was rather like a tin hut with a corrugated iron roof, with dressing rooms that were very uncomfortable – but it had a great atmosphere and was very popular. The audience seemed impervious to either the intense cold in the winter, or, in the summer, the very often quite debilitating heat.

I do remember one evening in 1984, however, when Frances Barber was playing the whore Marguerite Gautier in the Pam Gems adaptation of Alexandre Dumas' *Camille.* It was summer and there was not a breath of air, the audience and cast alike battling with perspiration. A woman sitting in the front row suddenly collapsed in a faint onto the edge of the stage at the very moment when Frances was doing the very dramatic death scene. Frances bravely carried on dying whilst the woman was carried out and revived in the wings.

I've talked before about the brilliant cast of *Les Liaisons*

Dangereuses, which included Lindsay Duncan, Juliet Stevenson, Lesley Manville, Fiona Shaw and Alan Rickman.

When, later on, they transferred to the Ambassadors Theatre in London, I visited several times and worked with them there – setting my table up in the rather strange green room affair. The room was hardly big enough to swing a cat. Actors made and quaffed tea around about me and the person I was teaching, but somehow it all worked out.

One day, they had a great surprise as they had no idea that Paul Newman and Joanne Woodward had apparently come unnoticed to a matinee performance. When they left, there was a bottle of champagne for every member of the cast with a note thanking them all, and saying that seldom had they seen such superb acting.

Lesley Manville was at that time a girlfriend of Gary Oldman and suggested to Gary that he should have some Alexander lessons. He was at the Royal Court and was having troubles with stress and back pain. I was teaching at home and so Gary came to see me there, and went on seeing me on and off for quite some time. On one occasion, he turned up at the same time as the actor Jim Hooper, who had brought Tony Sher's mother for an Alexander lesson under instruction from her son. Jim and Gary had a great time over coffee while I was teaching Mrs Sher. She came into the room asking if I minded if she took her wig off. I managed to take it calmly, to say lots of NO to myself. To my relief she was not bald but hadn't had time to go to the hairdresser.

Then Gary was cast in the film *Sid and Nancy* playing Sid. He came for help again, as he had to lose weight, a great deal of it, to really look like a drug addict and his energy levels were therefore very low. He would arrive at the front door as a Sid look-a-like with greasy spiked hair, contact lenses with pinpoint irises and torn leather jacket and trousers. Not a pretty sight. I reminded him that I had to live there so goodness knows what the neighbours would think. I put him on a nourishing brown rice, vegetable and fish diet with vitamin pills.

He said that he found the part difficult as he did not really know what the behaviour of a drug addict would be like. By chance at that time, for personal reasons, I had had a great deal to do with Al-Anon, Alcoholics Anonymous (AA) and Narcotics Anonymous (NA) and suggested that I took him to an open NA meeting. It was hysterical as we went with Gary looking as I have described. He was extremely nervous and asked what he should say when it came around for him to introduce himself. I told him just to say that he was Gary, a newcomer, and I would say I was a family member. He had a very friendly reception and, as always, at the end of the meeting everyone came up to us to make us feel welcome and offer words of encouragement. At a later date, Gary met up with the real Sid's actual dealer – and that then led to a meeting with the real Nancy's mother – so Gary gained great insights into playing the character Sid.

Another time, I was giving lessons to the actor Richard Vernon who had a very distinguished career in film and television. He appeared frequently in *Yes, Minister* and *Yes, Prime Minister* as Desmond Glazebrook and he had now been asked to play a much younger man, a young lover who was having an affair with the heroine of the play. This was quite a challenge because Richard was very bent and also suffered from severe back pain and needed to appear several years younger than he looked. I worked a lot with him using the wall exercise and it made a great deal of difference. I took before and after photos from the side to encourage him and tried to prevent him from always looking down at the floor. His response to this, which made us both go into fits of laughter, was to say, in his rich, fruity voice, 'I see, Sue, so you want me to walk in the dog shit.'

More excitement was generated in 1984 with Bill Alexander's production of *Richard III*. Antony Sher caused quite a stir with the way he played the title role – looking rather like a giant, evil spider, a terrifying monster manoeuvring himself around the stage on crutches. This was a real challenge, but in spite of constant offers to help him with his back – I could see what he was putting his body through in the performance and knew that Alexander could help him – he much preferred to take help from physiotherapy. We would joke about it sometimes and when he gave me his book, *The Year of the King*, the inscription read, 'With love to Sue, from the cripple that even you could not help'.

However, I taught many of the cast. Penny Downie who played Lady Anne, Patricia Routledge who played Queen Margaret, Christopher Ravenscroft who played Henry Earl of Richmond and Jim Hopper who played Sir James Tyrrel and the Ghost, were amongst those I taught.

That production received rave reviews and Antony received the Laurence Olivier award.

Watching him limp always in the same way inspired me to suggest to any actor who had to limp in the part, to swap sides so that using, say, the left leg all the time did not throw his balance out and become a habit and to go over to the right side sometimes would prevent that happening.

Patricia Routledge always complained about her feet and said that she hated them because they hurt and looked unattractive. I suggested that she should learn to love her feet, which was a direction that she never forgot. On one occasion I was in the Lyttleton in the front of the stalls and I turned around and saw she was sitting with a friend just behind me. Pat, in strident Hyacinth Bucket tones, introduced me to her American friend as Sue, her Alexander teacher, 'Who always told me to love my feet'. There was a great deal of head turning, not to look so much at me, but at Patricia, as they recognised that unmistakeable voice.

Pat was such a lovely person and an incredibly warm and funny woman. I will never forget her kindness when, one evening, I was sitting in the green room before going to yet another showing of *Richard III* and she came in and asked me what the matter was. I told her that I had just phoned my daughter, to find out her results and learned that she had obtained a first in Botany. I was, of course, pleased for her but feeling very sad as I just wished I were with her to celebrate.

'Are you coming to the show?', she asked. When I said I was she told me to go up and see her afterwards, which I did, to find that she had bought a bottle of champagne. She opened it and we drank a toast to my girl.

Then there were the Hamlets. I worked with Roger Rees in 1984 with his Hamlet, with Samuel West in 2001 and then with Toby Stephens in his Hamlet in 2004.

Toby was so reliant on his Alexander sessions that I was paid to go up specially on his press night, which made me feel very honoured. His interpretation of Hamlet was that of an overgrown schoolboy, with all the fears and insecurities of adolescence. This became blown up into a state of madness when the discovery of his uncle's treacheries combines with his passionate adoration of his mother.

Later, in 2008, Greg Doran's production of *Hamlet* came to The Courtyard Theatre. It featured David Tennant as Hamlet, Patrick Stewart as King Claudius and the ghost of Hamlet's father and Penny Downie as Gertrude. It was a sold out success. This was probably mainly due the title role being played by David Tennant, whose performance as the *Dr Who* time lord seemed a very good jumping off point for the most challenging and famous of all the Shakespearean characters.

I worked a great deal with Penny Downie and others in the cast, but could not persuade either David or Patrick to come for Alexander. David wanted to, as he had very bad back pain, but time conspired against us. Eventually he had to have an operation and take time off when the show went to London.

Juliet Stevenson and Fiona Shaw set up a campaign in the early eighties to get women directors into the RSC. Since Buzz Goodbody there had been a real dearth of them until in 1987 Deborah Warner directed *Titus Andronicus* with Brian Cox as Titus. I taught a great many of the cast, but the Isabella Bywater's set, dramatic as it was, created a great deal of dust, which affected the actors' voices adversely. The dust affected Brian in particular who was also suffering from a great deal of tension in one way or another. He was very anxious about his lack of fitness, so I sent him off to Dr Sham Singha, my doctor, to see if he could help. I warned Brian that he might have to do as he was told, dietwise, as he was a bit overweight. Sham put him on a week of nothing but grapes to eat. This meant seven lbs of grapes a day, no alcohol, no fags and nothing to drink except water.

Brian was very obedient and survived the week – and the ensuing weeks of raw foods too. It had the desired effect – his voice was back, he lost weight and generally felt a deal more energetic – and was able to tackle that extremely difficult part with great success.

Some months later I was walking down Barnes High Street where I live and I bumped into Brian, who also lived in the area. He was clutching a paper bag with grapes in it and his mouth was full of them. He had had to go back on to the grapes again apparently as the weight had crept back up, his energy was low and he needed to get back to strength to cope with another play that he was rehearsing.

The production of *The Rover*, directed by the legendary John Barton, moved in 1987 from Stratford to The Mermaid. I was teaching there and had a call for help from the stage manager asking if I could go in to help Jeremy Irons one Saturday as he was in trouble with his back. I went up, of course, and did my best to alleviate the pain. He had a pet rat, Miss Ratty, to whom he was devoted, who would sit in his pocket. She was very beautiful – a sort of silky brown and white colour – and surprisingly tame. She was so tame and friendly you almost forgot she was a rat. We dared him to have her sitting in his pocket in the show – she would have fitted in with his raggedy costume. I think he was sorely tempted, but it might have emptied the theatre pretty quickly, so Miss Ratty stayed in her cage in his dressing-room.

That was one of those many occasions when I just went to the 'rescue' but, perhaps foolishly, didn't ask for any money from the RSC for the trouble taken. I taught many of the *Rover* cast including Stephanie Beacham. Stephanie, of *Dallas* and *The Colby's* fame, had a great many lessons and was quite paranoid about me providing a receipt for each of her sessions. I found this amusing at only £8 a go. But I did as she asked.

Then there was John Wood. John, who died in 2011, came to me for a few lessons in 1998 whilst playing Prospero in *The Tempest*, directed by Nick Hytner. He was described by the critic Michael Coveney as 'sulphurous' and 'a craftsman of the mind'. I found John rather daunting to work with, as I did with so many of the actors, great and not so great. Indeed, Michael went on to say that 'John Wood's Prospero outshone even Gielgud. Such a simple name, such a complex actor. As with all great actors you know what they are thinking, all the time. John Wood has a brain on a stick and he wields it mercilessly.'

With many actors, especially the great ones, I felt that I wouldn't be able to teach them anything and frequently asked myself why were they coming to me anyway? However, I was always surprised at how they listened to my explanations, seemed to be very grateful for the guidance and would come back again and again for help.

John and I were to meet again later on in 1990 when there was a sequence of events which is etched very clearly in my memory. He was playing King Lear directed by Nicholas Hytner in a production at the RSC. At the very same time Brian Cox was also playing King Lear but at the National in a production directed by Deborah Warner.

John was in a great deal of trouble with his back, so he came to me for lessons practically every day when I was in Stratford. Then when I came back to London he would travel and come to see me in Barnes. I was still rather in awe of him, as he was rather a forbidding man, but he seemed to completely rely on me giving him lessons. He had me sit in on the rehearsals in the Ashcroft rehearsal room to watch what he had to do and then give him notes.

John was a chain smoker and was the only actor allowed to smoke in the rehearsal room. He claimed that he could not do without the cigarettes for any length of time.

One day he said to me that he thought it would be a good idea if I came to stay in his house whilst he was rehearsing instead of staying in my Bed & Breakfast. He pointed out that it would save me money and be much more convenient for lessons. It was winter time, so I agreed and followed him back down endless country lanes to what turned out to be the most magnificent Jacobean Manor House, which had been re-modelled in 1663. It was late when we arrived and neither his wife nor children were there. I have to say I felt rather nervous as it was so dark and gloomy. He made me a cup of tea in the kitchen by the Aga and then showed me to my bedroom. The hall was oak panelled, as indeed were all the rooms downstairs, and the bedrooms too I discovered – my room had a four-poster bed, dressing table and basin and a big window looking out over the garden, which of course I couldn't see until the morning. John bid me goodnight and said he was across the landing – and to come down and help myself to breakfast in the morning.

I had a very strange night with not much sleep but eventually managed a few hours' rest and woke early to the sun pouring in through the window. In the kitchen there was no sign of John – but he had left me hot coffee on top of the Aga, which I took out into the garden. There I found him sitting in a cloud of smoke at a table in the middle of the lawn, which was very overgrown and sparkling with dew. He was going through his lines out loud and waved vaguely in my direction. I wandered off to explore around the back of the house and grounds. It was very different in the daylight, not so forbidding, very fine and a sort of fairy-tale, dream house. The garden was wild and overgrown, but full of colour and flowering shrubs and I could have wandered around exploring for hours. The whole house and grounds had a very Chekhovian feel about them. Later John talked to me about how he could not really afford to keep it up and often had to take film work in America to finance it all. He described it as 'The most magical house in England' – and I could quite understand.

The next time I visited, John's wife, a little, warm generous woman, was there presiding over the Aga. She was a great cook and there was always a smell of deliciousness coming out of the kitchen. I went on to teach both of John's children at the RSC whenever I could.

It gradually became clear really why he wanted to see me so often – although I know I helped him a great deal – he was using me to find out what was going on in the Deborah Warner *King Lear.* I was in the most extraordinary position of teaching both companies at once. The two productions were so different from one another because Brian Cox and Deborah had decided to put Brian, as King Lear, in a wheelchair that he manoeuvred around the set 'with reckless gleefulness' at great speed, and I seem to remember multi-coloured balloons floating around, all of which added to the feeling of confusion and madness of King Lear.

John's performance, on the other hand, was described as stark and frightening, revealing his Lear to be the triumphant destination that he had been travelling towards all his life.

Then there was another moment that I will never forget. During a production of *Hamlet* where Virginia McKenna was playing Gertrude, I was teaching Virginia who was living near Godalming. We had much to talk about because she had border collies, as did I, and we both loved the breed for their intelligence and affectionate natures. I was watching the play one night – the scene where Ophelia is lowered into the grave. There was meant to be an opening in the floor of the stage for her to be dropped into and it didn't happen, nothing moved. Virginia with great presence of mind said, 'Bear her to the graveyard'. A couple sitting beside me said to one another, 'That's strange, I am sure that isn't in the text'.

There were so many hilarious moments – another I remember happened with an actor playing Brutus in a production of *Julius Caesar* who was wearing very tight, velvet pants. He bent over Caesar to stab him and precisely at the words 'Et tu, Brute', with his bottom facing the audience, there was a tearing sound and the pants ripped all the way up the back seam. Luckily he was wearing underpants, otherwise it could have been rather embarrassing for the poor chap – and certainly not something that was in the script.

10. Down Under

When I first went up to Stratford in 1982, Trevor Nunn was the Artistic Director who was much loved but hardly ever there, hence my being able to use his office and desk for teaching sometimes. However, he was often in London and it was suggested that when I wasn't in Stratford, I should go to teach at the Barbican for a couple of days a week. This was quite a challenge because once again this was the first time, for the Barbican, that there had been an Alexander teacher in the company. It meant I had to go through the process of getting to know the actors and the stage door girls and boys, who were invaluable to me for messages, putting my sign-up chart on the noticeboard and so on.

My room was the children's dressing room, which was many floors down under – in the bowels of the earth. It had air conditioning, poor artificial lighting and was completely lacking in atmosphere, as indeed was the rest of the building. Everything was underground and the only redeeming features were the auditorium and concert hall as both were comfortable and had excellent acoustics. The auditorium also had these rather dramatic side panels, which closed up and opened rather miraculously all at once.

I was given tickets to see all the shows as I had been in Stratford. This was my way of getting to know everyone as I would go to the green room after the show and chat to them all. I remember being rather thrown when they seemed to genuinely want me to tell them what I thought of their performances and give them notes. I felt flattered that they were interested in what I thought, me, who had remarkably little experience of the theatre and I felt unqualified to give an opinion. It was the same in Stratford and I had learned to say what I thought – but only if it was constructive – which could be difficult if it had been a poor production. Rather like when a friend asks if you like their new coat and it is perfectly dreadful. The only way out of the problem is to find one redeeming feature, maybe the buttons.

And then there was the food – the quality was very dependent on whether the chef was in a good mood or not – but that is probably the same the world over.

There were hardly ever any children in the shows, so I also shared with 'animals', which would usually be dogs. One day I went in to find a small Cairn terrier like dog fast asleep in a basket who seemed quite unfazed by my presence. Her owner, however, was quite hysterical and rushed in and threw his arms about saying that she needed her sleep, that I mustn't upset her as she had a show that night, she was very sensitive and must be on top form. I eventually calmed him down telling him that I was a dog owner and had been a dog owner all my life. He went away pacified – during all this time the dog had slept quietly on and never once opened an eye. However, the room was a meeting place and it was there that I relied on talking to actors, directors and stage management as there was very little choice outside the Barbican in the way of cafés – and even if there had been there was no time to get in and out in time for the next lesson or rehearsal.

One day I went in and was met by the strangest sight. The floor, which was imitation parquet, looked as though there was the Loch Ness monster or some giant snake writhing around underneath it. In fact, it was a leaking pipe and the whole thing had to be taken up and re-laid, which meant bringing in sandwiches and thermos flasks till things were back to normal.

What I enjoyed most about teaching at the Barbican was that I was able to continue teaching the pupils when the show came up to London from Stratford, which gave me longer with each actor and proved very valuable. This helped with the normal problem of not having enough time with an actor – unlike those pupils who are taught privately at home. This was, as I mentioned earlier, the reason I made my teaching CD to keep some sort of continuity and to try to help the actors to go on working on themselves.

Always there was the interference of the loud speaker calling actors to the rehearsal room – impossible to turn off or even turn down – and it could be very funny. One day there was a new play being rehearsed (I cannot remember the name or the director) and the call was put out for all those involved in the masturbating nuns' scene to go to Rehearsal Room 2.

This provoked hysterics, for my pupil and me and that was the end of a peaceful lesson – however laughter can very often be just as good a tonic for an excess of tension. And there was plenty of laughter – not only on that occasion but on many others. There are endless stories about happenings behind the scenes, some of which I'll relate as I go along.

Here is a tale attached to a play put on in the Pit, the small theatre in the round at the Barbican. I made the mistake of taking a friend who was not very appreciative of the material because in one scene a guy on a motorbike drove in and swung it around enveloping the front row with unpleasant fumes. One elderly woman sitting there started to cough violently. This was followed by another actor coming in, turning around in front of the same woman, dropping his trousers and exposing himself. At this point she had obviously had quite enough and stormed out in a fury.

On another occasion, I was teaching Trevor Nunn's Personal Assistant, Kate, who was determined to get him to have lessons as he was very stressed and had back pain. She also wanted him to see what a help the technique was for actors. He was directing *Les Misérables* and it was still in rehearsal – all taking place at the Barbican.

Kate eventually engineered a lesson. It was to take place in his office in the lunch hour and I took my table up there filled with nerves as I had never met him before.

What I dreaded was the explanation that I had to give of the basics of the technique. He looked completely exhausted so I dipped out of taking him in and out of the chair. As he lay down on the table, I went through the explanation at the same time as I gently encouraged him to let go, to stop all the activity and stress that he had displayed when I entered the room.

During the lesson he said nothing at all and this made me feel very nervous as I worried that I was not getting the message across. However, at the end I sat him up and he turned to me and said, 'This is excellent, we should arrange for you to work with both the voice department and the movement department as your work and theirs' are interdependent. The set of *Les Mis* is causing a great many problems and there have been several accidents, which the technique could help prevent'.

The tragedy was that the next week I was going on holiday and when I came back, *Les Mis* had moved to the Cambridge Theatre and the moment was lost. I however went on to teach several members of that company. Craig Schulman who played Valjean, came to me on a weekly basis as the strain on his voice playing eight shows a week was tremendous and he came to rely on those sessions – he said they helped him more than anything.

Another memorable production was *Midnight's Children,* in 2003. This was an adaptation of the book by Salman Rushdie and was directed by Tim Supple. Melly Still designed an extraordinary set. There were a great many Asian actors in the cast. One in particular I remember came for a lot of lessons. One day I asked him where he had trained. He laughed and said that he had not gone to drama school – he hadn't needed to as he learnt to act whilst working in his job as a barrister. He said that he had found it a very easy transition.

On the ground floor of the Barbican there was a large paved area bordering the artificial lake, on the other side of which was a convent school.

On the Barbican side there was a sculpture by Elizabeth Frink called the 'Running Man', which was a naked male figure with a rather large penis. This was facing the convent. I knew Liz Frink and noticed one day that the sculpture had been turned around to face the other way. I happened to meet Liz at another exhibition and asked why this had happened. She laughed and said the Nuns had requested the re-orientation – they said that the girls could not keep their minds on their lessons, they seemed to spend their times looking dreamily out of the windows over the lake and at the naked man.

On the whole, I really found working at the Barbican very off-putting due to the dinginess and lack of fresh air. There was air conditioning everywhere and no windows or balconies to go out and gulp in some London air. Even outside on the paved area surrounding the artificial lake, the air was full of traffic fumes. As always I made friends with the Stage Door where we could have a laugh and a gossip. This was also where I put up my list for the actors to sign up for lessons. Very often, I rang up Stage Door to find out what was on it as sometimes I would not be on till the afternoon and so did not have to panic about getting in early.

One indelible memory I have is about that wonderful actress and friend, Sue Fleetwood. Sue would come to me for lessons at the Barbican. There was one hysterically funny time when she asked me out to lunch at the macrobiotic/vegetarian restaurant in Old Street. This was at a time when Sue was wrestling with her health, not knowing quite what was the matter with her and she was taking very great care with her diet. Diet was always a big thing with me too and we had the most delicious meal of beans done this way and that with huge plates of unusual salads.

I had a full afternoon teaching at the Barbican and was suddenly afflicted with the most terrible wind – farting fits so bad that I had to keep going out into the corridor and breaking wind between lessons because the smell was so horrific.

I couldn't wait to get home where I drank litres of peppermint tea and sucked peppermints and charcoal tablets until the affliction subsided. I went completely off being a vegetarian and the macrobiotic diet.

I wasn't sorry when the huge decision was taken in 2002 to move the RSC from the Barbican. From then on, productions were in other West End theatres like the Novello and The New London. Rehearsals were in the Clapham rehearsal rooms and one or two other smaller spaces nearby.

I didn't like going to Clapham as teaching space was again

down under in the bowels of the earth and was a sometime costumes store. I very often had old coffee mugs in it and was either freezing cold or very hot and stuffy. The Clapham green room also left much to be desired and it only had a hot water urn and tea bags. The urns were very unreliable – either boiling hot or tepid – and very often gave the tea a funny taste. Ugh. We went out for food but luckily there was a Sainsbury's on the corner and several cheap cafés in the same road.

Going to Clapham meant less travel but it also meant going through the whole business again of making myself known to everyone. It was not nearly so easy finding out who was on the list, so I had to go in and, if no one had signed up for the first slot, just hang around. However, I managed to get permission to go into rehearsals very often. This helped enormously as then the actors knew who I was and would come and chat and sign up.

Stage Management there were a great help as it was a light and airy office and I could get cast lists printed out. From these I could write notes to the actors letting them know the times when I was teaching.

Once again I had to push myself to promote the technique. I was very aware that I needed to be sensitive as to my place in the scheme of things. Arrogance and behaving as though I knew it all would not have been acceptable.

One of my best times was a big production of *King Lear* in 2008 when the same company was running *The Seagull* concurrently. Ian McKellen was playing Lear and insisted that the company had group sessions of Alexander before rehearsal. Then, during the whole rehearsal period, I saw many of the actors individually for lessons in both Clapham and at Stratford. The productions were later taken on a world tour and when they came back, exhausted, I went to the New London once a week and worked with them there. I became very fond of them all (which was always the case) and almost went into a state of mourning when the show ended. Ian McKellen always had a lesson before the show. On one occasion he had a very sore throat and was very tired. I gave him the remains of a packet of Oil of Olbas lozenges to soothe it. I always carried them, along with that rescue remedy Arnica and many other aids to help in an emergency.

He told me that he had gone on sucking them throughout the performance and at one point during a particularly long speech the lozenge shot out of his mouth and into the audience. It was reported that afterwards it was auctioned on e-bay and went for £25. A good story. I have doubts about the e-bay bit, but the rest was certainly true.

Interspersed with working at Clapham, I often went to the Novello Theatre where there was a show that had moved to the West End from Stratford. It was always a palaver getting my teaching paraphernalia in place, but the wonderful stage management would lug the table up to the room where I was teaching. One time I taught in the bar on the ground floor, which was rather unpleasant as there was a strong smell of old booze and, in those days, cigarettes. It wasn't very congenial for teaching.

Another space I had was just underneath what I believe was Cameron Mackintosh's office at the very top of the building. It made me feel rather strange because, as I mentioned earlier, in another life I had run a nightclub and had gone to a party in the flat of Ivor Novello – the same flat now occupied by Cameron Mackintosh.

It had been an eventful night as the lift to the flat was very antiquated and only designed to hold four people. Six of us piled in to leave at about two in the morning and of course it stuck, luckily just above the ground floor. We managed to break out through the very thin wooden panelling. I slit my black velvet skirt right up to my waist and went home in a taxi feeling very sheepish.

Later I worked at the Novello with the very successful *Much Ado About Nothing*, which had been in the Swan at Stratford. Then the David Tennant *Hamlet* moved there as well and, although I did not work with him, I did work with many in the company.

It was quite difficult to fit in working at both the RSC in Stratford and Clapham and then the increasing time at the National – looking back I am not quite sure how I did it. Because there were so many upheavals at Stratford, whilst the main house and The Other Place were being re-built, whenever I went up my teaching space was altered and there was the problem of the table being located and moved. When, in 2010, I moved house to my little Victorian cottage in Barnes, where I think I will end my days as I love it so much, working at the RSC came to a natural ending.

The voice department was no longer responsible for arranging my times to go to Stratford and I decided that, whilst I was moving, I could not teach at both theatres as it was too much stress.

I feel sad about this, but I did have a wonderful twenty-seven years with the RSC where I learnt and experienced so much. If I find a suitable young teacher who is interested in the theatre I will introduce him or her to Greg Doran, whom I know well. When I met Greg just after his appointment as Artistic Director and congratulated him, he said to go up and see him to discuss starting Alexander up again. He would be very willing to help.

I don't regret a moment of those years and have enjoyed reliving much of it in writing this book. Even now, I see the actors I had taught years ago at the RSC turning up in productions at the NT so in a way I have never left.

11. The RSC After Trevor

Working at Stratford went through many phases over the years I was there. It was very often a struggle to keep up the pace because there was constant change and different companies every season as well as the feeling of excitement with the promise of success and fear of failure. It was impossible not to be affected and caught up in the whirl of activity. Terry Hands took over from Trevor Nunn in 1986. I, along with many others, found him rather a formidable character. I went to the company meetings if I was in Stratford at the time and screwed up my courage to talk to him about Alexander and to get his assurance that my work would continue. He was famous for his dramatic appearances in either all black with black wide brimmed hat and a sort of black cloak like garment or, dependant on either his mood or the weather, he would change to the same but all in sparkling white.

Nevertheless, I made an appointment to meet him and discuss my position. Surprisingly he agreed and was quite charming and understanding and seemed to recognise the need for Alexander Technique lessons for the actors. He even said he might try it himself, but of course it never happened. It was during Terry Hands time that my payment per lesson went up to £10 (plus my travel and costs). He said that I would be welcome in the rehearsal room whenever I wanted, a very generous offer that I took advantage of whenever I was able. However, there was one very upsetting incident which is indelibly burned in my memory. At the time, 1991, I was teaching many of the cast of *Love's Labour's Lost* directed by Terry and several of the actors asked me to go in and give them some notes afterwards. I had agreed as it could be really helpful to see what they were being asked to do and suggest ways of avoiding stressful movements and using the technique in moments when they were not actually doing anything.

So I crept in right at the back and sat in the dark watching the rehearsal, which turned out to be a run through. When they broke for lunch, I went into the green room and the theatre manager, Sonja, beckoned me out into the passage, her face red with fury. She hissed at me, 'Don't let me ever hear of you going into a run through without the director's permission, that was totally unacceptable. Have you no idea what a sensitive moment that is for the company? You might have upset them all.' I felt as if I was back at school and managed to say that the actors had asked me to go in and that Terry had said to go in whenever I wanted. But she flew off, still in a fury, and it was weeks before she spoke to me again. Meanwhile I told the actors and dear Sue Fleetwood, who was particularly close to Terry, what had happened. Apparently he had only asked who was in the room as he could not see as it had been so dark. He seemed quite unmoved by it being me. I also unburdened myself to Cicely Berry, who was always comforting, and it all melted away – but for me it was never forgotten.

A great event in the history of the theatre was the opening of the Swan Theatre built on the site of the old memorial theatre, which was burnt down in 1926. I watched its progress every time I went up to Stratford and it was exciting watching it grow month by month. One time when I went up, they were doing a tour around the nearly completed Swan and I joined the group. It was very interesting, but I suddenly realised that there seemed to be no dressing rooms. I questioned our guide who was showing us around and he looked confused for a moment. Then he said that he thought that the actors would be sharing dressing rooms with the main house.

Knowing what the state of those rooms were, how they were already cramped and dark, I was horrified – even more so as the use of computer technology was becoming a larger part of the running of the company and this meant that several of the dressing rooms were being converted into offices – so less and less room for the actors. However, the Ashcroft rehearsal room at the very top of the Swan was a triumph. It had turret like windows with window seats and a view over the Warwickshire countryside and river, which was so very beautiful. Here was a feeling of serenity and creativity and the actors found the auditorium a joy to work in.

Another apocalyptic change to the RSC was when Adrian

Noble, who took over as Artistic Director from Terry Hands, landed a blow on the whole company from which many of them never recovered. He ended the contract with the Barbican and the RSC lost its London home. Although it had been a rather hated venue for the company, another London home had not, and has never, been found. He had dreamt up a 'new' Stratford with a re-building of the main house and the creation of a 'Shakespeare' village. Although at that time the company was heavily in debt, he ploughed on ruthlessly, downsizing loyal company members from heads of departments to stage hands. In particular, I remember the manager who had run The Other Place for some twenty to twenty-five years, coming back from holiday to find that she was being told to re-apply for her job having had no prior warning.

After a campaign supported by many of the leading actors, this plan did not come to fruition. In 2003, Michael Boyd took over, while Adrian went off to direct *Chitty Chitty Bang Bang.* Michael reduced the debt in just one year and went on to direct 34 actors in seven productions of Shakespeare's monumental History Plays, which became a phenomenal success. It was an exhilarating time. I came to know the cast well, moving from Stratford to the Clapham rehearsal rooms and then later to the Roundhouse, taking my table and cushions with me. I was very fond of 'my boys' and, over the years, have met up with several again.

One was Geoffrey Streatfeild, a very talented actor. I remember him particularly as Prince Hal in *Henry V*. Geoff has also appeared in several plays at the National where he has had Alexander lessons with me.

I was always short of money as even charging the actors £10 a lesson was not very satisfactory. Sometimes I did not receive even that money as they were very broke, especially the younger ones just out of drama school who maybe only said one word (or not even that) in a production. However, when I could see that they needed help, I just had to support them, which was madness as there was no real reason why I should support the RSC.

With the changeover of artistic directors from Adrian to Michael, I was once more put onto a different footing. I wrote to Michael, introduced myself and said I hoped he would not get rid of the Alexander teaching and me. I still have his letter, it was so charming. He said, 'Of course, Sue, we will weave you into our lives'.

And true to his word, I was woven into The Histories Cycle plays that Michael directed. These were Olivier Award winning plays for which he became so noted, probably more than any of the other plays he directed during his reign at Stratford. The Guardian said it was 'One of the great events in modern theatre'. To be involved was indeed thrilling. From then on, I was paid £150 a day when I was working plus the B&B, travel and per diem for food. I was only in Stratford two days at a time, usually not more than once a month and then in the Clapham rehearsal rooms some days.

I went to the *Henry VI, parts I, II and III* performances, all shown on one day, in my case a Sunday, which was enthralling. Twelve hours in total – with pauses in between for breakfast, lunch and supper. For me, with my scanty knowledge of that era, I gained an insight into the processes of Medieval and Renaissance politics. Shakespeare gives us a flavour of those times from the top to the bottom of society, nobility, brothels, beggars, tavern life and all. I left in a state of euphoria and quite how I drove back to London, I don't know – I was probably in no state to have driven a car.

On one occasion at Christmas, there was a Carol Service at Holy Trinity Church in which there were readings and songs from the cast of the Histories – and HRH the Prince of Wales was coming by helicopter from Highgrove for the occasion.

We all arrived very early as it was going to be packed. I managed to get a good place with several of the actors and was longing for a 'good sing'.

However, proceedings were delayed as the helicopter was very late. There were apologies from Prince Charles as there were very few chairs and we were all standing, rather cold, looking forward to the mulled wine and mince pies that had been promised afterwards in the Ashcroft room.

Prince Charles moved around talking to the cast and the stage management. He suddenly turned and walked towards me where I was standing clutching a glass of wine. I was asked who I was and I told him that I was an Alexander teacher. I said that it had been suggested that I contact him by a friend of mine, an Admiral who knew Prince Charles from lunches at Highgrove, as the admiral was convinced that Alexander would help your Highness. I was not all that nervous as I had already consumed the glass of mulled wine.

I had remembered that Prince Charles had quite recently fallen off his horse during a Polo match and he was walking and standing, rather like the Duke of Edinburgh, leaning slightly forward with his hands together behind his back. This looked as if he was in some sort of pain, but he assured me cheerfully that he had recovered from the accident and was well on the road to recovery. He looked forward to my letter.

As if it was an afterthought, he looked me up and down and said, 'I must say you have very good posture'.

I wrote the letter with great difficulty spurred on by my Admiral's wife and with strict instructions to never put 'you' anywhere but instead 'Your Royal Highness', which made the letter look very strange as one has no idea how often 'you' is written.

I sent it, along with my CD with Dame Judi and me on the front, to St James Palace. I received a letter back from a secretary in which it was said that 'His Royal Highness wished to thank me for the letter and CD, but was too busy to fit in lessons. I should get in touch with the Back Pain Association and mention his name, as he was president and thought they would be very interested in my work.' Obviously my mistake was to send it to St James Palace rather than Highgrove.

I learned later that it is very much a mixed blessing doing something in a freelance capacity for the Royals. It is apparently considered such an honour that you don't get paid anything at all. I'm glad it didn't come to heaving my table all over country or London at my expense in order to fit in with the Prince, however nice he seemed to be.

12. National Theatre Studio

Among the wonderful cast of actors in *Les Liaisons Dangereuses* was Lindsay Duncan and she, like many of the actors, have remained friends over the years. I worked with her a great deal at Stratford, particularly during a period when she was having a very difficult time in her personal life. Despite her troubles, she was going from strength to strength as an actress and meeting up with her again at the National Theatre was to herald a changing point in my career. It happened when I went to see her in the 1988 production of Tennessee Williams' *Cat on a Hot Tin Roof* where she was playing Maggie. It was a thrilling production with Ian Charleson playing Brick and Eric Porter had been persuaded to play Big Daddy. I went to meet her in the canteen for a cup of tea afterwards. It was so good to see her and she said that what I must do was get in touch with Peter Gill, the Artistic Director, at the NT Studio. They wanted an Alexander teacher to work there and she had told Peter that I was, 'the only one'. Of course I didn't take her seriously and anyway I thought how could I possibly take on the NT as well as the RSC?

So, I did nothing. The usual feelings of inadequacy took over. I felt paralysed with indecision and the worry of committing myself to working with another huge theatre company.

A couple of weeks later, I received a message from Lindsay on the phone and a post card too, saying RING THIS NUMBER NOW. I felt quite sick with nerves as I could not see how I could possibly manage to teach at both these big companies.

With a supreme effort, I pulled myself together and phoned Peter Gill's assistant, Diane Borger. We arranged for me to have an interview the following week. This was 1988, when Peter Hall was just leaving and being replaced by Richard Eyre as Artistic Director.

However, Diane Borger was lovely and I immediately felt at ease. Diane had worked with Peter Gill as his assistant when he ran the Riverside studios. At the National she was really doing the same sort of job as well as working closely with Sue

Higginson who was the Studio manager. I explained how I had worked things out with the RSC, giving six introductory lessons to each actor and saying what I would need in a work space. I then went to meet Peter and it was arranged that I should start right away at the Studio, going twice a week (Tuesdays and Thursdays) and being paid for each lesson (I think it was £10). This amount used to go up £1 a year, which was hardly riches, but I could use the car park for free and all the facilities – and there was a constant supply of pupils.

The National Theatre Studio was the first purpose built theatre workshop in the country. It was built in 1958 when they had not considered the Alexander Technique teacher's needs. I had to begin with the most extraordinary work space. It was a very small wood lined room with a huge semi-circular pipe going up to the ceiling which took up most of the room. It had a window, which looked out onto the road, The Cut, and there was just room for my table.

I had a chair and a mirror in the passageway outside my room which led to the room next door. This was occupied by writers and another door led into a rehearsal room – so there was a great deal of through traffic. Once again very little peace but I did manage a bit of quiet in the couch room with the door shut.

The arrangement was that each actor could have six introductory lessons and I used the format that I had worked out in Stratford. There, no one particularly minded whether they had six or eight lessons or whatever, but in the Studio they were fairly strict and I had to carefully record the number each actor had as I was only paid for the number of lessons I gave.

My very first pupil was Tim Pigott-Smith, whom I knew from his part in the television programme *The Jewel in the Crown* where he played the sinister Ronald Merrick who had one arm bitten off by a tiger. He was, at that time, playing Trinculo in the final Peter Hall production of *The Tempest.* Once again I was extremely nervous, but need not have been because Tim was so easy going. We chatted along and I explained Alexander's journey to him. He said I had helped him a great deal and came back for many more lessons. Over the years I have often met up with him and Pam Miles, the actress and his wife. She also came to me for lessons in Barnes.

I always remember that Sue Higginson, the Studio manager, whom I did not meet until I started, showed me the work space on my first day saying, 'There you are Sue, here is your very own office in the centre of London'. I felt very proud and flattered, and so excited, to now be part of two of the greatest theatre companies in the world.

Sue Higginson had not been at the Studio when I first arrived as she had been to Spain with the Tony Harrison play, *The Trackers of Oxyrhynchus.* The play had premiered in the ancient stadium of Delphi in 1988 and was later performed at the National in 1990.

There had never been an Alexander teacher resident at the National Theatre previously, so it was new ground again and I had to adapt to another way of working. The Studio was a laboratory for the theatre where play readings took place, and sometimes rehearsals, for the plays to be put on at the NT. There was always a young writer in residence and a young director too. There were other writers working on new pieces and often studio productions of their plays were shown to other directors from theatres such as The Bush or The Court.

It was always very busy with an air of excitement. Peter Gill helped me more than anyone to understand the workings of theatre. He was always sitting at the table in the coffee area surrounded by eager young actors listening to his pearls of wisdom and the wicked gossip about his days at the Royal Court where he was Director in 1970. He is a great character, a quite unique director, and still comes around to my house and has Alexander lessons when the back is in trouble. On many occasions he has had me working with his productions and will send actors to me if he thinks they will benefit. Over the years I have grown very fond of him and have great respect for his work as a director and writer.

When Peter visited me at home it was usually on a Saturday

and I had to reserve the whole morning for him as he would first of all talk for half an hour, then the lesson, which was always just table work for another half hour or more. Then off the table still talking and when I suggested I gave him a lift home as he lived quite near, he accepted. And if I had said I was going to Waitrose, he would come too before going home, so that really did mean the whole morning. What a wonderful director. I really value the times I was with him and what I learnt from him, though I don't think he learnt much from me, just had some relief from his aches and pains.

Thankfully I never had anything to do with the politics and the relationships between the NT and the Studio. However, Peter left and Sue Higginson took over the running of the Studio completely. There was a different, more business-like air about the place. More people ensconced behind glass doors having meetings, more computers and less sitting around and communicating over coffee and sandwiches.

A great character was Harry, the sort of caretaker-maintenance man, who was a fixture and had had this role since the beginning of time. He had a room at the end of the Studio, which was his domain, with a strange sort of Heath Robinson contraption that he used to 'work out'. Although he must have been well over sixty, he had very muscular arms and torso of which he was very proud. One wall in the Studio was covered in his extraordinary paintings – they were a bit like mosaics – and when he wasn't working out, he would be painting. It was very important to keep on the right side of him if one wanted something moved or a radiator repaired or new light bulbs – in fact any odd jobs that one couldn't do for oneself. You had to catch him in a good mood and butter him up a bit before he would help you out. He was also in charge of the car park, about which he was always grumbling. But that was a very important part of his job, to grumble and make sure you knew who was boss.

From then on I was involved in not only teaching actors, but directors, stage managers and designers. I remember well Alison Chitty, who had many lessons. Her job entailed spending a great deal of time bending over a table, drawing and painting. Alison was a highly talented designer for theatre and opera and I grew very fond of her. She always looked so pale and wore either navy blue or black with not a speck of colour to relieve the overall effect. I said that I wanted to see her in emerald green, or peacock blue, which would have looked wonderful with her pale skin and brown hair. Alison thought about it and eventually said that she could not do that as she would find that it interfered with her work. She said that she would catch sight of the colours out of the corner of her eye and it would put her off her stroke.

Another designer, who made the most spectacular masks, was Vicki Harris. She and I eventually became great friends. At first, she was working on *The Trackers of Oxyrhynchus* when it came to the National. The costumes were spectacular, the trackers had extraordinary masks and huge phalluses strapped around their waists, which waved about as they moved around the set.

Vicki was setting everything up for the press night and, just before the curtain went up, hundreds of balloons in the shape of phalluses were meant to drift down from the flies and into the audience. The balloons duly arrived about two hours before curtain up. However, the balls, which were red, were huge and appeared on either side of a tiny white phallus. Vicki panicked and rang the suppliers to reorder smaller balls with bigger penises. They arrived just in time for the show to begin.

For me there was more involvement in projects, for which I have Sue to thank. It was through her that I went on several marvellous trips – South Africa, Lithuania and Ireland. I talk about those experiences, working with actors from different cultures, in a later chapter.

Because there were always several young writers working at the Studio, I very often taught them as they would spend their day, sometimes with hardly a break, crouched over a computer and getting completely lost in their own world. The result was very often acute back pain and the Alexander Technique could be a great help. It also taught me a great deal about how to deal with this sedentary way of being. I called them my 'head cases' as life was only going on in their heads and they were completely divorced from their bodies. There was no connection. I would work a lot with them getting in and out of the chair and suggested that they only continued sitting for twenty minute stretches, after which they needed to get up and walk around for a couple of minutes before they sit down again.

When sitting, I would remind them to have their feet spreading onto the floor not curled up in a bundle under the chair or legs crossed. The screen should be at eye level and the computer directly in front of them. Ideally they should have a chair that swivels, so that in moving from side to side to read something or to make a handwritten note, they can still keep their necks free and their backs lengthening. I would try to make them aware of their shoulder joints and, when lifting the arms from the shoulder joint, to let the elbow lead the arm away from the body using that joint. When typing, whether they could touch type or not, to imagine they have a coin balanced level on the back of the hand so that the wrist is not collapsed onto the key board or desk top. If this happens, the shoulders will drop forward, support of the back will be lost and there will be stress created between the shoulder blades and the lower back. I tried to get across the importance, during these two minute breaks or at any time when just resting and 'thinking', of taking a moment to just check through the whole person with the directions. Just thinking neck free will release it. The back lengthening, knees forward and away and feet spreading onto the floor thoughts will centre you and give a moment of awareness and presentness. A creative moment.

I had the great privilege to teach many, now famous, writers who were born at the Studio. Colin Teevan, Mark Ravenhill, Richard Bean and Jonathan Harvey, to name but a few. Probably most well known of all was Alan Bennett.

I think Alan only had about six lessons in the end. Our involvement started when I went to a talk he was giving about his latest book just before the book signing at the NT.

I was struck by how very tall he was and how collapsed his whole back was whilst sitting being interviewed. The queue for the signing was very long. A friend and I had a couple of glasses of wine and this boosted my courage to speak to him when my turn for the signing arrived. I told him that I was the Alexander Technique teacher at the Studio and that, should he have any issues with his back or neck etc., he was entitled to free lessons. He immediately looked very interested and when I went in the following week, he had signed up.

On this particular day, the room next to my teaching room was being used for rehearsals for a new work. Indeed, every available space was being taken up by two actors at a time going through their lines. The two actors next door were repeating just two lines over and over again, this way and that, and the two lines were:

'I see.'

'All you want to do is to get into my f…ing knickers.'

I thought that no way could I give a first lesson to Alan with that going on next door, so I rushed down to Sue and told her. They were moved immediately.

I often wished that I had made a recording of his lessons because we had such laughs. He was mostly telling stories about his parents as one or other of them had the beginnings of Alzheimer's and the things they said were so very funny. His stories were told with such love and kindness and in no way was he being derogatory.

Several years later he wrote two short plays, *Hymn* and *Cocktail Sticks,* about the relationship with his parents and his feelings about his childhood with so much truth, baring his soul to us all. I saw both of the plays and in a way, I found them the most touching of anything he has ever written.

Then lessons finished and, as happens, he was off the NT circuit for some time. When he was back with *Wind in the Willows,* and everyone was in the coffee area chatting, Alan suddenly extricated himself from the others, came across to me, asked how I was and then said, 'I always think of you in the mornings, and I think NO and tell my neck to be free.' It never ceases to amaze me that pupils remember the basics of the technique, long after their lessons have ended. So often I am not at all sure whether I have been making any sense to them when I'm explaining the principles. Often I have too short a time with pupils to be of any help, which can be very frustrating.

I had one more meeting with Alan when he was leaving after the press night of *The Habit of Art* when he once again asked how I was. He said that he kept telling his partner that he needed to come and see me, but so far that hasn't happened.

Jonathan Harvey, another young writer, came to me for many lessons. We got on so well – he had such a wonderful sense of humour and there was so much laughter. Jonathan was so obviously gay and was always camping things up, so one day I asked him about 'coming out' and if it had been difficult to tell his parents. His mother in particular had been very understanding and supportive. He lived in a large block of council flats and the main problem had been the neighbours who inevitably gossiped about him and his family, which had made it extremely difficult for them to cope.

Then in 1993, the play *Beautiful Thing* made the headlines. It was the story of two young gay teenagers on a Thamesmead estate. It was told with tenderness, a fondness for the inhabitants of the estate, and depicted the neighbours' intense disapproval and lack of understanding. Although homosexuality had been legalised since 1967, it was still frowned upon by much of the population. I realised that what Jonathan had been telling me was his own story, which he had then entitled 'Beautiful Thing'.

Sue Higginson was wonderful in the way she included me with so much that was going on at the Studio. There was great excitement one day as Sue and Diane Borger had managed to persuade Dirk Bogarde to come to the Studio. Dirk had just lost his long term partner and published

A Short Walk from Harrods. He had taken a lot of persuading as he was still grieving and Sue had found that the answer was to build up his confidence with a good supply of whiskey in her office beforehand.

It was wonderful to see and hear this famous actor, writer, icon, in the flesh. He had been asked to talk about working with various directors in films. I remember him mentioning Sam Peckinpah. Dirk said that he had had absolutely no sense of humour. Sam, he said, had only laughed once, when an actor had been in such a hurry to get dressed for work that he had stuck his 'cock' in the drawer whilst he was shutting it.

I was very interested to hear about the preparations he made for work. He knew that he never did the same take twice, each time it was always different. He added that there were always discoveries to be made and tried out during the performance.

Another very exciting meeting was with Billie Whitelaw, now a much older woman, but still full of energy and vitality. She was to talk to us about her time working with Samuel Beckett, the plays he wrote for her and her essential role as his muse. His reliance on her was almost total and he referred to her as 'the perfect actress'. Although she did not perform the initial *Not I,* she went on to do many performances and it became the part for which she probably received the most acclaim. We were shown videos, clips from those shows, the mouth, her mouth twisting, moving eerily against a black background, whilst Billie talked about her relationship with Beckett. It was almost surreal.

I have lost count of the *Midsummer Night's Dream*s I have been involved with. There was always a production at either the RSC or NT. But one has always remained in my memory, not for the performances or the clarity, but for the production itself. This was the 1992 production directed by the Robert Le Page, the celebrated Canadian director, a visionary and probably the most challenging and chimeric director of our time.

The set was muddy, to say the least. The stage was covered in it. The stage manager's real nightmare, not a dream.

I worked mainly with Sally Dexter, Titania, who suffered from a great deal of back and other aches. She spent much of the time with her almost completely naked body coated in mud and hanging upside down from a wooden structure.

It was very difficult to help her, other than bringing her back to some sort of balance after the experience.

My memory includes seeing the show from the third row of the stalls and getting covered in a fine spray of mud. Only the first two rows were given plastic sheets to cover themselves. I had on a new navy-blue, linen jacket, which I sent to the cleaners immediately afterwards as it had not escaped the mud.

Another time, I was rung by Tom Stoppard's secretary asking me if it was possible for me to give Tom some Alexander lessons. He was suffering a great deal of back pain mainly due to writing such a great deal at the desk. This meant that I would have to take my table to his flat in Chelsea Harbour. Of course I agreed, even though the thought of it was rather scary. Whatever was I going to talk to him about as here was one of the brightest writers of all with a fearsome intellect. Once again I felt I would not be able to cope with the conversation, as I was bound to come across as not too bright and uninformed. However, it never actually happened as he kept being called off to France, or somewhere else, and we were never able to fix a solid date.

Prunella Scales was an absolute scream to work with as not only is she extremely bright, but also very funny. She stood in front of the mirror and, taking a good look at herself, suggested she took off her clothes, as she didn't mind a bit if it was easier. I suggested that it might be a bit too much for the writers with John Burgess going back and forth into his room. Also the actors' attention would be diverted when going into the rehearsal room. 'Darling', she said, 'I don't mind a bit. Think of Ian Mac – he always strips down in the rehearsal room and he has a wonderful body'.

Anyway she was dissuaded and I really enjoyed working with her. But I was never quite sure whether I was of any help, as she said that everything would be alright if I just told her 'What to Do' and she would 'Do it'. I felt that I had not exactly got the message of Alexander across to her, so I just tried to relieve her aches and pains.

To finish off her six free lessons, Prunella asked if she could come to me in Barnes as she only lived just down the road in Putney. I asked Sue and she said, yes, just for the one time, as the Studio could not make a habit of paying for actors to be taught in my home. So along she came.

I was in fits of laughter again as she said, 'Sue, I really want you to teach Timmy (Timothy West, her husband) as he gets no exercise at all.' Donald Sinden, a great friend of the Wests', had suggested that they should go swimming together weekly in the Putney pool. Pru said that this would not do at all as Timothy had negative buoyancy.

In the end the idea of giving lessons to Timothy thankfully didn't happen. In my experience, if a partner tries to get their other half to have lessons, it never works. It has to come from the person themselves.

There was another instance of the partner telling their husband that they must have Alexander and signing him up whether he liked it or not.

This actor, whom we will call John, always looked very stiff and as if he needed to indulge in a bit of letting go. He turned up for his first lesson looking really miserable and very fixed with tension.

I struggled through the lesson as gently as I could, but he so patently loathed everything about being touched. When laying him out on the table he obviously felt very uncomfortable. At the end, I asked him gently whether he might feel that this was not really his thing. With great relief, he agreed and visibly became much less tense. I suggested that he should put all the blame on me and to say I didn't think I could help him, in case his wife gave him a hard time.

In 1995, Richard Eyre directed *Richard III* with Ian McKellen playing Richard to great acclaim. This production was later made into a film. Ian asked to come and see me for some Alexander at the Studio as he was having trouble with his shoulder. Once again I was very nervous. I tried not to display it and, as he had never had any lessons before, went through the usual explanation. Ian was completely silent throughout. I felt that I had made a hash of it and that he would never come back. At the end of the lesson I asked him how the shoulder felt and he said that it was much easier.

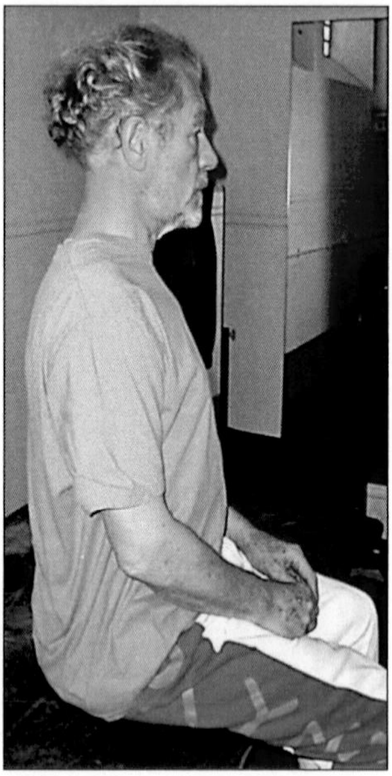

Sir Ian McKellen CH CBE after Alexander lessons

He sat on the edge of the couch and said he thought the whole of the company should have lessons – so what should we do about it? I realised that the reason he had been silent was because he was 'listening' and understanding, which in a first lesson is unusual. But then he is obviously a very special man. I was not used to pupils actually hearing and listening to what I am trying to explain in the first lesson. In fact, very often it takes at least four lessons before they seem to have an inkling of what's going on. Anyway we went straight down to see Sue and Ian asked for these lessons to be arranged immediately, which they were. I was in touch with the stage manager who then shipped actors across to the Studio. I also went into rehearsals at the NT to see what they were doing and where I could help, as always so useful for my teaching. The only person in the company who did not have lessons was Richard Eyre and it has always been a bit of a joke between us.

In 1989, during Richards Eyre's reign as Artistic Director of the NT, he directed Daniel Day-Lewis in *Hamlet* with Judi Dench as Gertrude. This production became infamous for the collapse of Daniel part way through. The cause was thought to be that he saw the ghost of his own father, Cecil Day-Lewis. Daniel later denied this and a more probable cause was put forward – *Hamlet* came along almost immediately after the highly acclaimed film *My Left Foot*, in which Daniel portrayed Christy Brown, the Irish playwright, poet and painter. Christy Brown, who had cerebral palsy, wrote holding the pen, paintbrush or pencil with the toes on his left foot – a very challenging role. I heard the full story the following day as Jeremy Northam, who was understudying Daniel, had to take over as Hamlet and was still in a state of shock. Jeremy said that it had been quite the worst night of his life, one that he hoped would never be repeated.

Meanwhile, the show had to go on. Richard Eyre, who was directing, was approached by Ian Charleson, famous for his part in *Chariots of Fire*, asking if he could be given the chance to take over as Hamlet. He had not long to live – and in fact had full blown AIDS. Richard agreed and, of course, this was a very well-guarded secret until Ian died just eight weeks later.

Tributes flowed in from all over the world, John Peter described his performance as virile and forceful, 'oozing intelligence from every pore'. In my teaching room, I used to hang posters of the shows that had been most important for me, or had pupils in them that I had taught. I hung one up of Ian and I went in one morning finding, to my great sorrow, that it had been stolen. When I went to find out if there were any more I was told it was unrepeatable.

Sue Higginson had lessons frequently. She was very tall and

tended to stoop as, 'everyone else seemed to be shorter', she said. What was wonderful about Sue was that she was always involving me in different situations for using Alexander. One initiative was a suggestion to young directors who were workshopping a new work or rehearsing a play to be shown to the Royal Court, The Bush or National. I would be asked to give group sessions before they rehearsed, which was very exciting. I had to learn different ways of coping with the different directors and adapting to what they wanted from me. I had to be very sensitive about how I helped the individual actors as the directors usually joined in with the group – on the whole they like to be in charge – so that if I were to suggest to an actor that they approach something from a different angle, there could be trouble. I remember Sean Mathias stopping me in mid-sentence saying, 'Stop there Sue, you're directing them. That's my job'. He said it jokingly, but I knew that he meant it.

For a few consecutive years, the Studio hosted the American Summer School, which entailed about fifty actors coming from all over the States for three weeks. During this time, they had sessions with teachers, directors, designers, stage managers and actors. They went to many productions at the NT and elsewhere, all paid for by their parents thankfully as it turned out to be a very expensive course.

Sue Higginson made space for me to teach these groups of students and suggested that I worked together with Helen Chadwick, a singer, composer and voice teacher. We worked with the Americans in classes of about twelve to fourteen at a time.

It was then that I really learnt such a lot from Helen, and she from me, about combining Alexander with voice. It was so exciting and having had only a little experience in Stratford with small groups and certainly not feeling at all confident, this was a new time for both Helen and myself to make discoveries. We planned the mornings in advance and discussed any problems that came up.

The Americans we met were very different from the Brits because they were longing to learn, willing to work and almost too enthusiastic. The down side was that they all had 'allergies' and big emotional problems too, which we had to take into consideration.

I would start off with sitting them down in a circle on the floor, take their names and, in my case, write them down as my memory is hopeless. Helen, on the other hand, could remember them all first time around.

I would ask them if they had ever had Alexander, which occasionally they had, as there are many teachers of the technique in America. I'd then explain Alexander's journey, have them lie down with books under their heads and talk them through gently moving their arms and legs, heads turning from side to side, breathing, whispered ahs, all with inhibiting and directing. Right away it was important that they had the right thickness of books under their heads. I would go around and adjust the books as either too high or too low could result in tightening of the throat and inhibit the breathing and voice.

As we progressed on to further classes, we would go through it again and ask them to speak afterwards. The change in their voices was always very marked – more resonant, deeper and relaxed.

I kept asking for feedback and questions, which we found very valuable. With all of them sitting down, we'd pick one student to stand with me and choose a text – usually about twelve lines of something they knew well. I would ask the others to watch carefully, maybe jot down their observations or remember what they noticed, voice wise, physically or emotionally.

We'd ask them not to discuss it with anyone sitting next to them, but to wait until the actor/guinea pig has been through the process again. This time we started with my hands on them, encouraging them to think through the directions, getting the diaphragm working and making sure that they were standing with the feet planted so the weight was evenly distributed and they were balanced.

Then he or she would give the same speech without further

preparation. The effect was always surprising and the feedback full of praise. The voice, general confidence and presentation seemed to have changed quite radically.

This experience of having the actors combining voice and Alexander, using the technique with their work, was very gratifying for Helen, myself and the actor. After all, it was how it all started with FM Alexander and now here was the proof. It usually prompted a great many questions from the pupils, which needed to be answered. I tried to be careful not to tell them what to do, but how to find the answers through using the technique themselves.

It works if you work it.

From then on, Helen and I did a great number of workshops with groups. Occasionally I would manage on my own, which was very good for me as I became more confident. I always found that the secret was to get plenty of feedback and make sure we had lots of laughs. I think it so important that working with Alexander should not be a strict discipline and getting rid of the feeling that 'you have got to get it right' is critical. It is much more about letting go, relying on changing the thought process and using NO moments to do that.

There were many occasions for having a good laugh. I remember teaching a group of young opera singers from Morley College who came once a year to work with directors and actors. I would get them singing and was amazed at the power in their voices, but working with them with the technique was very exciting. There was one very tall Norwegian bass baritone who had the habit of squeezing his upper arms in towards his torso. I suggested that he imagined he had balls underneath his armpits. There was a short silence and then I burst into laughter, and to my great relief, so did the group. From then on the ice was broken and we all learnt a lot from each other.

There were occasions when the Studio offered young directors the chance to come and work with actors, designers, writers, directors and voice teachers. I found myself giving them a morning of Alexander, which to begin with was very daunting as I sometimes did not have Helen with me, but that was good for me.

I would follow the same group format of sitting them down on the floor, asking their names and finding out if they had ever had Alexander before. The answer was usually no. When I asked if they had been to drama school, it was fascinating for me because usually the answer was also no. Several had never acted, some were dancers and others just wanted to be directors.

I decided it was important that these budding directors should understand what they were putting the actors through. So, after the initial explanation, floor and wall work, I would ask them to bring in a piece of text for the next session.

It was extraordinary because many of them could not even remember a few lines of Shakespeare. One even brought in a nursery rhyme, which made him look rather foolish. However, I battled on. I tried to get across to them how important it was for them to understand that all the actors were looking to them for direction. If the director were slumping around, looking flustered and not confident, there was a danger that the actor would not feel safe and secure with their director.

The feedback at the end was usually very encouraging. I would then feel that I had achieved something and helped them, leaving them with something to work on – and the offer to have individual lessons was always there. I did, in fact, teach several of the young directors on attachment who are now fully fledged. Some have ended up at the National, Bijan Sheibani being one of them, who did carry on his lessons when I went across to the National.

In 2003, Mike Leigh was assembling a company to take part in *Two Thousand Years*, which he had been given an extraordinary amount of time to devise as this was his method of working. I was giving lessons to Alexis Zegerman, a lovely young actress and playwright. She came in one day with exciting news. Not only had Mike Leigh asked her to be in *Two Thousand Years* but she had also been commissioned to write a play for Hampstead to be shown the following autumn. It was called *Lucky Seven* and was very well received both here and in the States.

Alexis wanted to continue her lessons with me, but came in and said that Mike had forbidden her to continue. He did not allow voice or movement sessions. I met him in the Studio one lunchtime and asked him what he had against Alexander. Very angrily he said, 'I don't want you interfering with my actors so keep your hands off them'. The last part was said with a bit of a smile, but oh dear, I kept well away from him after that.

Occasionally Sue Higginson would ask if I could give a particular actor some help, even if they were just passing through the Studio for a play reading or a workshop. It was in this way that the wonderful actor Michael Gambon came for just a few lessons prior to being Othello at Scarborough.

Sir Michael Gambon CBE

I was and am a great fan, but thought I will have a job getting this man to lose his really bad posture. As well as his fame as an actor, he was almost renowned for his very curved back and shambling gait.

Michael was, of course, absolutely charming and after my explanation he caught on quickly. He would go out looking completely different and having grown at least about four inches, which amused him greatly. He would stride out into the studio saying to Harry the caretaker, 'Look at me Harry, I'm heading for six foot'. Michael also had the longest fingers and toes that I can ever remember seeing on anyone, male or female.

Several years later, I opened the car park gates for him and he climbed out of the car saying, 'I am saying NO and keeping my neck free' – which made me feel really good.

Sometimes I would be asked to go over to the National itself to work just before rehearsals. In 1995, Sean Mathias directed *A Little Night Music*, by Stephen Sondheim. This was so exciting as it was a chance to work with a cast studded with well known actors. It included Judi Dench whom I had met before, briefly, at my brother Simon's wedding in Kew. He married a cousin of Judi's, Helen Craig, and I was able to remind her of this at the end of the first session. It started up quite a long relationship with her before she starred in films and became world famous.

I was invited into the rehearsals and found it quite overwhelming to sit facing the whole cast coming towards us singing and dancing the chorus numbers. I made copious notes so that I could help them individually with using Alexander for breathing and voice. However, in a large group it was more difficult as I sometimes only had forty-five minutes to go through the great many ways of using the technique. As for the actors working on themselves, I continued to find the wall a great help in allowing them to feel their backs and what was happening when they took a breath, spoke or sang.

Having worked with Judi in *A Little Night Music*, she asked me if I could go over again to the NT to work with her during Rodney Ackland's *Absolute Hell* where she was playing Christine, who ran this seedy nightclub in the heart of Soho at the end of the second world war. It was described in The Independent as not only an archaeologist's treasure, but one of the most moving plays to hit London at that time. It said, 'It was the story of a "world weary" hostess of a drinking club where members gather to drink, escape, dream, and bitch, dream and destroy'. This was in 1991 and watching this, along with knowing all the other parts she had inhabited, I marvelled at her ability to play any character that she was given with such conviction.

Judi had several projects on the go and was getting very tired. I would go up to the dressing room with my table because there was no time for her to come across to the Studio. It very exciting to work with her and an opportunity to get to know her much better.

The last time I worked with Judi was in *Amy's View* by David Hare at the Aldwych when she was also filming, doing another episode of *As Time Goes By* and then going back every night to her home in Sussex. This required a great deal of stamina and quite how she did it was difficult to imagine.

Judi's dressing room at the Aldwych was for the leading actor, so she had used it many times in the past when working with the RSC and it was filled with wonderful memories.

She was such a generous woman and how we did laugh. Her fun loving spirit was always there and however tired she was, her sense of humour seemed to be unfailing. The lessons always ended up on a light-hearted note.

When I made the CD for my pupils to work with, she agreed to have a photograph of herself with me on the cover, which we set up at the National in Rehearsal Room 3. Somewhere I found the strength to ask her if she would do this. I don't quite know how, but Judi came in during a rehearsal, joked with my friend the photographer and, as usual, everyone fell in love with her.

After that I did not work with her again. She became a 'film star' and was off to the Oscars where she received an Oscar for her performance as Queen Victoria in *Mrs Brown*. I do remember her being so thrilled and excited about going. She had offers from all the leading designers to dress her for the occasion, Versace included, which she had declined as she thought the dress might be frontless or topless. Instead her chosen designer was Nicole Farhi, the wife of David Hare, who designed her the most beautiful dress for the ceremony.

Richard Eyre's revival of *Guys and Dolls* in 1996 was a roaring success – but funnily enough I cannot remember who I taught on that show. I am pretty sure I helped Henry Goodman, who created an unforgettable Nathan Detroit, as I taught him and his wife (a dancer) at Stratford. Clive Rowe, playing Nicely-Nicely, was always saying he was coming for lessons but thankfully never did. He was, is, rather large and I feared for the strength of my table.

One day there was a great surprise for me at Stage door. A huge package had been left for me, a large cardboard box about five-foot tall – with my name on it.

The staff on the desk were dying to know who it was from. So was I – and when I opened the note on the top, I saw that it was from John Heffernan. I told Stage Door it was from Colin Firth, just to shut them up. John was apologising for all the lessons he had missed or had had to cancel.

It was a large and very beautiful plant with no indication of the name – and I have never been able to find out – but it has dark green leaves and very graceful white flowers and is still thriving in my bathroom.

I had taught John through several of his performances at the NT and he is a fabulous actor. To begin with, we had quite a job with his posture. He was tall and gangly and inclined to stoop and look rather apologetic. All that has changed quite dramatically. His performance as *Edward II* proved that he is a very versatile actor who can be incredibly funny. He also played Hastings in *She Stoops to Conquer*, where he plays a whimsical fop who goes into ecstasies over the prospect of owning a gold coat. The play was also extremely moving, although unfortunately that production received very mixed reviews.

I gave lessons for quite some time to Mark Ravenhill who was our writer on attachment to the Studio.

Mark had become well known with his play *Shopping and Fucking,* written in 1996 for the Out of Joint theatre company. He then went on to write many more and is now with the RSC as their literary manager.

One day, Mark asked me if I would go up to one of the studios and watch him go through his latest play. It was called *Product* and, as he had never acted before, he wanted me to give him notes and generally help him with his voice and movement. He was taking this to the Edinburgh Festival and said he felt extremely nervous.

The play was a satirical monologue pitched to a silent actress who has fallen in love with a suicide bomber. Mark said that having written the script it made him cry, so he had to produce it. It was said of *Product* that it was society's desperate need for narrative and for closure after 9/11, an intelligent and immediate discussion of the media's response to terrorism.

Then in 2005, The Studio building became Grade II listed. This coincided with another change. Ed Mirvish of Mirvish Productions, who was the main funder, decided to withdraw his commitment to the National Theatre, even though he and his company had supported the NT since 1984. There then followed a period of uncertainty when everyone felt that they were going to lose their jobs and the Studio would be no more.

Yet another change was that Sue Higginson left, which for me was certainly a great sadness as she had always been a wonderful supporter of Alexander and had many, many lessons herself. So now, even thought I had fought so hard to keep Alexander going, I could see all my dreams of keeping it as an accepted part of the National falling apart.

After Sue left, during the inter-regnum when they were deciding on a new manager, Paul Miller took over. He was a very good director and very popular with everyone, but we all worried about the next boss and who it might be. Everyone kept a watch on who went in for interviews. Eventually Lucy Davies filled the space. She was a very popular choice and was very approachable and easy going.

For several months, there was still anxiety about jobs. However, at the eleventh hour, money-grants appeared, from where I didn't quite know and the National had somehow raised the money to secure the Studio for itself. Lucy Davies then found herself overseeing the refurbishment of the building. This was very extensive and meant we had to move to temporary premises in Brixton while the work was taking place.

Life became fairly chaotic, certainly from my point of view, as once again it was rather like working for the RSC. I found myself working in strange corners of the building with lack of light and privacy, dragging my table from one place to another – I hated it. I had very few pupils as they did not know where I was, so Lucy kindly suggested that I should see if there was room for me at the National itself. She told me to get in touch with Rosie Beattie who was the head of stage management. They had a room that was used by a masseur and chiropodist/ reflexologist. Neither of them were employed by the National, but had been generously given space for their practice.

It just so happened that one of them had given up a day and Rosie said I could use it on behalf of the Studio, who would still pay me rather than the National. So I put my list up outside the green room next to the rehearsal schedules where everyone could see it. In addition, information was given to every company employee in their welcome pack.

Immediately, the response was very encouraging and soon the list was full and overflowing. The teaching room was right in the centre of everything, just by the canteen, green room and Rehearsal Room 3. I began to gain confidence as once again I was seeing a new set of faces.

In this way, my life began in the heart of the National Theatre, which is where I had really wanted to be – and another dream seemed to be coming true.

13. In the Heart of the National

When I found myself in the National I noticed that there were many, many links with the past as actors that I had taught sometimes twenty years ago in one guise, returned in another. Plays likewise – you find that you have worked on several *Hamlet*s or *Lear*s. So, in writing these chapters, lives intertwine, friendships are renewed and this triggers memories, all with Alexander as a constant.

Working in the National Theatre I have been continually teaching Alexander, building relationships and the trust of all those I have worked with, maybe in the past and now in the present. My memories here are not necessarily written chronologically but very much as things come to mind.

There is nothing quite like being part of a working theatre where you are surrounded by a huge company of actors, writer, directors, designers, musicians and stage managers all with one purpose – to create and perfect some of the greatest shows that British theatre can produce.

Gradually I was introduced to the permanent staff, the people running various departments and I often had lunch with them, the press office staff in particular.

Alexander was open to everyone who was a member of the NT, so people from all areas of admin came for lessons. Everyone was so friendly and seemed to be glad to see me, so I very quickly felt part of it all even though I was still being funded by the Studio.

Lovely Lucy Davies, the Studio manager, had promised me a new room for when everyone returned to The Cut and I was to choose the colours. She asked me to talk to the architect about what chairs they should buy and what would be good for peoples' posture, back problems etc. Sadly, this never happened because, in 2007 Lucy left, we never quite knew why, and she was replaced by Purni Morell from the literary department.

Then one day I was told that, at the end of the month, the

new refurbished Studio building would be ready for all of us in Brixton to move into. It had all been very well done and was beautiful compared with the old scruffy rooms that we had been used to for many years, which we had all been rather comfortable with.

I was expecting to go back at the end of May when I received a call from Purni wanting a meeting with me at the National. She said it was to discuss my coming back to the Studio. It turned out to be one of the worst days of my life. She sat down, introduced herself and said that the Studio was now going to be run in a very different way. They were no longer going to be able to afford 'pastoral activities'. This meant no more Craniosacral practitioner, who had been working there for a few years and no more Alexander. I would be paid until the end of July and that was the end of it.

I was so shocked that I couldn't say anything at all to start with. Then I composed myself sufficiently to be able to say that I had worked there for twenty years and she couldn't just do that with so little warning and that it was really appreciated by all the performers and that I had taught all the leading actors as well. But she was immovable. The one concession was that I could still use a room at the Studio, but everyone would have to pay me individually. The Studio could no longer support Alexander.

I immediately rang through to Rosie Beattie, who had become a friend, and Trish Montemuro, also a friend and head of a team of stage managers. Tearfully, I told them what had happened. Rosie immediately said that I was to speak to Nick Hytner and to Nick Starr – and if that didn't work, she would help me start a protest campaign with the actors, which could be presented to Nick and Nick. I should also go to the head of personnel. Rosie and Trish were pretty sure that Purni could not just fire me without their consent.

After a large drink with Trish in the green room, I went home and spent most of the weekend composing a letter to the Nicks. I included one of my CD's with the photo of Judi on the cover. Having asked another friend, the director Jane

Howell, to run through it with me, I kept everything crossed and gave it to stage door to deliver to both Nicks – and sat back and waited.

I heard nothing, so e-mailed Nick Starr. I received a reply which said he was looking into the situation and would get back to me. Then, coming into the theatre one day I ran into him and he said cheerfully, 'Sue, the good news is that you're on, pop up to the office and we'll chat.'

So in 2007, with relief and excitement, I really did move, permanently, into the National Theatre.

There, actors could just slip in if they were not needed in rehearsal or at lunchtime before the show. Before, there would not have been time to come across to the Studio, so it was by far the best place to be. This became apparent because my list was always full to capacity and there were complaints that no one could get a place. This prompted me to ask Nick Starr for another day and after a bit of delay, I was given Thursdays as well as Fridays. Then with being asked to teach the puppeteers in *War Horse*, I taught one more day, this time it was Tuesdays. More of that fascinating experience later.

My teaching room was the Quiet Room right next door to Rehearsal Room 3. I requested a mirror and two chairs to work with and brought in a stool which I used against the wall as an extension of the wall exercise.

I always thought it was rather amusing to be called a 'Quiet' Room. On the passage walls were two quotations, one from *Hamlet,* 'The rest is silence' and one from *As you Like It,* 'Silence is the perfectest herald of joy'. But it was incredibly noisy. It was next door to the drum of the Olivier stage, there was fierce air conditioning which made strange noises and very often screams and shouts could be heard if there was a noisy production in the rehearsal room.

Then there was a vast safe up in one corner and an even bigger cupboard and the decoration, if you could call it that, was vile. Everything seemed to be 'shit brown', furniture, carpet and sofas. Later on when I became much more established I complained and was thrilled when around they came and I was able to choose the colour of the paintwork, the carpet and the new sofas. I chose a new mirror, a blind at the window and a notice board. I also framed posters of shows that I had worked on and put them on the walls.

The only problem was the safe which was incredibly heavy. They didn't know how to move it or what was in it. Eventually we realised that the NT priest had occasionally taken communion in the room and so thought that it could possibly contain the chalice. However, on trying to locate the priest it turned out that he had died. The only choice left was to 'blow it up', which I was invited to watch. Sadly, there was nothing in it, no hidden treasure. So it was removed, leaving a more peaceful environment to teach in.

The big advantage of the Quiet Room was that it was right next door to all the traffic going to and from the green room and the canteen – so it was very easy to find. My lists for pupils to complete were put up next to the rehearsal schedules so they could not be missed. I also put up notices saying when and where the Alexander lessons were, pinning them up on the notice boards just outside Rehearsal Rooms 1 and 2.

I asked for the cast lists from Stage Door and would write a short note to all the actors and put it in their pigeon holes. When they started rehearsing, I just wanted to make sure they realised that they could get free lessons. This information is always in their welcome pack, but often they are so carried away with starting at the NT that this is forgotten. Otherwise they will remember just before the run ends – and so miss out on all or some of their six lessons.

Gradually I came to know all the stage managers and many would come for lessons. I could then ask to go into rehearsals, which, as I've said, was always very valuable.

Because Alexander was a new addition to the theatre, I found I had to publicise it in the most sensitive way. I was constantly aware that I was a small cog in a big organisation. My confidence was still fragile since my initial shock with Purni

Morell, which in a way was a good thing. Gradually, however, I became bolder and as I saw all the shows, I would go up to some of the cast when they were in the canteen, chat to them about the show and introduce myself – and in this way encouraged them to come for lessons.

I then became even bolder and thought that it would be very useful if I could persuade directors to have Alexander. They would then be able to encourage the actors to do the same when they saw the value with their work. Whilst in the Studio, I had taught Ian Rickson, Polly Teale, his wife, and then Paul Miller, who later used me in two of his productions to give group sessions.

Sean Mathias, as I have said earlier, always used me to work in his productions. Many of the actors came to me afterwards for individual sessions. I have already talked about Judi – but there were others.

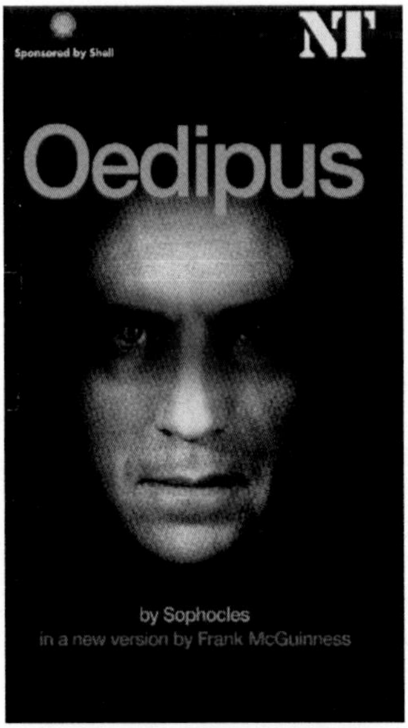

Oedipus, in 2008, was a much publicised production directed by Jonathan Kent starring Ralph Fiennes as Oedipus, Clare Higgins as Jocasta and Alan Howard as Teiresias, with the music written by Jonathan Dove. I taught many of the cast and several of the very strong, all male chorus.

In particular, the lead tenor Darren Fox, who had a wonderful voice, came for many lessons. I much enjoyed working with him and he too laid great store by the lessons. He was a quite delightful man and extremely talented. Darren was complaining of a tightness in his chest and a certain amount of pain, usually after singing.

I was very puzzled by this as I could feel with my hands a

blockage there, which was difficult to shift, even after using whispered ahs, breathing and voice with wall work.

Then, I came in one morning to find everyone in a state of shock. Darren had had a heart attack and died almost instantly. Mercifully not during the show, but because he was the lead, he was very difficult to replace with such minimal notice.

I went to his memorial service in The Linbury at the ROH where we heard a recording of him singing in the Pearl Fishers. I managed to get a recording sent to me by Darren's singing teacher, Arwel Morgan, who happened to have given me a few lessons. We met up after the service to share our sadness at losing such a lovely, talented young singer.

Later in 2008, there was a production of *The Year of Magical Thinking*, a memoir of the journalist Joan Didion. The book was about the death of her husband in 2003 and the illness of her daughter who died in 2005. It had been adapted and resulted in a one-woman performance by Vanessa Redgrave directed by David Hare. Vanessa gave a deeply felt performance, with moments of raw anguish. She showed the importance of being able to let go of devastating experiences, like that of Joan Didion.

Whilst Vanessa was in rehearsal, I saw her in the canteen one day and sat with her and chatted. I told her of my work as an Alexander teacher and, as is my wont, gently ran my fingers down her very curved back as she was sitting rather slumped over the table. This resulted in a series of lessons during which I came to know Vanessa well. She is a tall woman, but even so, quite soon her whole body seemed to change. It was quite miraculous and she grew about two inches. Not only that, the lessons seemed to be making a great deal of difference to the tensions that she was experiencing. Eventually, when she had begun the show, I would give her a lesson before nearly every performance.

We had a shared many laughs over her smoking habit. I noticed how she would pull down into the cigarette whenever she was on the balcony, inhaling deeply and losing the two inches of height immediately. I suggested she smoked the 'Alexander' way, which meant that she did not pull down when she drew the smoke in, but lengthened up opening out her lungs. Then exhale, still lengthening, until the air was completely expelled.

Vanessa Redgrave CBE after Alexander lessons

On the opening night at the party afterwards, Vanessa took me out on the balcony to meet Corin, her brother. In the same year, 2008, he was going to do a one-man performance of *De Profundis* reading the letters from Oscar Wilde to his lover Bosie, which he had written from prison.

I'd met Corin earlier when he played Lear at Stratford. It had been on the occasion of my first meeting with Vanessa when she took me up to congratulate him after the press night. I found it a very moving performance. He was following in his father's footsteps – Michael Redgrave had played Lear in 1953 to great acclaim. It had been said that his was one of the most powerful ever. Understandably Corin had agonized over taking the part, but he certainly triumphed over the fear of playing that demanding role, which was given a very different interpretation from that of his father's fifty-one years earlier.

At the National, *Honour*, a play by an Australian writer Joanna Murray-Smith, was one of the other times I saw Corin accompanied by a superb cast of actors including Eileen Atkins, Catherine McCormack and Anna Maxwell Martin. Roger Michell directed this heartrending story of a marriage breaking down and an older man's infatuation with a younger woman.

The night I saw it in the Cottesloe, there was a major breakdown of all the electrics. The audience were left for about twenty minutes or more in mid-performance while the lights were repaired. The actors deserved extra stars for the way they continued the story in such fine style that we, the audience, felt that there had been no break at all. It was certainly an evening to remember.

Vanessa insisted that I should give Corin Alexander lessons as she said that it would help him so much. When he started rehearsals for *De Profundis* our lessons began.

Corin had been very ill. He had been diagnosed with prostate cancer in 2000, but seemed to be managing fairly well although he did suffer from back pain. I felt that he was finding the prospect of this one man show rather daunting. Neil Bartlett had written the play and it was non-stop with no interval, so a lot of lines to remember.

The director Richard Nelson eventually noticed the effect that the lessons were having, that they made a great improvement to Corin's performance, his speaking and confidence. Richard said that, if possible, he wanted me to teach Corin before every performance.

For Corin, remembering his lines was the main worry. But in a way, if he was pausing a bit, it felt as though he was thinking out loud. It seemed that he was searching for the words to best express the writing of a letter, which some say was the greatest love letter ever written. Corin's performance was both gentle and moving, and he received rapturous applause from a packed house at the Lyttleton.

This was not to be the end of my time with Corin because his next, and final, work was *Trumbo* by Christopher Trumbo. This is based on the letters of Dalton Trumbo and is the true story of an American journalist blacklisted for refusing to testify at an investigation by The House Un-American Activists Committee into Communist influences in the USA.

The play was directed by John Dove and performed at the Jermyn Street theatre in March 2009. On the opening night, Corin dedicated it to his niece, Natasha, who had tragically died in a skiing accident a week before.

In the lead up to *Trumbo*, again Vanessa arranged for Corin to come for lessons at the NT. I would get there early to work with him before I started teaching actors at the theatre. It all became rather worrying though because his memory seemed to be failing. I would be closely in touch with Kika Markham, his wife, to confirm that he arrived and I would ring her when he had left. She would let me know when he arrived back safely as he insisted on taking public transport.

During this time, Corin had his 70th birthday party, to which I was invited. I offered to read a quote from Plato about music as Corin was a great lover of both. I was extremely nervous, but read it half way through the proceedings, which was when the talking and speeches had ended and the music began.

> *Music is a moral Law. It gives a soul to the universe,*
> *Wings to the mind, flight to the imagination,*
> *A charm to sadness, and life to everything.*
> *It is the essence of order and it leads to all that is*
> *Good and just and beautiful, of which it is the invisible,*
> *But nevertheless dazzling, passionate and eternal form.*
>
> Plato

Corin and Kika then sang some songs together from the shows and I was amazed at the quality of Corin's voice. When he was singing, his voice was impeccable, the memory faultless, completely different from his normal speaking.

This gave me the idea of getting him to bring his ukulele into the National so we could work with that whilst applying Alexander. I asked him to bring it into the next lesson but, of course, he forgot.

I went to Matthew Scott, the head of music, and explained the situation to see if they could lend him one. Apparently they hadn't one, but Matthew said, 'We will buy him one', which I thought was a lovely gesture.

The morning before Corin's next lesson, quite early, I had a phone call from Kika to say that Corin had died peacefully during the night, with the family at his bedside.

For Vanessa this was yet another tragedy, having just lost her beloved daughter Natasha. To then lose her brother, to whom she was so very close, was almost as if she was reliving *The Year of Magical Thinking.*

I went to Corin's funeral, which was at the actors' church in Covent garden, and it was crammed full of so many, familiar faces. The tributes were incredibly moving and the vicar insisted that we should feel free to applaud, which lifted the tension and it really did feel like a celebration.

During the service there was a sudden silence. We saw a bed being wheeled up the main aisle with Lynn Redgrave, youngest sister for Vanessa and Corin. She had been fighting cancer but despite this had flown over from the States especially for the funeral.

Lynn was helped off the bed and up onto the stage to say her goodbyes. To remember her days as a child with her brother, which were full of fun, as she obviously adored him. She then quoted a sonnet, which she had off by heart.

Corin went off in the horse drawn carriage with the congregation singing, 'Good byee, good byee' and then many of us went off to The Ivy for the wake.

A week later Lynn Redgrave died, another devastating blow for poor Vanessa and her family.

The Collaborators written by John Hodge in 2011, was a great success with a dream casting of Simon Russell Beale as Stalin and Alex Jennings as Bulgakov.

It was a play about Stalin's attempt to get into the head of Mikhail Bulgakov who had been commissioned by Stalin to write a play about Stalin's life, whilst reporting back to Stalin every day so that his progress could be watched and approved of by the dictator. Eventually Stalin lost patience and decided that he should write the play himself, whilst Bulgakov should take over the running of the country, which he described as being a 'tedious job'.

I taught many in the company, but one young actor, Pierce Reid, remains in my memory as he was extremely tall and spent most of his time in a cupboard at the side of the stage. He had to keep darting in and out to report on happenings. His back became extremely painful, but after a large number of Alexander lessons, and especially wall work, the pain eased. A complication was that his head was right up on the ceiling of the cupboard and he had a tendency to bang it, nearly knocking himself out. We considered asking the designer Bob Crowley to change the headroom for 'The proletariat in the cupboard'. But we thought that Bob would say to stop having Alexander – it was a cheaper option, so we didn't ask.

The Amen Corner was another production that I had a considerable amount to do with. Directed by Rufus Norris in 2013, it was a revival of James Baldwin's gospel drama, which debuted in 1954.

Some reviews described it as 'other worldly'. The music and the singing made me want to get up and dance, sing along, laugh and cry. It was a fantastic evening.

Inevitably there were problems with voices. There were injuries too as the set was very tricky with lots of different levels to manoeuvre whilst singing and dancing.

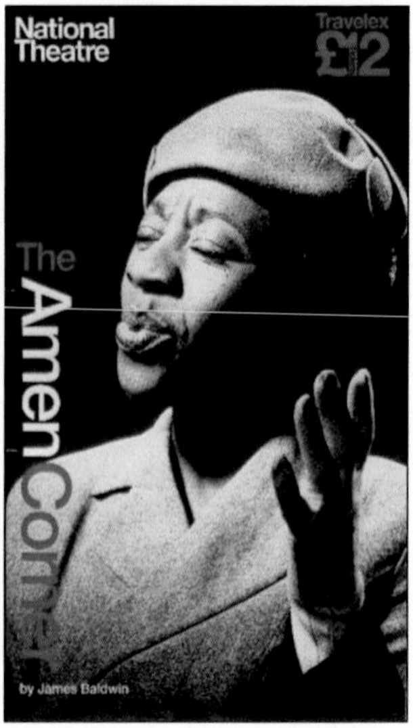

I never worked with Marianne Jean-Baptiste who gave a very memorable performance as the priest, but the ensemble, the musicians and singers, came dancing along.

The renovation of the National had begun and I was now in a tiny dressing room, which had a window overlooking the square in the centre of the building, Room 201. This became my home for a year and during the very hot summer it was lovely to look out of the window and wave to everyone in their dressing rooms across the square.

One of the actors, when she left, donated her window box filled with geraniums, which Sarah, the Chiropodist, and I kept watered and pruned throughout the summer months.

There was a trumpeter who came for lessons called Byron. He would play out into the square just before the show and would be replied to by other musicians who joined in, and the singers too, leaning out of their windows into the hot summer air. I loved hearing all the old standards pouring out of that trumpet. He was really a jazz musician and very talented. I love jazz so it was a delight to listen to him.

Byron was having great trouble with both his back and his breathing. I asked him to bring his trumpet along so I could see what he was up to, what tensions he was creating when he played.

It was very exciting as Byron, to my amazement, latched on to NO and waited a moment before launching into playing. He was such a full on, energetic guy that it was extraordinary.

I worked with him against the wall where he played the trumpet and went through the breathing. His sound changed and he was astounded that all this happened effortlessly, no 'trying'. He was such a great achiever, but began to realise that there was no need to tense up to put all he had into every note.

He went around telling everyone how he had been transformed by Alexander, and singing my praises, which was quite embarrassing.

In that production, there were many of the singers that came for help and amongst them was a very short, round woman with a lovely alto voice. One day she was due for a lesson and as usual knocked on the door. I waited before opening it, and saw her sitting cross legged on the floor with two children seated either side of her.

They all looked up at me with smiling faces and she said, 'I have brought my grandchildren. They will be very good'. They were so sweet and I ended explaining to the elder one the principles as she was early teens and just beginning to slump. Then I had to take a photo of them lengthened up and looking so pleased with themselves.

I was next called to help the chorus of women who were all losing their voices and suffering from various aches and pains. I was asked to give them a group session on the set, which was, as I have said, very difficult to manage. They were at different levels and getting in and out of rickety chairs which sloped this way and that. It was quite a challenge as I had to briefly explain the principles and then have them singing as they got in and out of the chairs. The main problem was that they all went on talking whilst I was trying to be heard. It was very funny in retrospect, but in such a short session I felt I could not really help and it was a bit frustrating.

In 2009, there was great excitement over a production of Racine's *Phèdre*, directed by Nick Hytner. Helen Mirren, in the title role, was back on stage playing the Athenian Queen harbouring secret desires for her stepson, played by Dominic Cooper.

Margaret Tyzack, playing Oenone, took many lessons and this for me was a very special time. Maggie had big problems with her back but was hilarious to talk to. We had so many gossipy jokes to share that I very often had to stop her talking so that I could help her with her pain and her understanding of the technique. To my mind, she was the best thing in the whole production, she was such a professional and a very steadying member of the cast.

Dominic Cooper kept almost threatening to have lessons, but would never actually book one like everyone else. Then one day I was in my room waiting for a pupil to arrive and he appeared at the door, flung himself onto my table and said, 'There you are – please sort me out'.

I protested, said I was fully booked and would not submit to his charms. Whereupon the next pupil came and generously gave up his time for the cheeky boy. That, of course, was the last time he came.

When *Phèdre* went to Greece, *Mother Courage and Her Children,* directed by Deborah Warner, came into the Olivier. While they were in tech rehearsal, the noise from the drum was very intrusive in my 'Quiet' room. Nothing could really be done, but Deborah, in a very commanding mood, instructed the poor stage manager to stop the helicopters flying low over the NT as it interrupted rehearsals and then shouted at the poor girl drummer to play more quietly, forgetting that she was deaf.

The final straw came in the first preview. Deborah marched onto the stage and told the audience that actually they were not quite ready to go through the whole performance – only the first half. So if they wanted to go away and re-book she was sure that they would get their money back. The poor box office was thrown into chaos. Since when Deborah has not directed anything at the NT.

Every Good Boy Deserves Favour came to the NT in January 2009. Tom Stoppard's black comedy, which was originally performed in 1977 at the Royal Festival Hall, was a collaboration with André Previn who composed the music. Tom Morris and Punchdrunk's Felix Barrett were directing.

The play was attacking the Soviet Union's practice of treating political dissent as a form of madness. Two men share a cell in a psychiatric hospital. Alexander, a political prisoner played by Joe Millson, and his cell mate Ivanov, who is genuinely mad and hears a full orchestra playing in his head, played brilliantly by Toby Jones.

In the National Theatre's production, the orchestra was the Southbank Sinfonia comprising some 35 young classical musicians, many of whom came to me for Alexander sessions along with some members of the cast. These were Joe Millson, Bryony Hannah, who played Sacha the son of Alexander, Dan Stevens the doctor and Bronagh Gallagher the teacher.

I had in the past taught a scattering of musicians. Some at the RSC and privately a flautist, a violin player and intriguingly the player of a tuba, the youngest of the brass instruments. The tuba player was a very young boy, sent to me by his father who was very worried about his back pain. He also had bad posture, which was very noticeable when he stopped practising.

With this pupil I did achieve considerable success. However, as he was still growing, he would need to carry on with lessons for some time. But he moved away and it became impossible for me to help further.

However, back to *EGBDF*, *Every Good Boy Deserves Favour.* Teaching many of the young musicians was an opportunity for me to learn a great deal about helping them to apply the technique while playing. A musician has this very close relationship with their instrument, almost as if it is their sibling or child, and I would ask them if they had given it a name.

In many cases they had, but if not I would encourage them to do so (was it male or female?). I think it helped them to be able to refer to it as Poppy (a cello), or Tommy the Trumpet and so on. For both me and them it was very exciting as, after they had played to me, it was easy to see where the unnecessary tensions were. As with any situation, the use of inhibiting and changes in the mental thought process brought about inevitable reactions; the sound they were creating had more resonance and flow. Breathing, of course, always plays a large part of the process and I found that I needed to take them back to the Alexander principles, which helped to get the back and the diaphragm working. They were then able to let go of all they had been doing with the shoulders and upper chest. This had an almost miraculous effect on them, their confidence in the sound they were making and how they were feeling physically and mentally.

I had feared that I would have to be able to play an instrument, (I can only play the piano a little) to be of any help at all, but that was not so. Several of the musicians came back to me after the play had ended for help. One, Dan Shilladay a viola player, brought me his new viola to help him learn her ways, which I was very touched by.

It was a thrilling experience watching *EGBDF* and listening to the almost Shostakovian music, which I went several times to observe. Then, as often when the production ends, there is almost a period of grieving, letting go of all the pupils after the experience of being so involved with them all.

In 2010, *Danton's Death*, by George Buchner and Howard Brenton, starred Toby Stephens. I met up with him again after his Hamlet at the RSC in 2009 where I had been summoned up to Stratford specially to give him a lesson before his press night. Before I talk about Danton, I must mention the various members of the cast in *Hamlet* whom I taught. Polonius was played by Richard Cordery, who was always a challenge as he was a very big man, tall and always enthusiastic about his lessons. Sian Thomas, who was a constant pupil and became a friend when she came to the NT for many productions there. I remember also Greg Hicks, who played the ghost and grave digger. He reduced me to a fit of the giggles and infuriated the rest of the cast by slowly, excruciatingly slowly, coming down the steps from within the audience dragging a very heavy chain. Then very slowly up the steps onto the stage, adding at least a quarter of an hour to an already long play.

However, back to *Danton's Death* in which Toby played Danton. He played it with such charm and endeared us all, only to horrify us by his beheading, which was incredibly realistic. So much so that Maggie Smith, his mum, said she was unable to look – it was so shocking.

Toby was a delight to teach. He would arrive for his lesson before time and sit cross legged on the floor in the passage outside the room patiently waiting for his appointment. He was just about to become a father for the third time and was so proud of his brood, talking about them constantly. He arrived one day with a bottle of champagne for me as a thank you. He shared how he had decided not to drink any alcohol himself as he felt that he might inherit the alcoholism of the legendary Robert Stephens, his father, which showed remarkable strength of character and intelligence. He was a charmer, a lovely man, and I really enjoyed meeting him and helping him in what was a very difficult part.

In 2011, Jonathan Miller staged and directed Bach's *St Matthew Passion*, which was produced in the Olivier. There was, of course, a great deal of controversy about such an attempt, thinking that this would detract from the purity of the work, but the production was highly acclaimed. Once again the Southbank Sinfonia were used – a forty-piece orchestra of young musicians playing with conviction, conducted by Paul Goodwin. The chorus were drawn from the Guildhall School of music. I taught many of the musicians again, and some of the singers, and for me it was once more a great learning process.

Also in 2011, there was a production of Sean O'Casey's play *Juno and the Paycock*. I taught several of the cast. I don't know what it is, but I just love teaching the Irish actors.

I love the accent and their sense of fun. They are so articulate, seeming to be able to express their feelings quite naturally, both men and women. I worked a great deal with Ciarán Hinds, who played Captain Boyle. He had damaged his back during a rather disastrous press night performance. Firstly, a door failed to open at a crucial, emotional moment in the play and this resulted in curtain down whilst it was mended. The audience thought it was meant to be funny so at first there was laughter, but then silence as they realised that what had happened was an accident. Then on another occasion, Ciarán fell through a door when he was drunk. I hasten to say that he was acting, but he unintentionally slipped so heavily that he damaged his back. I then helped him to recover using some Alexander. We had many chats as he was a great friend of Liam Neeson, married to Natasha Richardson who had died so tragically. As I had previously had so much to do with Vanessa and Corin, there was lots to talk about.

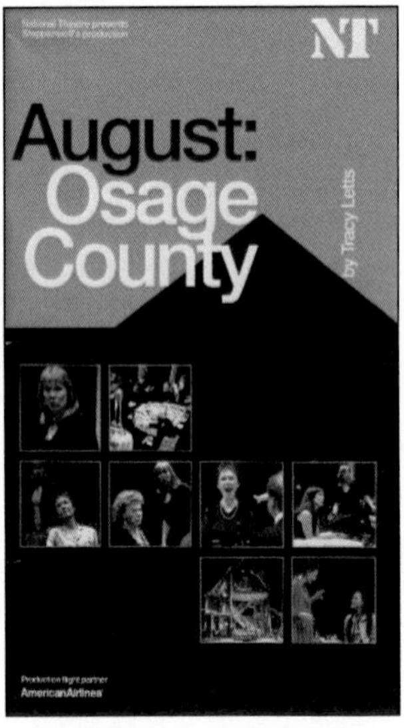

The Steppenwolf Theatre Company from Chicago brought two extraordinarily powerful plays to the National. In 2008, it was *August: Osage County,* which had an all American cast and it was a joy for me to work with practically all of them.

It is the story of a mid-western family at a critical point when the patriarch mysteriously disappears. This brings out all the supressed anger, envy, violence and hatred that up until then had been hidden. I found that I was dealing with the psychological effects that the parts were having on the actors. Like many Americans, they were not afraid to talk about their feelings. I was almost in a state of mourning when they eventually left and must have seen the play three times.

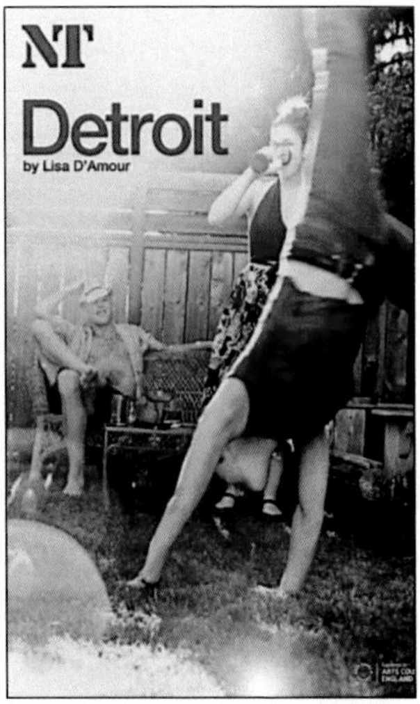

Then in 2012, the next play from the Steppenwolf Company, but this time with an English cast, was *Detroit*, by Lisa D'Amour, described by The Telegraph as an American *Abigail's Party*. It is a brutal yet hilarious play set in the suburbs of that city and it centres around the relationship between two couples. Ben and Mary, who are a typical couple trying to keep up with the Jones', dustless and doylies, and the new couple Kenny and Sharon, who have lived a rootless existence in different cities with their only real focus being drugs. Through barbecues fuelled by bouts of drinking with their new neighbours, the fragility of their relationship is exposed.

Kenny, played by Will Adamsdale, is constantly trying to go on the wagon and is the most difficult character to interpret. I worked with Will a great deal because he had probably the tightest shoulder and neck muscles I ever had to address. Will, at just one year old, had fractured his skull and was very pulled down with his head over to one side. He was a well known comedian, but as is often the case, very gloomy and lacking in self-worth.

The physio had told him that he would never have more than thirty percent movement in his neck. I helped him to turn much more than that without any pain. His physical and mental state was exacerbated by the part – we had many chats about his life – about recovery from addiction, which was his part in the play. We also worked at leaving 'Kenny' behind at the end of the evening, not taking him to bed…not feeding himself with negative messages. Later I saw him in a play at the Royal Court, which he had devised himself. He was very funny and I saw a completely different side to the man.

In 2014 another Sean O'Casey production, written in 1928,

was *The Silver Tassie*, a rarely performed anti-war play about the destruction and terrible waste of the First World War. In this the cast was almost entirely Irish and I worked mainly with Ronan Raftery. He played the much maligned hero Harry Heegan, who came back from the war wheelchair bound. Ronan's main problem was with his wrists and shoulders, caused through manipulating the wheelchair, sometimes at top speed, around the stage. His back was suffering. We did a great deal of work to help him use it correctly, giving the back directions to lengthen and not keeping it rigid. Also, as he had much to say from this unnatural position and his voice was being trapped, breathing was very important. He made many, significant changes and it was very rewarding for both of us.

In 2011, there was great excitement generated with the NT production of *Frankenstein*, directed by Danny Boyle. The part of The Creature and Victor Frankenstein alternated between Benedict Cumberbatch and Jonny Lee Miller, both actors managing to show a different side to The Creature's character and the emotions with which he was battling.

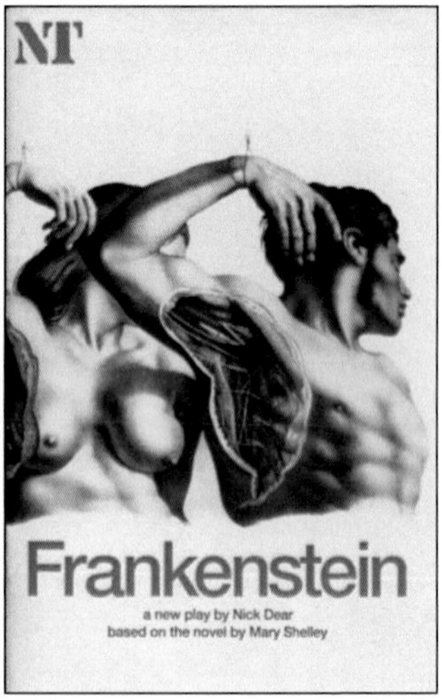

The staging was brilliant. I found that Benedict's interpretation of The Creature showed a longing for female companionship, which was tragic, especially when his attempts to get the love he yearned for sadly failed.

I was quite frightened of Jonny Lee, he projected emotions strongly and was very menacing. Jonny didn't come for lessons.

Karl Johnson, a wonderful actor, played De Lacey, the blind father of Felix, with sensitivity and caring. It was he who inspired The Creature to speak, and to listen to poetry and music as De Lacey strummed his guitar. The Creature's first words were, 'Bugger off', learnt from the beggars he had first encountered earlier in the play, which inevitably earned him rounds of laughter.

I worked with Karl and we achieved a great deal when he brought his guitar into the room. We went through breathing and singing, at the same time not forgetting that he was meant to be completely blind.

The experience of working with Benedict was exciting for me and not too intimidating as I had met him several times with his parents, who were friends of mine. I first worked with him in Thea Sharrock's superb production of Terence Rattigan's *After the Dance*. This was a 'lost play', so rarely performed, but heralded a season of Rattigan in the West End.

Benedict had had some Alexander lessons at LAMDA (London Academy of Music & Dramatic Art), but found my way of teaching slightly different. If there was ever one lesson that I would like to have been filmed or recorded, it was the lesson he insisted I gave him in the make-up room.

Ben was completely exhausted and asked me to get stage management to take my table up to the room where he and Jonny prepared for their roles of The Creature.

I had never been into that room before. It was quite small and over the walls and shelves there were samples of hair and skin, and swatches of colour. Photographs of the two actors in their various guises and mirrors were arranged so that all sides of the person could be seen simultaneously.

In came Benedict, to my horror in full make-up. He was practically naked with scars and stitch marks all over him, the few wisps of hair on his nearly bald head were gluey, and his shiny, slippery body covered in grease.

I laughed and asked him if he honestly thought I could be of any help to him, to which he replied, 'Of course you can, just straighten me out and relax me. I'm exhausted, that's all I need'.

I did the best I could by gently turning his head and freeing his neck and shoulders till he nearly dropped off. But suddenly, with two pizzas, in came Jonny who sat down at the end of the bed and proceeded to eat. Ben wearily roused himself saying that was just what he had needed, me, to sort him out. With much laughter about me being in the room alone with a near naked man, I left them to get ready for the show.

Benedict Cumberbatch CBE in rehearsal for *Frankenstein*

Shakespeare at the NT was obviously not so common as the RSC and I have to say I missed it very much. Some of the most outstanding productions for me were *Much Ado About Nothing* with Zoë Wanamaker and Simon Russell Beale as Beatrice and Benedick, *All's Well That Ends Well*, *The Comedy of Errors* with Lenny Henry and *Hamlet* with Rory Kinnear.

I also had a great deal to do with *Othello* with Rory Kinnear as Iago and Adrian Lester, Othello.

The production of *King Lear* with Simon Russell Beale as Lear was also a very exciting time and I will talk about some of these productions separately.

In *The Comedy of Errors* I taught Lenny Henry, who came up to me in the canteen and asked for lessons, laughing and making himself very tall and straight. He is a large man anyway but it made me smile.

Previously, he had done some Alexander but felt that he did not understand the psycho-physical connection and was fascinated by it.

This great big, jovial actor, whom I had always connected with comedy roles, turned out to be hiding inside a sensitive and nervous human being.

Lenny turned out to be very insecure about doing Shakespeare but his Othello directed by Barry Rutter, first for the Leeds Playhouse and then later at the Trafalgar Studios, was a resounding success.

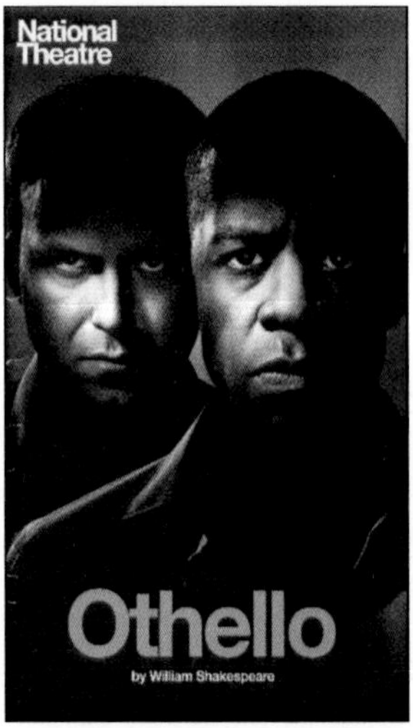

He graduated with a BA in English Literature in 2007 and gained an MA in television screen writing at Royal Holloway. He is presently studying for a PhD on the role of black people in the media. What energy, he never stops. It was a real pleasure to work with this lovely, generous actor.

In 2009, *All's Well That Ends Well*, directed by Marianne Elliot and set by Rae Smith, included the actress Michelle Terry to whom I became very attached. She has proved to be an extremely talented actress who was wrestling with the very difficult part of Helena. George Rainsford was the rather handsome Bertram, Clare Higgins played the Countess Rosillion and Conleth Hill played Parolles.

I didn't know the play at all as I hadn't seen it during my years at Stratford, but I felt with Rae's wonderful filmic set, it was rather like a fairy tale. I worked a great deal with Michelle and supported her as much as I could. I also gave her lessons later on where she shone in many other productions. In *Comedy* she and Claudia Blakely as Luciana and Adriana were superb, how we laughed at their scheming and manipulations.

Where Michelle really came into her own was in Dion Boucicault's *London Assurance* playing Grace Harkaway together with a star cast. There was Simon Russell Beale as Sir Harcourt Courtly, Paul Ready was his son Charles Courtly, Fiona Shaw as Lady Gay Spanker and the last stage appearance of Richard Briers playing Mr Adolphus 'Dolly' Spanker. 'Dolly' was a joy from start to finish. I must have seen it three times at least and every time my stomach ached with laughter.

After *London Assurance,* I spent more time working with Paul Ready as he was in several plays at the NT and a very talented, versatile young actor.

In JB Priestley's *Time and the Conways* in 2011, Paul played the sisters' brother and one review said, 'The most compelling performance was from Paul Ready as the nerdy brother who found happiness in decent, ordinary dullness'. I found it such a moving performance that it brought tears to my eyes and made me look at several things within myself in a very different way.

Then in 2013, there was *Othello* directed by Nick Hytner, with Rory Kinnear as Iago and Adrian Lester as Othello. The production had rave reviews and I enjoyed it so much I went four times. I had worked with other Othellos at the RSC – Ben Kingsley's Othello with David Suchet as Iago and Niamh Cusack as Desdemona and then Willard White's Othello with Ian McKellen as Iago and Imogen Stubbs as Desdemona.

Previously I had never really understood the jealousy of Othello over Desdemona and her suspected infidelity with Cassio. His sudden rage and fury with Desdemona had seemed unreasonable to me when she was so patently in love with him and thrilled to see him back from the war.

Nick had brilliantly placed the play in a war setting with his army uniforms. We were right in there in the atmosphere of the army camp with the troops welcoming Othello back from the war where he had triumphed. We could understand Othello's exhaustion and his need to be left to rest with his young bride. To then have Iago needling away about Desdemona's behaviour in his absence became too much for him to deal with in his exhausted state. It then made sense to me – his sudden insecurity, mistrust of his young wife and the fury of being betrayed.

I seemed to become very involved with that production and taught many of the actors including Lyndsey Marshal as Emilia and Jonathan Bailey as Cassio. Jonathan and I had a great breakthrough with his voice. He had such an important part, but his voice was becoming strained. I had noted that he was very prone to throwing his head back when speaking and so causing a lot of tension in the throat. By going through the text with Alexander breathing, he managed to overcome the habit during the run, which was a great achievement for him.

I had worked with Rory Kinnear before as Hamlet and here he was giving another spellbinding performance as Iago. He again managed to find time for lessons, mainly just to help him let go of the tensions of such a demanding part. He and Adrian had done their training at RADA so it was not a case of first lessons. I did manage to get Adrian to come for just two or three lessons, but he was fairly reluctant. To my distress, he seemed to have had a poor experience of Alexander and he said it was too negative. I was really upset. I would have liked to have explained that, of course, it is in no way a negative experience but rather the opposite, very positive. But this was just before the end of the run, so the opportunity didn't arise.

Jeannette Nelson, the Head of Voice, recommended that I should work with Olivia Vinall, a young actress who played Desdemona. She was a thread that ran through *Othello* and then *King Lear* where she played Cordelia, requiring two very different performances.

I became very attached to Olivia and she became a friend as well as a longstanding pupil. She is beautiful, smart and very sensitive. I think I helped her overcome a great many fears and Alexander gave her confidence in herself. Her performances resulted in rave reviews for her Desdemona with one critic referring to her as 'almost unbearably poignant'.

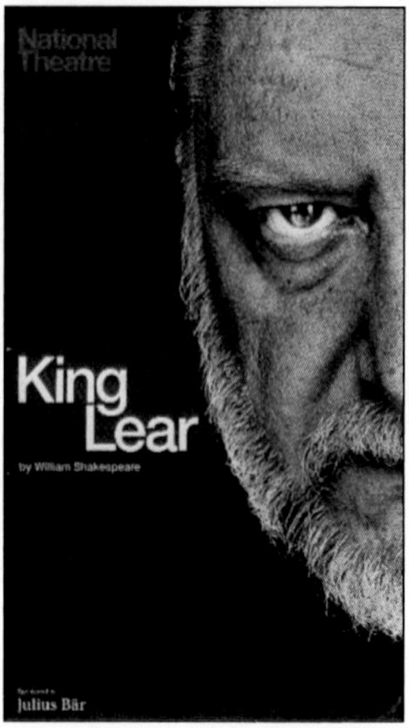

Playing Lear's daughter Cordelia was a very different part and Olivia said that it was an emotional challenge. Simon Russell Beale, playing Lear, apparently looked rather like her actual Dad. Although her parents do not come from an acting background, they love Shakespeare and actually chose her name from *Twelfth Night.* They were however looking forward to seeing her in something where she does not die.

That of course happened shortly afterwards when Olivia was asked to play the lead in the new Tom Stoppard play, *The Hard Problem.*

Dear Olivia came through my door bursting with excitement at the prospect of spending yet another year at the National and the opportunity to be in this long awaited play from Sir Tom Stoppard, one of our leading writers. This was his first play for the National since *The Coast of Utopia* in 2002, so there was a great deal of nervous anticipation.

The Hard Problem was a very different challenge. It was about the conundrum of human consciousness. Olivia plays Hilary, a young psychologist who is working for a brain science institute. She has real problems accepting that brain activity explains emotions such as sorrow and eventually rejects the theory and departs for New York to study philosophy.

I always read any play by Tom Stoppard before I go to see it because I fear that I won't be able to understand a word of it. This time I was fascinated by the subject as much of the content related working with the unconscious, which I studied when I had been doing my counselling course. Also pertinent was my reading of Jung and Freud and in particular a book called *Molecules of Emotion,* by the scientist Candace Pert, PhD.

Candace had studied the emotional connection to the body and the bio-chemical links that exist between consciousness, mind and body. I was intrigued and by chance saw Tom in the canteen. After asking him if he had read it – and he hadn't, I gave him a copy. According to the stage manager, he sat gobbling it up whilst in rehearsal. I never knew what his opinion of the book was, but was content to know that he had read it.

I gave many lessons to Olivia during *The Hard Problem*, which helped to see her through this role that was so different from Desdemona or Cordelia. Again she said how much Alexander had helped her. Olivia showed in her intelligent performances that although still a very young actress she had the versatility to cope magnificently with any part that was thrust in her path. She has a great career ahead of her and I certainly hope I manage to see her again at the National before long.

Olivia Vinall, Cordelia and
Simon Russell Beale CBE, King Lear

In all the Shakespeares I taught many of the cast, especially those from *King Lear*. In this play, as well as the main characters there were thirty supernumeraries, thirty huge young men with very heavy legs. Luckily it was impossible to fit all of them in – so I managed not to do my back in and resort to the osteopath, which might have been on the cards.

It was terribly funny because they all seemed to have their supper in Rehearsal Room 3 next door to the Quiet Room where I worked. There was very often a strong smell of chicken curry streaming out from underneath the door, which permeated me and the poor pupils.

I managed to work with all King Lear's daughters, Olivia as Cordelia, of course, while Anna Maxwell-Martin played Regan and Kate Fleetwood played Goneril – all brilliant young actresses.

Simon Manyonda played Oswald, which I always think is a thankless part as he is so badly treated in spite of his loyalty to the King. I worked with him when he was in *Greenland* and several other shows – he is a very talented young actor. What I really enjoy at the NT is when the actors come back into another show. Then I can carry on working with them as I did with Simon in Caryl Churchill's *Light Shining in Buckinghamshire*. This time we had a sort of breakthrough in his lessons, it all seemed to suddenly make sense.

At the National, when a pupil does come back for another show, they are, of course, entitled to another six lessons. I know that FM Alexander wanted everyone to have fifteen lessons on the trot, so I am often surprised when I look back in my notebooks and find that when pupils have had about fifteen sessions then something really seems to stay in there. It is as if the seed has been well and truly sown.

I met up with Lesley Sharp first of all during *Uncle Vanya* whilst we were rehearsing in the NT Studio and I was working with the cast in groups before rehearsal. Working with Lesley individually, however, came much later in 2008 with *Harper Regan*. This was a very disturbing Simon Stephens' piece where

Harper leaves home to see her father before he dies and in that journey explores her troubled relationships with her husband and her daughter.

Lesley, playing Harper, found it an emotional challenge and, first working through it in rehearsal, then to play this part night after night did show up in her body physically. Lesley was a very special woman and very open about how she felt and what the Alexander was doing for her. The next challenge was when she played Helen, a very different mother in *A Taste of Honey*, Shelagh Delaney's taboo breaking play set in the 1950s. Bijan Sheibani directed this 'zestful production'. Again it was a very upsetting part, emotionally, for Lesley. She coped magnificently and, for me, was a joy to work with. When she talked about how she felt, her tensed up body responded by letting go of all the unnecessary tension.

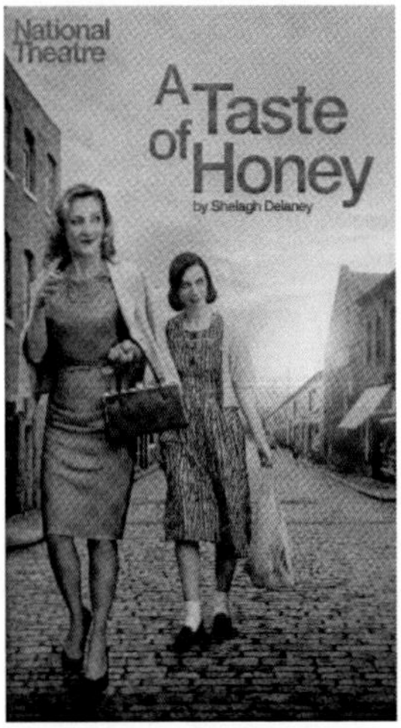

A Taste of Honey had been rarely seen since its debut at the Theatre Royal, Stratford East in 1958 and was brought to the National in 2014. Lesley gave a dazzling performance as Helen, the mother with Kate O'Flynn as an excellent Jo the daughter. Lesley captured the character of Helen, with all its complexities, wonderfully. I helped her to learn to leave Helen at the end of the performance, which was a challenge for this very sensitive actress.

Then there was *A Small Family Business,* by Alan Ayckbourn, the high energy farce with dark undercurrents of family feuds and deception – yet both funny and tragic. I taught several members of the cast, in particular Gawn Grainger and Amy Marston. Gawn had been 'sent to me' by his wife Zoë Wanamaker, with strict instructions to sort him out. I first taught Gawn in *A Woman Killed with Kindness* in 2011, so it was great to see him back again at the top of his form.

How we did laugh and gossip but, whilst that was going on, I did manage to teach him how to reduce his unnecessary tensions. He made a great many changes to his habitual ways of moving, not only in his work, but in daily life as well. To prove to Zoë how well Gawn had done I took a before and after photo of his transformation.

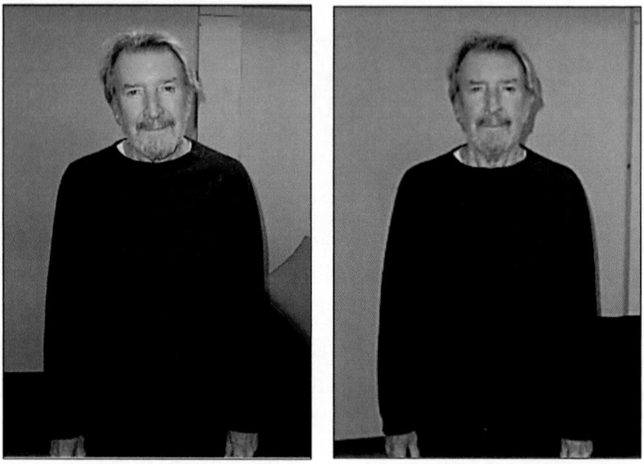

Gawn Grainger, Before and After Alexander

Amy's part was Harriet Ayres. Harriet was an obsessive spinster whose love of her dog, that never appeared, was touching and sad as there did not seem to be anything else in her life that mattered above the dog's well-being. We had many lessons, and talks, and I think she found Alexander extremely helpful in her work.

I first taught Henry Goodman at the RSC in the 1983 production of *The Comedy of Errors* where he played Dromio of Ephesus, for which, in 1984, he won an Olivier.

I worked with him again in several productions. In the 1999 *The Merchant of Venice* directed by Trevor Nunn, where his Shylock was mesmerizing, he received great acclaim. I was reduced to tears, which I confess does not often happen to me in the theatre – it is usually films that have that effect on my emotional responses where they are not very far from the surface.

When performing in *The Holy Rosenbergs* in 2011 at the National, Henry came for lessons once more. He was finding the role of David Rosenberg, the father of a son who is killed fighting for the Israeli defence forces, very emotionally draining. The tension it generated was giving him a great deal of neck and shoulder pain. Further tensions were created in the play when his daughter, who is a lawyer for the UN investigating war crimes in Gaza, returns and her presence at her brother's funeral is going to produce anger and unrest amongst the Jewish community where the family live.

Once again it showed me how important it is to talk to the pupil, to encourage them to share the difficulties they are having psychologically and help them not let these feelings affect the body physically.

In June 2015, Patrick Marber returned to the National with his first play since 2001 called *The Red Lion*, faultlessly directed by Ian Rickson. One review said that it was Marber's night, at fifty he had found his voice again and it roared.

To my delight, Ian became a regular once or twice a week pupil and introduced me to the cast. He also invited me in for the first run through so I felt very involved. Ian seemed to really take Alexander on board this time and together we made many discoveries. What was so interesting about him was that he really loves actors and that can be a rare thing in directors. I began to realise this through hearing what the actors have to say about their relationship with the director. You could see that the actors love being directed by Ian and he seems to draw the very best out of them in return.

We were to work together again with Wallace Shawn's new play *Evening at the Talk House*, where once again I became very involved with the cast and the play. The delightful Joe Mydell came for lessons and we worked out that we had first met up in *Angels in America* some 20 years before, where he played Belize and had won an Olivier award for best supporting actor. The dear man kept bringing me beautiful avocados from his local market after I had remarked how delicious they looked when he was eating them for his lunch in the canteen.

In August 2015, Gawn and Patrick Marber were back again in Patrick's version of Turgenev's *A Month in the Country*, shortened to *Three Days in the Country*. The play received rapturous reviews describing it as, 'an elegant dance, where the wit of the dialogue captivates as it moves between comedy and anguish, reminding us of love as an impractical joke'.

I loved the play, but I couldn't understand the set.

Amanda Drew, who played Natalya, was insecure because she did not feel attractive and sexy enough. We had to put a stop to that. We worked on building her confidence and to really inhabit the beautiful woman she was, and is, and be proud of herself.

Gawn Grainger was back again as the German tutor and I had more sessions with him and Lynn Farleigh, who played Anna. I have taught her on and off over the years, together with Cassie Raine, who was ensemble and understudying Amanda.

Mark Gatiss, playing Shpigelsky, the 'doctor of misdiagnosis', who received ovations practically every time he appeared, was hilarious, especially when he sinks to his knees to propose to Lizaveta. An attack of lumbago prevents him from rising again and he has to crawl across the stage in the most undignified way. I met him in the corridor one day and suggested that Alexander is very helpful for bad backache, which made him laugh saying it was all an act. Sadly, I never persuaded him to come in for a lesson, as it would have been so interesting to talk to him, such a great actor.

Towards the end of 2015 and the beginning of 2016 my teaching became even more interesting and special because I was working with four plays, not only with the cast but the directors as well.

In November of 2015, Polly Findlay directed the first *As You Like It* at the National for twenty-six years. I seem to have given lessons to Polly on and off for some time, but usually more off than on. During *As You Like It*, I saw a great deal of her and found that she is a delightful girl. I say girl – I am sure she is more than nineteen – but she looks so young and because of that it is difficult to believe that she has directed so many, highly successful productions at the National, the RSC and elsewhere.

Her *As You Like It* is one of those successful productions and had one of the most unusual sets. It transforms the opening scene, an open plan office with everyone eating sandwiches and tapping on their computers, into the Forest of Arden in a dramatic explosion. Tables and chairs crack apart and are whisked skywards, becoming a forest of trees like a huge prickly bush above the action below. The ensemble is perched on the branches making wonderfully realistic bird sounds blending in with the melancholy swell of the music.

My work was mainly with the ensemble who were having many problems. They were, for a large part of the play, staying up in the branches leading to many physical aches and pains. I went twice to the show taking children who had never been to a Shakespeare before and it was a great success, an excellent introduction to the Bard.

The handsome Simon Shepherd had many lessons and he seemed to understand the Alexander process from the word go. It was fascinating to hear that his dad, Ben Shepherd, owned The Dirty Duck, 'The Duck', as it was colloquially known, in Stratford-upon-Avon from 1959-1986. Simon said that he lived there until he was about eight and then moved to Snitterfield when Pam Harris came in as manager.

> 'He was a real gent, my Dad, and it was an amazing place to grow up in. My parents always had seats 18/19 row G in the stalls on 1st nights and when we were old enough we went with them. So I saw the famous Peter Brook whitebox *Dream*... I was about 11 and loved it! Not too surprising that I became an actor I guess.'

I wish we'd had time to gossip more about Stratford as I was there from 1982 until 2010 and there were lots more memories we could have shared. The show closed. I missed them all as is often the case when I go into a kind of mourning state. I have to remind myself that, more often than not, these actors come back again and then we can resume the lessons where we left off.

The celebration of The National Theatre's *Fifty Years on Stage* was on November 2nd 2013. The excitement during the preparations for this very special evening seemed to permeate the whole building many days and weeks before. When the rehearsals began, the dressing rooms on either side of my teaching room were filled with the actors taking part in the grand finale.

It was going to be such an enormous invited audience that the staff were only going to be able to go to the dress rehearsal and, as I was only a freelance member of the NT, it was highly unlikely that I would be able to go to either the show or the party afterwards.

I had been teaching many of the cast in Nicholas Hytner's highly acclaimed *Othello*. Lyndsey Marshal and Olivia Vinall were particularly upset that I had not received a ticket. But at the last moment Lyndsey, to my delight, magically produced one. I then went to one of the most enjoyable evenings of my life.

I shared a taxi with my friends Wanda Ventham and Tim Carlton who were as excited as I was. As we ploughed our way through the huge crowds at stage door, Wanda and Tim were signing autographs. We eventually managed to get to our seats.

Nick Hytner took the stage and spoke about his time at the National and what it had meant to him. He spoke movingly of the staff and the support they had provided during his term as Artistic Director. I wish it had been recorded, because I had never heard him speak with such feeling. My tears started then and continued on and off throughout the two and a half hours with no interval. The cheers for Nick were so long and prolonged that it was difficult to get the show on the road.

Nick had directed the show. It was more or less a chronological history with film clips of Paul Scofield in *Amadeus* and Nigel Hawthorne in *The Madness of George III* and Michael Bryant as the Fool in *King Lear*.

Alan Bennett was one of the biggest stars of the show, not only as a writer, but as an actor as well. He stepped into the shoes of the much missed Richard Griffiths to play the schoolmaster in a riotous scene from his *The History Boys*. This brought tears of laughter.

Among the stars was Judi Dench who was profoundly moving. She revisited her Cleopatra with an extraordinary depth of emotion and went on later as Desiree to sing Send in the Clowns from *A Little Night Music.*

Maggie Smith revealed the high definition, comic glory in the 1964 revival of Noel Coward's *Hay Fever*, directed by the author.

Splendid too was Michael Gambon and Derek Jacobi in roles originally played by Gielgud and Richardson in Pinter's *No Man's Land.*

I could go on relating all those special moments and performances but if anyone wants to see the evening in more detail, it has been recorded on a splendid DVD.

The show ended with a witty epilogue from *The Habit of Art* by Alan Bennett superbly delivered by Frances de la Tour.

And afterwards the party…I eventually managed to find my bed in the early hours, feeling very tired and privileged to have been part of such a unique and wonderful evening.

In 2004, *His Dark Materials*, the Philip Pullman book adapted by Nicholas Wright, became a sensational success for both children and adults. It was about two children wandering through a series of parallel universes in search of the Republic of Heaven.

During their journeys, they encountered fantasy creatures, witches and armoured polar bears who, on stage, were represented by puppets handled by the actors.

The puppets were devised by the company Blind Summit, which helped the actors manipulate them. It was complicated and exhausting. I was not nearly as involved as I should have been, but the actors that I did help found Alexander very useful. They sometimes needed to bend and run with the puppets, so learning to use monkey and coming back to use the wall exercise in between times, was very useful for them. In addition, they had to simultaneously use their voices which contributed to the tiredness that would overtake them.

There were so many shows that I worked on during the Nick Hytner years, but I will only mention those that I had most to do with.

In 2006, *The History Boys* was an outstanding success and is probably Alan Bennett's most popular stage play ever. I taught a lot of the boys, some briefly. I do remember Sacha Dhawan, who came often, as he was finding Alexander helped him a great deal.

This also meant a meeting up with Frances de la Tour again – she was playing Mrs Lintott – which was lovely. She was outstanding as usual and very funny.

Coram Boy also in 2006, directed by Melly Still, deals with eighteenth century attitudes to illegitimate children. It was put on as a Christmas show. The advice that this was not for the viewing of children under twelve was for very good reason. It was a very dark and distressing tale – not exactly a Christmas romp. I did however take my twelve-year-old grand-daughter who found it very thought provoking. We had a lot to discuss afterwards.

I know I taught several in the cast, but I remember in particular Eve Matheson playing Mrs Milcote. I worked with her at the RSC many years back – she had that wonderful head of golden-red curly hair. I found that many of the actors suffered from the stress of their parts. There was very little joy to be found in the play where Eve's part was to play a very sad woman. It was difficult not to be affected by playing it night after night.

Then in 2007, *The Man of Mode,* by George Etherege, was chosen to cheer us all up I felt. It was a restoration comedy with the ever versatile Rory Kinnear as Sir Fopling Flutter, for which he received an Olivier Award.

Then came the phenomenal *War Horse,* directed by Tom Morris and Marianne Elliott of the Handspring Puppet Company in South Africa. As I worked on that production extensively, until the show came off at the New London in 2016, I have written a separate chapter about that fascinating work with the puppeteers.

The highly regarded director Howard Davies directed many, many shows at the NT over the years. The ones I remember most are the Russian plays.

The first was *The Philistines* by Maxim Gorky in 2007, which to my mind did not have a long enough run. I loved it and taught several of the actors – Mark Bonnar, Maggie McCarthy, bless her and Ruth Wilson, who is a very talented actress. I tried to work on Alexander with breathing and voice with her as she had rather a small voice. Ruth's career seems lately to have been mostly film and television, but voice projection is more difficult when working on stage.

The next Russian play, in 2009, was *Burnt by the Sun.* The Russian translation means 'Wearied by the Sun'. The story depicts a Red Army officer and his family during the great purge of the late 1930s in Stalinist Soviet Union. Like a classical Greek tragedy, it takes place in the space of one day.

Rory Kinnear and Ciaran Hinds with Michelle Dockery were the star performances and I taught several of the cast.

In 2010 Mikhail Bulgakov's *The White Guard* was Howard Davies' third Russian play. It is Bulgakov's semi-autobiographical account of pro-Tsarist forces in the Ukraine during the civil war of 1918/19. Bulgakov was very much a dissident in Tsarist Russia at that time. His story is seen through the eyes of the Turbin household who are cloistered at home and so disorientated by what's going on, without any of the usual news from outside.

It had a very large cast of which I taught several actors. I remember in particular Pip Carter, who made me weep with laughter. He transformed during his Alexander lessons and I have photos to prove it. It was rather amusing, because I don't think he quite realised what a difference they made. But I gave him copies of the photos to encourage him.

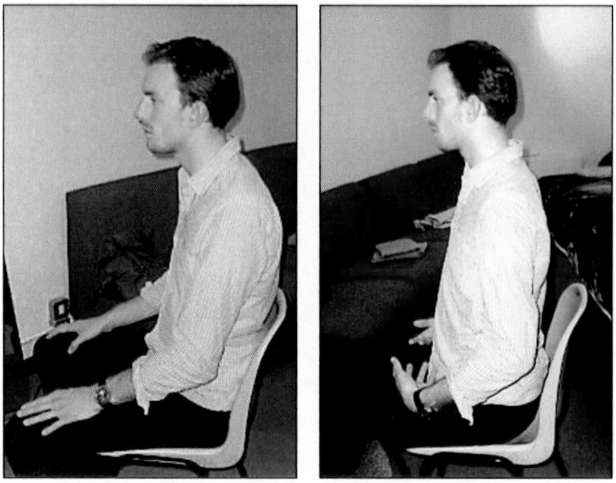

Pip Carter, Before and After Alexander

All in all, it was a cracking start to the new season of plays at the National with Howard Davies in his very best form, as usual never putting a foot wrong.

Musicals at the National

In 1989 along came *Ma Rainey's Black Bottom.* This was the first musical that I was involved with where several of the musicians needed to learn their instruments from scratch. This was a bit of a challenge for me, in particular the trumpet player, but the technique helped a great deal with his breathing. I never managed to get my hands on the great Clarke Peters, who didn't have to learn the piano as he was a natural, the notes and sounds just poured out of his fingers. Hugh Quarshie was Levee and Clarke Peters was Toledo. Hugh I had taught at Stratford and I worked with several of the others. It was a great show.

In 1990, Steven Pimlott directed *Sunday in the Park with George,* the Sondheim musical with which I was involved. It was my first Sondheim and I met and taught the inspiring Philip Quast, with whom I fell in love instantly. Philip, who played George, was a challenge as he was a very large. He wasn't fat, he just had a very big frame to go with his powerful voice. Philip had never had Alexander before and found it very useful. He had had a great deal of trouble with his back and various other aches and pains. However, after lessons, his voice became even more resonant. He was very excited by it as he was of course Australian, like FM Alexander.

Another pupil from the cast with whom I worked was Maria Friedman. I first met with her briefly in *The Ghetto* in 1989. In 1990, with *Sunday in the Park with George,* where she played Dot, she was suffering a great deal from nerves and had other problems in her life, which we spent a great deal of time discussing. She was then able to let go and let that wonderful voice flow out into the auditorium. Then later, in 1997, there was *Lady in the Dark*, where she played Liza Elliott and was nominated for another Olivier award.

I had been an ardent follower of *The Forsyte Saga* so it was very exciting to work with Nyree Dawn Porter, who was playing Yvonne in *Sunday in the Park with George.* Nyree lived near me in Barnes. After the show had ended, she became so reliant on her lessons that she came to me privately at my home. She also sent her daughter who lived with her at the time. I remember one very dramatic moment in *George* which had a most beautiful set designed by Tom Cairns and gave the impression of being a Pissarro painting. There were very tall trees in the foreground along the banks of the river and one evening one of them fell down in the middle of the performance with an almighty crash, narrowly missing poor Nyree.

Others in the cast whom I taught and remember in particular, were Di Botcher, playing Frieda and Gary Raymond as Jules, whom I knew as a friend.

In 1992 came *Carousel*, which meant that I again met up with Patricia Routledge and I think it was my first encounter with Janie Dee. Patricia had the most wonderful voice, which flew out into the auditorium effortlessly. She was trained as a classical singer and came to me for many lessons. She was such fun and we laughed and laughed, but I didn't interfere with her breathing as there was no need. Her voice production was faultless.

In 1998, I taught many of the cast of Trevor Nunn's *Oklahoma,* but in particular I remember sending a note to Maureen Lipman who was playing Aunt Eller – Sue Higginson had also suggested that I get in touch with Maureen. I asked her whether she would like some Alexander sessions as I had seen in an article that she and I had shared the same doctor for back pain. I said that the Alexander Technique could really help. I received a really unpleasant reply, via Sue, saying that, 'She had no intention of being controlled by anyone, thank you very much'.

Sue H and I had a good laugh over that one.

My Fair Lady in 2001 was a 'wow'. I must have seen it about four times. Both Alex Jennings and Martine McCutcheon received 'Best actors in a musical'. When the show moved to the West End, she was replaced by Joanna Riding (who I thought was much better) who finished the run. I had great pleasure in taking my eldest grandson, Samuel, to his first musical and also giving him his first Italian meal. He was absolutely spellbound by it. He was about nine years old and it was exciting for me to see his reaction. I had given him many theatrical experiences since the age of four and just hope that he remembers them as I do.

In 2003, Cole Porter's *Anything Goes,* perhaps my favourite musical of all, also moved to the West End. Susan Tracy, who played Mrs Evangeline Harcourt, was a long term pupil of mine and a friend who was an endless supply of £20 tickets when the show went to Drury Lane. I think I ended up taking friends for about five performances during the run.

One evening there was 'a happening'. The set of the show was an ocean liner and most of the action took place on the deck where the sailors danced, sang, played deck games and so on. Susan, who always minced around holding a small Yorkshire terrier, suddenly slipped on a rubber quoit, which was lying on the deck. She shot forward right off the stage, the dog left her arms and flew into the audience. The dog was quite unharmed and Susan, like a true actress, recovered, went back on stage having collected the dog (who seemed quite unperturbed). And all this to roars of laughter from the audience, who thought it was all part of the show.

Susan was not unharmed though and although she carried on bravely, it was found that she had in fact fractured her leg. She had to miss several shows before coming back and carrying on. Afterwards I gave her follow up lessons.

Nicholas Hytner took over as Artistic Director of the NT in 2003 and, after starting with *Henry V,* he then saw the potential in the controversial *Jerry Springer: The Opera,* loosely based on the Jerry Springer Show in the States. It contained 'Judeo-Christian themes, extensive profanity and surreal images such as a troupe of tap-dancing Ku Klux Klan members'.

This was a British musical written by Richard Thomas and Stewart Lee and, in spite of street protests and the organization Christian Voice trying to bring blasphemy charges against the show, it won four Olivier Awards. The magistrate's court refused to issue a summons, a decision that was later upheld by the High Court of Justice.

The standard of singing was outstanding. I found myself involved with much Alexander work helping to prevent voice strain. The show was all singing with very little speaking. Many of the actors were extremely large and were expected to dance as they sang, which they found exhausting. I was again worried that my table would not stand up to these weighty beings, but it stood the test, thank heaven.

I had very little to do with *The Light Princess* in Jan 2014 with music by Tori Amos and Samuel Adamson. I was sorry about this as there were some wonderful puppeteers in it, but none that I had worked with previously. I found the music was a disappointment as there were no catchy tunes, none to sing along with, which for me is an essential in a musical. It did look spectacular though and was a great production.

In September 2014, I was involved with *Here Lies Love*, which had taken New York by storm and came hot from Broadway. It was the opening show at the Dorfman, 'a life-giving, roof-raising, booty-shaking blast of pure joy', was the marketing description.

The music was by David Byrne and Fatboy Slim and the show traced the astonishing journey of Imelda Marcos, first lady of the Philippines, through her meteoric rise to power and subsequent descent into infamy and disgrace. Imelda's shoes were not mentioned.

The set was a stage manager's nightmare. It was constantly on the move, incorporating the audience with the actors. The audience were encouraged to dance along and were given little chance to sit throughout the performance. I went three times with my teenage grandchildren, who loved it, and I would have gone again if there had been a chance.

I taught many of the cast, who were mainly Filipinos, and delightful. They had superb voices, in particular Natalie Mendoza who played Imelda, but sadly I only gave a couple of lessons to her. I gave more lessons to Mark Bautista playing Ferdinand Marcos, who was a beautiful dancer as well as a singer.

I have never seen such energy as demonstrated by Martin Sarreal, playing a disc jockey, and he was singing and swinging to the music practically non-stop. I gave him several lessons to help loss of voice, which I noted was all to do with throwing his head back and losing support from his back with all the jigging about. He also had a bad habit of putting his head right over to one side. I made him sing in front of the mirror and watch his head gradually go over. We listened to his voice when he was shutting his eyes with his head off centre – and then going forward and up – and the difference was very marked. The voice immediately had more resonance and tone. It was exciting for us both to see that just a few lessons and use of the CD, could do the trick.

Sunny Yeo was a very tall, mobile girl. She too had several

sessions as she was suffering from back pain. I did a great deal of breathing and wall work, while singing with the exercise.

Kok-Hwa Lie, who was inclined to get very tight in his body, needed to be helped to get back to balance and basics after the show. None of these performers had ever had any Alexander and it was rewarding to see how much it helped in such a show where there were no quiet times. It was very difficult to help them to have 'No' moments, to just think neck free, but they were beginning to manage and saw the benefits.

14. Directors and Groups in Rehearsal

The director Sean Mathias, then partner of Ian McKellen, had for many years been a great believer in Alexander and felt it would be very beneficial for his actors. He asked me to give group sessions before the rehearsals started in several of his productions. I recollect one time, when he was directing the legendary Pam Gems' adaptation of *Uncle Vanya*, which was being rehearsed at the Studio with a star studded cast. Ian McKellen was Uncle Vanya, Janet McTeer a magnificent Yelena, Antony Sher as Astrov, Eric Porter as Serebryakov and Lesley Sharp was the hopelessly in love Sonya.

I only managed to have two tables in the room, so the rest of the cast had to lie on the floor. I talked them through inhibition and direction as they moved and explained the breathing process. At the same time, I went from one to the other making fine adjustments to their heads and bodies. One day Eric was late and there was a lot of joking as he had just had his hair cut rather too short. I had saved the table for him and I would always bring books for everyone to put under their heads. That particular morning, I had turned out a book from home with a photograph of Eric as Soames in *The Forsyte Saga* on the front. That had been many years ago when he was a very handsome young man. I said, 'Eric, I have something very special for you to put your head on today' and handed the book to him. He took it from me, looked at it, sat up very straight on the edge of the table and proclaimed in that wonderful voice, 'I want my life back'. Everyone clapped. It was not until I went to the first run through that I realised this was one of his lines as the professor in the play. He thought he was very ill and, as he lay back in the chair on stage, out came that line again, 'I want my life back'.

It had been rumoured that the production would go to Moscow, in which case there might have been a chance that I could have gone too. Sadly, the money could not be found and it did not happen.

I've already mentioned holding group sessions before

rehearsals for another of Sean's productions, *A Little Night Music* with Judi Dench as Desiree. In addition, there was Siân Phillips as Madame Armfeldt, Patricia Hodge, Joanna Riding and Laurence Guittard. I would go across to the National twice a week at 9.30am and I would take them through lying down, a bit of wall work and breathing. After the sessions I would go into Rehearsal Room 1 to watch them. There were occasions when it was quite overpowering to sit there with the whole company dancing towards us, at full throttle, singing at the tops of their voices, full of joy. I often felt tearful and there was the feeling that I was part of the whole thing. When teaching a large group, we used the passageway for wall work because there were seldom any suitable bare spaces in the rehearsal rooms.

Another production that I worked on with Sean was the wonderfully successful, and funny, *Design for Living* at the Donmar Warehouse in 1994 with Rachel Weisz, Clive Owen, Rupert Graves and Paul Rhys. There was no room for my table anywhere, so it was group sessions on stage and individual lessons in the bar. I remember trying to give Rachel a relaxing lesson on one of the benches in the bar as there was nowhere else, but it was so narrow she kept nearly falling off.

Then there was *Les Parents Terribles*, a French farce by Jean Cocteau, where once again I gave mostly group sessions in the rehearsal room. My table was moved to the room and, taking it in turns, I laid the actors down for individual 'goes'. The cast included Frances de La Tour, Sheila Gish, Jude Law and Alan Howard. Alan was the only one who would never join in. When Alexander work was taking place he would go into a corner of the room and turn his back on us all.

One memorable play, also directed by Sean, *Marlene* by Pam Gems, was rehearsing in the Studio. The play was set in 1969 in Paris when Marlene Dietrich did her very last performance. Siân Phillips was playing Marlene. She was magnificent and watching the run throughs it was almost impossible to tell that it was not actually Marlene Dietrich singing, 'Falling in Love Again' and 'La Vie en Rose'. Siân would come for individual lessons and before the rehearsals I would do a group Alexander session for the cast. Pam, who was a large woman with a great sense of humour, insisted on joining in. However, when they all lay on the floor with books under their heads she cried out, 'Girls I will never be able to get up from here. You'll have to help me back on my feet'. Of course, she received assurances from us all. When it came to me talking them through getting up, dear Pam floated up like thistledown. No one was more surprised than Pam and she was given a round of applause – in fact a standing ovation.

Many years later I spoke to Siân in the canteen at the National where she was rehearsing *People* by Alan Bennett. Siân, at 80, immediately recalled the *Marlene* moment and also told me that she had kept all my Alexander notes and still referred to them. I was both amazed and flattered. I asked her, when she came for a lesson before the tour, what her secret was. How was she able, at 80, to take a leading role with probably eight shows a week and all that that involves and still look about twenty years younger?

She simply said that she had given up multi-tasking and this had left her mind clear and able to focus.

I am still trying to take the same advice. I suppose I should use Alexander to be in the present moment, to have what I say are 'No moments', so making it impossible to do too many things at once.

The last time I worked with Sean was when Trevor Nunn was Artistic Director of the National. Trevor asked Sean to direct *Antony and Cleopatra* with Alan Rickman as Antony and Helen Mirren as Cleopatra. Alan Bates was to have been Antony but he had to cancel at the last minute due to an injury. I would give group sessions, but mostly I gave individual lessons to Helen and Alan. I seem to remember it was in the most peculiar corners of the rehearsal rooms when nothing else was going on. They were both a delight. Alan, of course, I knew from before at the RSC, but Helen was surprisingly nervous. I remember getting her vitamin pills to help her through, although apparently she had played Cleopatra a long time previously, so learning her lines was not too formidable.

The production however was not a success for several reasons. The design of the set was quite complicated with exits and entrances confusing both the audience and the actors. The reviews were terrible although it did not seem to deter the public. It remained booked out for the whole run.

I think Sean felt it was a bit tough of Trevor to give him the challenge of *Antony and Cleopatra* for his first Shakespeare. There was one incident in the production that wasn't publicised, the escape of the snake. Helen had a real live snake wound around her neck and at the end of one show, it escaped, never to be found again, dead or alive, poor thing.

Paul Miller is another director who always asked me to do group sessions. He was such a generous man and directed several plays at the National Theatre. Much later on he ran the Studio for a while when Sue Higginson left and they were looking to appoint a new Studio manager.

Paul received great acclaim for his direction of three plays that were plucked from the NT's Connections series: *DNA*, *The Miracle* and *Baby Girl*. For all these I worked with the cast in groups. It was a bit of a challenge as the average age must have been about nineteen or twenty and they tended to talk to one another whilst I was trying to explain Alexander. I had to be rather strict. It was like teaching a lot of unruly teenagers and not an enjoyable experience because I suddenly felt awkward, although I tried not to show it.

Paul always gave me a very complimentary introduction, saying how well known I was and that I was his friend. This always made me blush a bit as I found being complimented in public rather embarrassing.

The production of *The Enchantment* that he also directed, which unfortunately did not get good reviews, had very impressive casting. Nancy Carroll was pregnant at the time and had to have the dresses made to be adaptable for her tummy to expand. She was previously such a slight build.

My pupil Ray Newe, who played the Postman in the same production, was very tall – well over six feet – and was also extremely nervous about his lines, which were actually the key to the whole play. We went over and over his entrance and preparing for it, using Alexander and breathing until he felt much more confident. I was there on the press night and one review, probably the only good one, was praising him, saying that there was a glorious cameo by Ray Newe as the postman. He delivered his two lines with such finesse and aplomb saying, as he handed over the letter, 'For Miss Louise Strandberg', then after a pause 'Afternoon' – and with that one word he almost stole the show. There was such cheek within it and a glint in his eye, the theatrical hors d'oeuvre and, as the audience would discover later on, the turning point in the whole play. This was really thrilling for him and, after all our hard work, he gained confidence. It was lovely for me as well as I indulged in a bit of reflected glory.

I remember the Director Katie Mitchell, who had a great many individual sessions with me, asked me to do a group session with the cast. I realised almost immediately that she could not cope with someone else interfering with 'her actors' when she stepped in and almost took my place. It was, in retrospect, very funny but only to me. No one else saw the joke as they were so used to Katie directing operations that it seemed perfectly natural, so I said nothing at all and did as I was told.

When I was at the Studio in 1993, Bill Gaskill was directing Pirandello's, *The Mountain Giants.* I had heard stories from a great many of my actors about being directed by Bill. He was a great director but rather terrifying. I would have them coming to me to be calmed down and given confidence as he was a perfectionist and did not suffer fools gladly. To my astonishment, Bill himself came to me for a series of lessons. I discovered that he was actually not at all frightening, but rather nervous and unsure of himself. He was a delight to talk to and very receptive to the technique. I learnt so much from his vast experience of the theatre world. I hope that he found the lessons as valuable to him as his knowledge was to me.

I worked with the young Bijan Sheibani at the Studio when he was a Director on attachment and afterwards at the National, where for some time he was an Associate Director. Bijan was given, unfairly I thought, three major plays to direct right at the beginning of his work at the NT.

First was *Greenland* in 2011, a collaboration between four writers: Moira Buffini, Matt Charman, Penelope Skinner and Jack Thorne. It had very mixed reviews – mainly because it was difficult to direct a play encompassing four differing opinions.

The second was Arnold Wesker's *The Kitchen* was revived at the National and has held a special place in my heart as, having run a restaurant myself, it brought back many memories. The frenzy of serving sometimes hundreds of people, ovens breaking down, staff not turning up, the zillions of things that go wrong and the total exhaustion at the end of the day.

I also saw the original production at the Royal Court and have to say I much preferred this one and the show was a great success. I had a great time teaching many of the girls, the waitresses, who had to teeter around in stiletto type heels.

This illustrates another aspect of the excitement of teaching the actors. We have to devise a way to use Alexander to help problems with the set or the costume. I always ask them to bring their shoes or costumes in. Then we can work with them being worn.

Then there was *Damned by Despair*, Frank McGuiness' adaptation of Tirso de Molina's play. The title really says it all. It was a devil of a play to direct and closed before the end of the run through lack of support.

Bijan has directed two shows since then. There was Erich Kastner's *Emil and the Detectives*, the Christmas show of 2013, which would have been a challenge for any director as it involved 180 children in three teams. When the show was on things were pretty chaotic behind the scenes. And then in 2014 he directed *A Taste of Honey,* which I mentioned earlier.

Ian Rickson and Polly Teale both came to me first at the Studio. Ian has subsequently directed *The Red Lion* in the Dorfman at the NT. He had a lesson every week right through the rehearsal period and we built up a great relationship as he was rehearsing right next door to the Quiet Room. Ian is so in tune with his mind and body. It was fascinating for both of us to work on his state of 'presentness'. Actors respond to the state of the director and will quite unconsciously take their cue from him.

If the director is stressed or sitting at the table in front of them slumped and not appearing to care about the actor, he will create the wrong atmosphere in the room. The overall impression of Ian is that he loves the actors, he cares about them and listens to them. They in return respond by opening up and giving their very best. Without exception they really love working with him.

Jeremy Herrin, the Artistic Director of Headlong, is another director with whom I have really enjoyed working. I first met Jeremy when he was directing *This House* at the NT. Stage management sent him to me in desperation. He was so stressed, he couldn't keep still and I really had a job on my hands.

At the same time as *This House,* he was preparing to direct *Wolf Hall* and *Bring Up the Bodies* for the RSC, which followed on from *The Tempest* at The Globe.

I remember one day Jeremy said that he was going to meet Hilary Mantel, the author of *Wolf Hall* and *Bring Up the Bodies,* to discuss the plays. He was rather dreading it as she was reputed to be quite an alarming woman to deal with. I joked with him and said she probably only came up to his navel as Jeremy is extremely tall, well over six feet even before Alexander so she would find him quite formidable as well.

These directors have always been highly intellectual and, if they are men, I find that it is a job to stop them intellectualising their problems rather than listening to their bodies and minds. It has been the same with writers whom I have previously referred to as my 'head cases'. They have been completely out of touch with their bodies – unless perchance they are hurting.

Jeremy understood and applied my explanation of the technique. It was exciting to see how he would quieten down and experience stillness, whilst resisting the need to move and twist about to relieve the tension.

Jeremy's latest play by Duncan Macmillan, *People, Places and Things* was, is, an extraordinary play about addiction and the central character's struggles with re-hab, her parents' reaction to having a daughter who is an addict and then to her eventual recovery, sometimes temporary, sometimes ongoing.

It is mostly set in a re-hab centre, with fine performances from all the cast dealing with a maybe familiar process to some, but nevertheless a very painful experience to watch and perform. Not many laughs.

I read the play and told Jeremy of my involvement in the drugs and alcohol scene. Jeremy suggested that they took advice – and I gave lessons to most of the cast. My experience of addiction, dealing with people close to me suffering from this illness and learning to manage with this extremely difficult situation, helped me to help them. From then on, I felt very involved with the production, which turned out to be a phenomenal success. During the shows, Denise Gough gave an extraordinarily believable and moving performance, about which Jeremy said, 'A Star is Born'.

As with *The Red Lion* and *Evening at the Talk House,* working with this play was once more a very special experience. The directors had made me feel that I was part of the whole production and could see how useful Alexander can be to the actors, the director and anyone else connected in this exciting process. I felt very privileged.

In 1993, with the production of *Sweeney Todd,* Declan Donnellan, the director, and Nick Ormerod, his partner and designer, would come for their lessons together. Each would sit outside my teaching room at the Studio waiting for the other to finish their session. I found it rather touching, but was not quite sure whether they had actually taken on board what I was trying to explain.

I taught Jonathan Kent at my home in Barnes for some time, while he was just acting. This was before 1990, when he joined Ian McDiarmid as joint Artistic Director and together they transformed the Almeida into a major producing theatre.

I enjoyed teaching these directors enormously although it can be a bit nerve wracking. I always have to overcome feelings that I am not intelligent enough to cope with conversations about the theatre, that my opinions are not important or of interest to someone who is obviously much better educated. So I have had to become quite good at brazening it out. I think I might have been quite a good actress after all.

However, I do remember once getting annoyed with Adrian Noble whom I was trying to encourage to take lessons as he was suffering from aches and pains. Having watched him in rehearsal, he was forever twitching, never still for a moment so I knew the technique would help him. Emboldened with a glass of wine, I said to him that I felt should he have lessons. If he did, there would be no need for any of the actors to come for Alexander sessions. However, it was noisy and luckily I don't think he heard me as he might have been offended – and I would have regretted it.

I never forget the London press night of *Pericles*. I talked to Adrian's son, who could only have been about 7 years old, and asked him how he had enjoyed the play. It was so sweet as he looked up at me and said, 'Thank you for asking. I enjoyed it very much, it was my first Shakespeare'.

I've mentioned all the directors that I have actually taught, but I have to mention Peter Brook who came to the Studio to do a three-week workshop with actors. I felt I had to introduce myself – I was a great admirer of his work – and it seemed to me that he must be aware of the Alexander Technique. When watching his productions, the 'presentness' and 'stillness' of the actors was so completely what I had hoped to be able to achieve through my teaching. Anyway I bravely went up to him because I had another connection that I wanted to make him aware of.

Peter had directed the *Lord of the Flies* film and my cousin, Tom Gaman, had been picked out of his class at school to be the character Simon. When I had lived in the States with my cousins Tom had been a delightful five-year-old. He had been very solemn, with, I seem to remember, very large ears, which did not detract from his beauty. He was a gorgeous little boy.

I said to Peter that I felt I must tell him that Tom Gaman was my cousin. Hearing this he shrieked, 'This is marvellous,' he said, 'I must contact him'. Peter was making a documentary in which the cast of *Lord of the Flies* all go back to the island and meet up after forty years of having been apart and getting on with their lives. It had been commissioned by the BBC and, 'We can't find Piggy', said Peter.

It was very exciting, Piggy was found, the film was made and I went to the first showing in the Studio. There was much merriment and excitement – so I never regretted my boldness in approaching the great Peter Brook – although I didn't manage to give him a lesson – he probably didn't need it.

Ian Rickson was working as an Assistant Director on a production with Rufus Norris, the Artistic Director of the National. I was teaching Ian and he said he was going to propose that Rufus come to see me for lessons. At the press night of *People, Places and Things* I decided to approach Rufus and tell him I had been working with Ian and many of the cast. I suggested that maybe we could arrange for him to come and be de-stressed with a bit of Alexander. He enthusiastically agreed and said that I should go to his personal assistant, who was starting in three weeks, to fix up a regular appointment for him.

As you can imagine, I was thrilled. I feel that this is what I have always wanted – to work with the Artistic Director and so secure the future of Alexander, which I have fought so hard to make an accepted part of the programme, for all members of the National Theatre.

15. War Horse Company Puppeteers

One day I was summoned to Rehearsal Room 1 at the Studio by the director Tom Morris. Tom had always threatened to come for lessons but never made it – and it was a bit of a joke between us. So I was amazed to be confronted with the very first Joey horse puppet, a larger-than-life horse. *War Horse* was starting at the National Theatre.

Inside were three puppeteers, one in front holding Joey's head, another one as the heart and at the back of the horse the 'hind' working his hind legs. It was an amazing sight. Tom wanted me to see what the puppeteers were up against. He thought that these guys were going to need my help.

Little did I realise that this was going to be the beginning of some very exciting work with the puppeteers. I worked with the puppeteers for the show, which is now a worldwide success in Japan, Australia and America – a theatrical phenomenon, right up until the final London party before going on tour in the UK.

I became fascinated by the extremes of tension, stress and energy that were used to manipulate the two big horses, Joey and Topthorn and then baby Joey where again three puppeteers were needed. The Mustering horses, where the puppet is just the top of a horse, has a single puppeteer underneath. The horse has to be manipulated when they charge into battle, collapsing as they die. There are places in the background where, with the clever use of the lighting, they appear to be fully grown horses. It also creates the effect of there being a large group of horses when in fact there are no more than half a dozen. Those puppeteers also do 'hoofing', meaning that they have to kneel down low on the ground and work the hooves of the horses when they are in full gallop. I could immediately see that they would need a great deal of help and Alexander lessons would be of great benefit.

I was able to inspect the harnesses of the puppeteers in Topthorn and Joey. I noted that the heart puppeteer had very little support for their backs and were continually bending over from the centre of their spine so hardly using their hip joints for movement at all.

I talked to the girl who was fitting the harnesses and suggested that a wide elasticated band of about eighteen inches was inserted into the back of the harness. This way, the puppeteer had support whilst still allowing them to bend and reducing the risk of collapse in the centre of the spine. I felt that otherwise the strain would, and of course sometimes did, result in injuries.

To my relief, this was taken seriously and the adjustment was carried out. As far as I know, the modification is still used with the many horses that have been since made.

When teaching the puppeteer, one of the first things I ask them to recognise is where their hip joints are. For nearly all pupils this is a revelation. They will point vaguely to their waists or the tips of the hip bones. As I explained in Lesson 3, that junction in the body is so vital. The hip must hinge when bending, sitting or walking as otherwise people will unfortunately bend from the waist (the lumbar area). The lower back will then suffer and, for many, end up being painful as a great deal of strain is put on the lumbar and sacroiliac area.

War Horse then moved from the National to the New London theatre and I started to go up there for an afternoon to teach. Lovely Charles Evans was the theatre manager at the time. I had known him since Stratford days, so he made arrangements for me to give an introductory session before the show to as many of the puppeteers that we could muster. This group session would take place on the stage. As usual, I would then give a brief explanation of what Alexander is all about, they would lie down and I would talk them through using inhibiting and directing. I arrived early, went into the green room for a cup of tea and a chat with them and then I would go onto the stage where puppeteers were often rehearsing various moves with the horses. This was so useful for me because I could begin to see what they were doing with their bodies whilst manipulating these extremely heavy horse puppets. I was especially interested in the horse noises that all three puppeteers needed to make and I felt sure that I would be able to help them with their breathing.

Charles showed me the room where I was going to be working. It had plenty of mirrors, in fact the walls were surrounded with them, and he asked me if I would mind if there was a lot of horses in there as well. Baby Joey was across the end of room, around the walls were Joey and Topthorn heads and there were legs and bits of horse hanging from the ceiling. It was a rather strange atmosphere to work in as you would suddenly find Joey's eye fixed on you. I would turn his head around so that he was looking in the other direction.

I really liked working in amongst the cast and being able to just go through and watch them rehearsing. Sadly, this arrangement came to an end and the management decided that the puppeteers would have to come to the National for their lessons. I then had to ask for more time for their sessions – which was a complication. In the end it worked out that I had sessions on a Tuesday as well as Thursdays and Fridays to fit in NT actors and the War Horse company.

In October 2010, Handspring Puppet Company brought the show *Or You Could Kiss Me* to the Cottesloe. It had life sized puppets and only one animal – a rheumy old dog. The story was of a gay couple in a lifelong relationship. Adrian Kohler and Basil Jones, amongst others, were puppeteering.

It received nothing like the reception that *War Horse* had. This was rather disappointing as the puppets were so lifelike, you felt that you could shake their hands and they would respond.

During the run, I managed to give several lessons to Adrian Kohler. This was very exciting for me, as Adrian almost immediately understood what was going on and how the Alexander Technique would be invaluable to the puppeteers. He generously wrote a letter of encouragement, to all puppeteers, in which he shared how Alexander had helped him and suggested that they all took advantage of lessons.

Adrian wrote:

> 'I found that the alexander lessons were of great benefit to a puppeteer.
>
> I came to the technique late, towards the end of the run of *Or You Could Kiss Me* at the National Theatre, so only had five lessons, but am writing this to say how much I benefitted from them. Craig Leo, veteran of *War Horse,* urged me to go. He always looked delightfully relaxed after a lesson. A relaxed mind and body is something you can take with you into the run up to a performance, but this is not the main reason to have lessons.
>
> Warming up before a performance gets the body focused on the heavy physical work ahead, but the mental preparedness for me has been more difficult. When the play is new, I carry several fears about: Will I get everything right, how will this particular audience be? In the thirty seconds or so before my cue light, my mind can become a jumble of anxious thoughts. I found this a perfect time to apply the lessons and do a few simple exercises that Sue taught me. Instantly my mind relaxed and cue-light fear disappeared.
>
> In other parts of the performance, when I had less to do and found my mind wandering, another quick Alexander reminder brought everything back into place.
>
> When a new play becomes one you do for a long time, there will inevitably be moments when, for whatever reason, you don't feel like appearing. You can then call on the technique to clear your head.
>
> I imagine it should also be very useful for rehearsal when you feel exposed and raw. I have yet to see whether that works, however, I'm convinced that a lot of injury could be avoided if these techniques were known, say by horse teams, when preparing to do a bout of very physical moves. I imagine too, that within a team, this knowledge would help to deal with group tensions should they arise.

So take a series of lessons. They build on one another. Talk to someone who regularly attends Sue's lessons. It's not about how to get out of a chair, its about how to sit well in your life.'

I am going to add here some feedback from two of the leading Puppeteers, both the head of Joey, who have benefitted so much from the technique.

Nicholas Hart wrote his thoughts and sent this to me, which was very gratifying for me as his teacher.

'The principles of Alexander Technique, if manifested in your puppeteering body, can manifest in the puppet itself.

An awareness of the space in your own body will inevitably lead to an awareness in your puppet's body too. This allows you to discover and explore a whole new world of micro-movement, a term coined by the Handspring Puppet Company to express the slightest movements of a puppet that best reflect the slightest movements in real life.

If I, as the head puppeteer, think of my neck to be free, head to go forward and up, I actively see the head of my puppet becoming free, his head moving forward and up and I am able to achieve greater control. I can focus not on the physical demands of puppeteering, but on the story and the character of the puppet. I can breathe life into the puppets thoughts and objectives.

The puppet is heavy. It requires a lot of strength to prevent it from becoming a 'dead weight' on stage, but the idea of strength can often manifest itself as whole body tension in certain areas like the shoulders for example.

This tension has become so habitual through life that we no longer notice it, it feels normal. I have learned through practising Alexander that the strength needed to hold Joeys head is achievable through lengthening and widening. You can discover strength in a free body, in a spine that lengthens and widens, instead of compressing and narrowing in an attempt to engage the wrong muscles. If you allow the weight of the puppet to travel down your arm, into your body, and down through your heels into the ground, you are allowing gravity to hold the head for you.

The deep, strong breath I discover through practising the technique allows my voice to resonate louder and clearer, despite the intense physical effort I have to exert. I am grounded, with my spine stacked, so I have greater control over my voice, the horse noises that I need to make, and the puppet I am controlling.

You have to actively practise Alexander regularly to reap its benefits, it is not purely physical. You have to open your mind in addition to your body. The only way to stop the impulse to tilt your head backwards when speaking is to replace the impulse, the habit – to replace the impulse with the thought 'No' and instead allow the neck to be free and your head to move forwards and up. This approach allows you to eventually reach a point where during a performance, you can conduct regular check-ins with your body and thinking 'No' to superfluous tension without forcing relaxation.'

And then Gareth Aled's thoughts emphasising the key Alexander directions:

'Puppeteering the head of the horses is as much of a physical challenge as it is an acting one. You need the strength and stamina to technically meet the demands of the play, but at the same time, a specificity, a sensitivity to detail to clearly tell the story. It is sometimes hard to feel that you are succeeding at both.

Acting is a huge exercise in listening. Having performed the play many times I have realised that I do my best work when I am able to strike a balance between relaxation/realise and tension/engagement. It is a type of "front footedness" which enables an ease, a presence and a focus to the work that I do. Once I have gained control of my body, the detail and curiosity I strive to deliver will naturally follow.

For me, during performance, I "check in" and focus on several main questions:

- Are my head & neck free?
- Are my shoulders released?
- Is my back lengthening and widening?
- Is my lower back arching or is it supported?
- Are my knees locked or released?

During a performance, in the moment, you can't possibly give yourself a full evaluation, but using these shortcut questions gives me an adequate awareness.

Finding and maintaining alignment between Joey's head, heart & hind is a constant challenge, however aspiring for this in my own human body naturally translates to the puppet.

The Alexander Technique has therefore been an imperative in my journey thus far and for the work I continue to strive for.'

As these actors have to work every day, sometimes doing nine shows a week, they have a unique opportunity to work on themselves and all the time are making new discoveries.

As I mentioned earlier, the puppeteers make all the noises that a horse would make in whatever situation they are placed, be it frightened, galloping, in pain or whilst just grazing or eating. I noted sometimes, when breathing and making horse noises, they were not using their diaphragms and this meant that they were gulping in air using the upper chest. The process was started by tightening the neck and throwing the head back, which shortened the whole body. I found that working against the wall and giving the puppeteers an awareness of their backs against the wall while breathing and using the technique worked wonders, which they could then take on into movement.

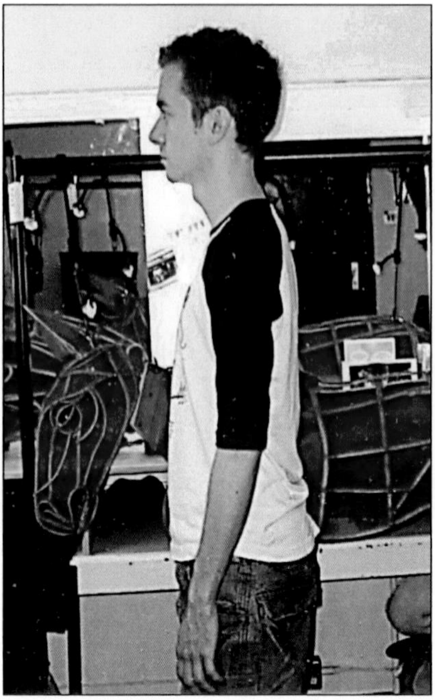

Toby Olié, hind of Joey, taking a lesson with baby Joey

The breathing and horse sounds were then heard by the audience as if the noises were coming from inside the horse, while at the same time the puppeteer felt much more in control. If I shut my eyes, the horse whinnies and frightened screeches were so realistic that it really felt as though there was a live horse in the room.

As well as the puppeteers, I worked with the Song man or woman. You will know if you have seen the show that this is quite a scary part, as they have to play an accordion, which is very heavy, and sing out all alone, centre stage. During lessons, I would have them singing and playing from the wall, or going through the wall exercise both before and after the show to help them back into balance.

It is the same with the puppeteers – it is vitally important for them to do some wall work and lying down with inhibition and direction at the end of the day to make sure they leave the show behind. By doing this they notice habits or tensions that have begun during the performance and they will be more aware next time they are in the show.

In the penultimate year of the show Nick and Gareth inspired many of the other puppeteers to come across to the NT and have help with Alexander. Even though there were countless accidents and subsequently huge medical bills for the NT, I am thrilled to be able to say that not a single one of my pupils ever suffered from a self-induced injury. I battled away during the whole of the ten or more years to try to emphasise the benefit of Alexander to the company with only some success. However, I did manage to keep the lessons going and teaching them gave me huge pleasure – especially when the puppeteers told me how much it had helped them.

I will never forget the last night in London. Just writing and thinking about it makes me emotional.

On the evening of 12th March 2016, a platform performance, *War Horse: The Final Farewell,* was staged. The author Michael Morpurgo was joined on stage by Basil Jones and Adrian Kohler, who had designed the original puppets, Tom Morris and Marianne Elliott, the co-directors and Rae Smith the designer. Then there was Adrian Sutton, whose score won him Olivier and Dora (Toronto) nominations and Songmaker John Tams. The line up included Toby Sedgwick, director of movement and horse choreography and Nick Starr, who was co-founder of the London Theatre Company with Nicolas Hytner in 2015.

Everyone shared their stories of the creation of this amazing production. Michael Morpurgo spoke fluently. He had had initial doubts that this audacious plan would ever work, but had obviously been proven wrong. *War Horse*, his book, had been spectacularly interpreted by actors with puppet horses and was reducing audiences, even grown men, to tears throughout the world. He ended the platform to huge rounds of applause.

Afterwards the final performance of *War Horse* at the New London theatre took place. This was followed by a party, which went on far into the early hours, where there were tears and laughter with the sharing of memories of this unique experience – working with one of the most talked about plays that the West End, indeed the world, has seen for many years.

16. Actors in Other Countries

Travels with Ben Kingsley

In the days when the Almeida had Sunday matinees, we often used to go and have lunch there as well as going to the play. This was really lovely to do as in those days there was nowhere near as much traffic and it was easy to drive there and park. I had been teaching the director Alison Kingsley while I was in Stratford and she insisted that I meet Ben, her husband who, she said, badly needed Alexander. I was duly introduced, he seemed interested and said he would be in touch the next time I was in Stratford.

About two months later, he began having lessons and it proved to be the beginning of working with Ben for about four years. This was 1986 when Ben was in several productions at the RSC. The first was *Othello,* with Ben as Othello, David Suchet as Iago and Niamh Cusack as a very young Desdemona at the beginning of her career as an actress. It was especially gratifying working with Ben as he took Alexander and really used it with his part as the Moor. He said that what he would like to achieve was to think 'no' in between each syllable.

I found it a very exciting production. I was very closely involved, as I taught Ben and Niamh every time I was up there as well as several others in the cast – although not David Suchet. I went up on press night and, at the party afterwards, when I congratulated Ben on his success, he generously said, 'I think there was a little bit of you in there, Sue'.

Ben would come to my house in Barnes for lessons whenever he was in London and he became a friend as well as a pupil. I was very excited when he said that he was going to Brazil to work in a film called *The 5th Monkey*. Would I like to go out there and carry on with his lessons?

Never having been to South America before, or at this stage anywhere else very far from Barnes, I didn't know what to expect. I was having to say a great deal of NO to keep myself calm.

Brazil

Ben arranged for me to join him once they had started shooting. I was to work with him and with any other members of the crew who would like some Alexander.

The 5th Monkey featured four chimpanzees with Ben supposedly being the fifth. I was flown out business class, which was bliss. It was my first experience of luxury on a long haul flight and I could have quite happily stayed on board for longer than the six hours as it was so comfortable. However, we had to stop in San Paulo for two hours, which slightly marred my good spirits, but eventually we got to Rio where there were two very jolly looking Brazilians waving a flag with, 'Lorry for Kingsley' written on it in huge letters. It took about two hours to get to Parati, an idyllic small town on the river mouth with a bay full of little islands with palm trees. The streets were cobbled and there was practically no traffic. Its beauty often attracted film crews.

I was staying in a small hotel with the crew and Ben had a little house down one of the streets nearby. I was taken straight to the film set to be greeted by everyone and then, thankfully, went to my room to recover.

Everyone was up about 6.30 and had breakfast at 7.00. This was delicious, with a choice of little pastries made with cheese, homemade bread, piles of fruit, mango, papaya, pineapple – nothing ordinary like apples or pears. The best coffee I had ever tasted – and there was ham or crispy bacon and egg if you needed extra protein.

Then off to the jungle, which is where practically all the filming took place. It seemed to be full of the sort of plants that I almost seemed to recognise – because I might have had them at home on the dining room table as house plants. Of course here they were gigantic, towering above us up to the sky.

What made my days were the chimpanzees. Each one had their trainer holding their hand and sitting beside them whenever we stopped, which was often as there was much hanging around. One of the chimps belonged to Michael

Jackson and was called Bubbles. He was probably the largest of the four. The youngest and smallest was so lovable and called Land Rover, though quite why I never discovered. They had a big trailer in which they travelled to and from set staying in Parati in the evenings.

While we were waiting for developments the chimps were a great source of amusement. The trainers would play games of catch with them and send them right up to the top of the tallest trees to fetch things like coconuts or bananas.

One day Boone, the head trainer, smoking incessantly as he did, was standing with his chimp beside him. Boone had a way of holding the cigarette between the third and fourth finger and I saw the chimp watching him curiously. The chimp then picked a cigarette out of the pack lying on the floor at Boone's feet, carefully placed it between the exact same fingers, put it to his lips and took a deep puff – and then looked rather disappointed when there was no smoke coming out of the end.

I had to again get used to teaching in extraordinary places. Ben had his own caravan, where I had no table so it was chair or floor work only. In the hotel, where I gave various members of the company lessons, things were easier as there was a suitable table in my room. I had to very much just teach whoever was there in front of me. There was inevitably a lot of stress around, so it meant a lot of listening and calming down. This was where my counselling course proved very useful.

I spent quite a bit of time with Boone's girlfriend when we had some time off. On one occasion we went to a local zoo, which was very upsetting. Although the animals were well fed, their cages were too small and often needed cleaning, so the smell was unbearable. We wandered on and rounding a corner came upon a cheetah. It was simply tethered to a post with no surrounding fence. At first he appeared to be sleeping, but opened an eye and, seeing us, rose to his feet and walked towards us. We thought he might be hungry and looking for food, so we made a quick dash for the exit, which luckily was not too far away.

On another occasion, Ben and I went walking into the jungle. Quite suddenly, we came upon a little clearing with a couple of huts. There were goats, donkeys and vegetable plots with a fire burning in the centre, which had cooking pots strung over it. Neither of us spoke any Portuguese and their English was minimal. However, we managed to find out that it was a family who had lived there for many years existing on what they could grow. To see other human beings was quite a rare occurrence, but, when they realised we were friendly, the rifles were put down and they offered us food and water which we politely declined. They seemed to be sorry to see us go.

I fell in love with Brazil, the scenery was stunning and I really felt that I was part of another culture. Looking out to sea, there were little islands dotted around, some of them minute with maybe just a couple of palm trees on them. Ben decided that, at the weekend, we should hire a boat and sail out to one for lunch.

The island we went to just had a couple of huts with a cluster of trees on the top and down by the water's edge was a restaurant, if you could call it that. It had a counter with a cooking arrangement behind and a very friendly cook who told us what there was on the menu. It was the inevitable prawns, crab and salad, brought to us in great style, with beer and fruit for pudding.

It was idyllic. We swam, sunbathed and generally relaxed until the sun began to go down when the boatman arrived to take us back.

As we landed, a small crowd began to follow us chanting, 'Gandhi, Gandhi', much to Ben's annoyance as he had hoped that here he would not be recognized. However, this began to be a regular occurrence. He found himself signing autographs and talking to his fans, when he had hoped to be able to travel incognito so far away from the big cities.

One evening we heard that a puppet company (hand puppets) were doing a show. They were meant to be famous in Brazil, so Ben and I went along to watch as we both loved puppetry. It was held in a very small, dimly lit hall, but luckily we arrived early and had good seats. It was very popular and when the show started there wasn't an empty seat anywhere.

There were two stories, both of which were rather sad. The first was a love story, a story of unrequited love. It was so sad, and, with an accompaniment of haunting music, so beautifully told by the puppeteers with their long delicate fingers that I found I had tears in eyes.

The second story I found more difficult to understand (the characters were speaking in Portuguese), but again there was not much joy or laughter and with a death at the end. This story didn't move me so much although the quality of the work was just as impressive.

We were told that we must visit a waterfall in the jungle. So very early one morning, we went there and found a huge flat rock with a completely smooth surface in the middle of the river at the top of the waterfall. Here we could sit and listen to the noises of the jungle, watch the birds and the fish and take in the beauty of it all. We came back several times to the same spot. I felt I needed to remember this place, to keep it in my heart forever.

Inevitably the filming was coming to an end and it was time for me to go, but I will never forget my last morning. The car taking me to Rio was coming to the set. That day they were filming halfway up a mountain and there I was, all packed up and ready to go at 7.30 in the morning.

I wanted specially to say goodbye to the chimps. The trainers and Boone said, 'Right guys, come and say goodbye to Sue. She's going today'.

One by one, they jumped off the trailer and stood in a line in front of me. Then each of them held out their hand and vigorously shook mine. When it came to Land Rover, Boone said, 'Come on Land Rover, give her a kiss'. Obediently the baby chimp leapt into my arms, put his arms around my neck and kissed me on both cheeks.

Land Rover saying Goodbye to Sue

That completely finished me off, the tears came streaming down. I climbed into the car and we all waved until they were out of sight. I felt immensely sad at leaving that very special place and wanted to stay until the end of the filming. But it was not possible, I had to get back to work at home.

Generously, Ben had arranged for me to stay in a five-star hotel in Rio for two nights before my flight. I was rather nervous, but it turned out that two of the American producers I had met in Parati were staying there as well. They suggested that we meet for dinner that evening.

I had a great room overlooking the beach. In the afternoon I went down with my costume and plunged into the sea as it was so hot. The beach was stiff with beautiful people, some not so beautiful, but I had managed a bit of a tan so did not feel too out of it. It was exciting to be in Rio, but I was a bit wary of wandering around on my own. I had been warned of pickpockets, so had bought myself a denim jacket with zip up pockets on the inside, which took a bit of getting used to.

I had also been warned to never go too far from the hotel to just walk around. And at night, to go everywhere by taxi. That evening I met up with the producers and we went off to have dinner with some friends of theirs in a sumptuous flat. It was right on the top floor overlooking the sea and Rio at night, an amazing sight to see. The following day I was left to my own devices. In the morning, I went on the beach again and in the afternoon took a taxi ride around the city with a well-informed driver. He delighted in showing me through the shanti towns, which were more horrifying than Soweto, a town I was to see later in South Africa. They seemed to go on for miles with the ramshackle huts so close together. The children looked very undernourished and were playing around in the dirt seemingly unhappy and uncared for. In Soweto, I found that the families, and the children in particular, looked happier.

I did walk around the hotel and look at a few of the shops, which were very expensive and not particularly inviting. The pavements were full of beggars. I came upon a very handsome young boy, who could not have been any older than seventeen or eighteen, who had no arms or legs – it was horrific. The limbs had been taken off just above the elbows and before the knees. He was smiling hopefully at all the passers-by. Just as I was about to put some money in his cap, an ancient old woman, who looked very poor and like a beggar herself, came up to him. She said something in Portuguese as she put money into the cap before shuffling off down the street.

That evening I had dinner in a local restaurant with the producers again. They insisted on treating me and we gossiped about the film. They seemed to have many problems with it, the money needed to market it and so on. I had heard whispers about this when I was in Parati, but thank goodness it was nothing to do with me.

The next morning, I was off home, full of memories from a very full experience and vowing to come back some day. So far I haven't managed it, but then who knows what fate has in store.

The 5th Monkey, I am afraid, never progressed further than being made into a video, which was sad. I gathered this was because there was not enough money to market it. I wouldn't have missed being involved with the film making in that magical setting for anything. Thank you Ben.

Austria

In 1990 there was a movie made of the book, *The Children,* by Edith Wharton. Tony Palmer directed it with a very starry cast including Ben Kingsley, Kim Novak, Geraldine Chapman, Britt Ekland, Donald Sinden and Rupert Graves.

Once again, Ben asked me to join the cast in a hotel near Salzburg. This was not just to teach him, but also to work with many of the cast. It kept me busy and there was not nearly as much hanging around as there had been with *The 5th Monkey.* Anyone who has ever been involved in the shooting of a film knows that it can be interminably boring as things sometimes move very slowly. I had never been to Austria, so we went into Salzburg several times where I went to Mozart's birthplace and the museum with his piano. However, there was no time to do much other than look in the shops, which were rather mouth-watering. I did have a couple of lovely meals in the five-star Hotel Goldener Hirsch, where Ben insisted on being given a table even though it was apparently totally booked out.

I declined a visit to Berchtesgaden, which I saw in the distance through a mist. It looked so very gloomy and forbidding. In spite of the cloud that day, the weather on the whole was beautiful and clear, which we needed for the filming as a great deal of it was outside. For the inside shots, an amazing house and grounds had been hired. The owner was a middle-aged woman, who was completely attired in the Austrian fashion with Tyrolean green hat, fitted jacket, trousers and high boots to finish off the effect. The hat was worn both inside and out and we were regaled constantly with tales of her tragic divorce, interspersed with warnings about the value of the furniture and knick-knacks that lay everywhere. In fact, I don't think I had ever before seen so much kitsch in one place. She was pleasantly bonkers and was always grabbing me for a chat, mostly about her plight. She was trying to direct operations and was worried about anything being broken or damaged.

The house was surrounded by fields and trees with mountains

in the distance. Grazing the fields were llamas and vicunas that the owner took great pride in. There were also a couple of horses and several uncontrolled dogs, which were a bit of a nuisance as they kept coming onto the set.

Rosemary Leach, acting as Miss Scope the teacher, worked with the children. They were a bit unruly so she got rather exhausted. Most of the filming with them seemed to be in a studio and it was there that I gave the majority of the lessons.

Kim Novak, who played Rose Sellers, had starred in many, many films and came for several sessions. She had a number of pet animals, some of them exotic, and it was very interesting talking to her. She was passionate about all of them as well as being a rider and owning several Arabs that she kept on her ranch in Oregon. This was a talking point, as having been a rider myself, I could give her hints about using Alexander with riding. There seemed to be no end to her talents. She became known as a poet, artist and photographer all of which she continued to practise until these interests eventually took priority over her acting career.

Britt Ekland, whose career stretched from 1960 to 1988 on stage and then television to the present day, had sessions too. Britt was fluent in English, French, German and, of course, Swedish her native language. I remember having many talks with her about physical fitness and the application of the Alexander Technique. Britt later made a fitness video.

Both these women were so beautiful and I found it strange to be with them, teaching them and being treated as an equal. They showed a genuine interest in 'me', which, given bouts of uncertainty about my self-worth, I found humbling.

Siri Neal, who played Judith, was very young and, I felt, a bit overwhelmed by working with these stars. I think I helped to give her some confidence in herself as she was very talented and, with a wonderful head of brown curly hair, very pretty.

This was another great experience of being thrown into the unknown, having to adapt to unforeseen circumstances and teaching in strange places, which I came to enjoy. I was meeting people that I would never normally come across. This taught me to communicate with different personalities and to get the Alexander message across in a very short space of time.

Again it was with great thanks to Ben, now Sir Ben Kingsley, he was knighted in 2002, for without him I would probably never have experienced working in the world of film.

Lithuania

The Studio director Sue Higginson was responsible for setting up trips abroad. It was exciting for actors, directors, designers, stage managers, writers and teachers to work with the equivalent skills in theatre companies abroad.

Our first trip was in 1992 to Lithuania. We were invited there by a young director Dalia Ibelhauptaite, who was very enthusiastic that the National should make a cultural visit to Vilnius. She put the idea to Sue. From then on the project grew, and then became a reality, and became a never to be forgotten experience for us all.

Dalia had started the Young Theatre Company at the age of fifteen. She worked in the Vilnius State Theatre, which was instrumental in making arrangements with other theatre companies in Vilnius.

There was great excitement when we set off from Heathrow. We had been warned that it would be cold as, although the end of winter in England, it was still winter in Lithuania. We had heard that there were several shortages there – like coffee, tea, loo paper, soap, tampax and of course chocolate and sweets. Impossible to imagine, but no fruit and certainly no vitamin pills or aspirin.

The team also panicked when it was rumoured that there was no wine, only vodka, but it turned out to be a leg pull – although the wine was disgusting. We took as many bags of sweets as we could squeeze into our suitcases, as presents for them all.

The cheapest way to go was via Warsaw, so the journey was

long and tiring. When we arrived, we were hungry and thirsty. So first and foremost, encouraged by Antony Sher who had been there before, we headed for the nearest bar. We sat drinking neat (they appeared not to have tonic water) 'Stoli', an abbreviation for Stolichnaya, the very delicious Polish Vodka, followed by a huge plate of chips.

On the way, the day in Warsaw was a great bonus as the sun was shining and it happened to be a public holiday. We had a five hour wait, so obtained visas to go into the town. It was fascinating to see the old town, which had been completely rebuilt after the war. Apparently some of the leading architects in Warsaw had realised the likelihood of an imminent invasion and had set their students to work to draw up plans for the rebuilding of the city if disaster struck. When disaster did strike, the result was a magical re-construction of the old city buildings and churches, quite indistinguishable from the past grandeur of the pre-war Warsaw.

Our welcome in Vilnius was ecstatic – the Russians had only recently left and no one had met any actors from the West for many a year. This proved to be the pattern throughout our stay, whenever we met a new group of people. There was always a reception, usually with tea and homemade cakes, and then we were driven to our hostel, which, along with the food and transport, was funded by the Lithuanians. They insisted on making this trip as comfortable as they could for their visitors, in spite of existing on very low salaries themselves. This was very touching and made it extra difficult to say how much we appreciated their generosity. No one we met spoke English, so we had to work with interpreters throughout our stay.

We were then driven to our hostel, which could be described as their equivalent to The Sheraton, very 1930s. The rooms were very rudimentary and everything was brown – including the water that came out of the tap. It was stone cold until it had been running for about ten minutes. Then it turned yellow and was much hotter.

I have to say I was dreading the bed. It was a very narrow wooden bench with a warm, clean duvet, but I suppose anything would have done that first night. There was a four hour difference and we had to be ready to set off at ten o'clock the following morning.

I slept.

The first day was beautifully sunny and bright, but freezing cold. We were collected from the hostel and taken to a hotel for breakfast, which to our horror was enormous. Three fried eggs plus potatoes, bread and jam, mineral water (tasting of salt) and tea – now that was excellent. I had horrendous indigestion for the first few days, but eventually we were able to say that we could not eat quite so much and, to our relief, the portions were cut down. But most importantly we did not offend their generosity.

Aristides, a rather good-looking young man, was our constant minder who spoke practically no English, but was always smiling and helpful.

Sunday, our first day in Vilnius, had been planned as a day of 'rest' for us, which entailed a very tight schedule of seeing the sights of the city. Although it was far from restful, I wouldn't have missed it for anything. Our time after this was so full, we would never have had time to visit the churches and university and walk around the old town, which was very beautiful. Many of the buildings were painted in lovely pinks and yellows and it was heartening to see that so much restoration had already taken place. Some of the churches that had been turned into cinemas were now back to churches again. There were still a few tanks behind high barbed wire fences, lurking like ghostly monsters, which had a sinister air about them.

At one time, there had been forty synagogues and now there was only one. We met a marvellous 75-year-old priest, who had been in Siberia with a wonderful sense of humour and a feeling of serenity about him. He showed us the catacombs, and photographs of himself as a young man in Siberia.

Apart from the very occasional car going by on the cobbles, the whole city was so quiet as there was no aircraft noise and no other traffic.

In the late afternoon, we were taken to the 'Artist Palace', inside the French Embassy, where we were to be working. We first met the interpreters, who I think were all as nervous as we were. There seemed to be about twenty of them and, as I was going to be working on my own most of the time, I was allotted my own personal interpreter, Maria.

Having interpreters was to be a challenge. Lithuanian is said to be the oldest language with no resonances of German, French or even Russian, though Russia is virtually next door. Its roots are in Sanskrit and apparently there are also traces of Finnish.

Maria was one of those people who are always so helpful and energetic that you get exhausted by just being with them. Not exactly what one wants when teaching an anxious, rather depressed, and repressed, Lithuanian actor, how to relax. She followed me everywhere, even to the lavatory.

It was all sorted out eventually and I ended up with a lovely, more suitable girl called Irena.

The French Embassy was a knockout – huge ballrooms with chandeliers and moulded ceilings with grand staircases. The embassy functions were at one end and we were working at the other. I had a small room to teach in and we had asked for a stool to be in there. Sure enough there it was, a very high stool specially made by another Aristides. It was so tall the pupil would have needed stilts to sit on it. What could I say but, thank you.

That first Sunday evening we were to dine with Dalia's parents. This was a big occasion for them and preparations had been going on for some time. All Lithuanians live in flats, and very small ones too, often with several members of the same family sharing the one bedroom.

We again had a wonderful reception. They had made a very long table stretching right down the middle of the very small room, which must have been a bedroom. Quite how it happened I don't know, but twenty or more people sat down around it.

The table was piled high with food, including a traditional Lithuanian celebration tree cake, known as raguolis, and the champagne and cognac flowed. This was followed by the speeches. Speeches, of course, took twice as long as usual because of having to be translated. There were lots of tears too. Dalia's father, who was obviously so proud of his daughter, soaked several handkerchiefs and, frustrated at not being to be able to communicate verbally, kept filling up the cognac glasses.

Lithuanian tree cake known as raguolis

I found the answer to stopping him filling up mine, as I cannot drink the stuff, was to fill my glass with neat tea from one of the large teapots on the table.

It was a lovely, extraordinary evening, and very moving to be on the receiving end of so much love and generosity from people who have so little in comparison to us. At the end, we were all given little presents of pottery bells, which are characteristic of their local craft.

The next day was the start of work and I don't think I have ever worked so hard in my life. The days were so full, it is difficult to know where to start to tell the story.

We worked out that it was impossible to give every actor an individual lesson (there were forty-five, plus interpreters and students from the conservatoire). So the plan was for Helen Chadwick, a singer and voice teacher, and I to work together with groups. We had worked together before at the Studio and it had been a very successful combination. That first day, we saw every actor that we were teaching. They were split into groups and pupils moved between voice sessions and the acting and movement workshops.

This meant that we were working from 9.30 in the morning until 9.30 in the evening, all the time with an interpreter, which of course slowed the process up considerably.

I must say it was extremely rewarding, because those actors who started the week looking rather forlorn, anxious and repressed had, by the end, totally changed. They had opened up like flowers and became very alive in their bodies. They found their voices and confidence and it was a joy to see.

I managed to give individual lessons to about a third of the actors. It was extraordinary to see how they were so unused to being touched, and had become so vulnerable, that the tears of relief would flow and my box of Kleenex emptied very quickly. They were so longing to be shown a way to release all the pent up tension and I was frustrated not to able to do more in the very short time we had.

Every evening, there was a reception of some kind which usually entailed going to the theatre. The first working evening there was a reception held in the Art Gallery. There were some young musicians, a saxophonist and two violinists, who were excellent. They were from the Moscow Conservatory where Ashkenazy had studied.

Antony Sher returned back from a weekend in another part of Lithuania where he had been searching for his roots. Three of his grandparents were Lithuanians and he was trying to see if there were any remaining relations left. On his return, he wrote an article for The Independent newspaper about his experiences.

Antony had also been playing Astrov in the National Theatre production of *Uncle Vanya* and to honour this the Lithuanians put on their production of *Uncle Vanya* for us. It was very long but a lot of it was very funny. Yelena looked very like a young edition of Barbara Goalen, the fashion model, and spent a great deal of time looking at herself in a mother of pearl hand mirror. The three servants suddenly broke into a song and dance act, sliding across the stage in snow boots for no apparent reason.

We were given head phones, which were meant to translate into English, but they were very unreliable and faint, and as we knew the play I found it easier to discard them. I had expected that I would most probably drop off to sleep in *The Nose* by Gogol, but stayed awake as it was so funny and very well done. Another play, *The Square*, which was based on a documentary by someone called Yeliseyeva, was excellent.

The fourth theatrical experience was a gruelling evening at the equivalent of their National Theatre. The play was the *Marquis de Sade*. On this occasion, there were no headphones but you really did need to know what was happening. The four women stood like statues, with little or no action for the entire evening, and only very occasionally talking. Again it was very long, I was sitting next to Tony, and I was dozing off. I suddenly felt a heavy weight on my shoulder – it was Tony dropping off too. Sue Higginson, who was sitting opposite me, had the most wonderful head of blonde curly, wavy hair. I noticed that it was all over her face, and her head was dropping forward, obviously concealing her nap.

The final party was very emotional with lots of speeches which took twice as long as normal. They all sang folk songs and danced with great enthusiasm. The Lithuanians had lovely singing voices and were led by Cosmos, a very attractive, but very drunk, leading actor. One of the interpreters had a wife who was reputed to be a leading fashion designer and turned up in an amazing dress. It was a violent turquoise with a huge skirt, rather like a crinoline, and she had great difficulty getting around in it and being sociable because you couldn't get near her to have a conversation.

I wanted to give Irena, my interpreter, a present for being such a support all the time I was there. I knew she was extremely poor and lived in a small flat with her parents, brothers and sisters. Her job was secretary to the French ambassador for which she was paid the equivalent of £15 a month. I was horrified to be told this and became all the more determined to give her something. However, to find a shop in the old town was extremely difficult. At the time of the Russian invasion, the inhabitants had made their living rooms into shops meaning that there were no windows onto the street and therefore difficult to find.

I eventually managed to find a gift shop of sorts and bought Irena a very pretty bracelet. When I gave it to her, she was quite overcome. She said nobody had ever given her a present since she was a little girl. Her response was, 'Sue, that is so kind of you. I really don't need anything at all'.

That rang in my head, never more so than when we arrived back at Heathrow and saw all the mounds of sweets, trinkets and useless goodies that we take for granted. It made me feel slightly nauseous.

I was so very grateful for that experience. The impression that those courageous, uncomplaining and generous Lithuanians made on me, after everything that they had suffered during the Russian occupation, will be with me always.

South Africa

In the winter of 1994, Barney Simon, the Artistic Director of the Market Theatre in Johannesburg, came to visit the NT Studio, prior to our trip later in the spring of that year. Barney, the son of Lithuanian Jewish parents, founded the Market Theatre in 1976. It was the first multi-racial cultural centre in the country where Barney produced controversial plays in front of a multi-racial audiences. He was in constant threat of arrest. We saw slides of the theatre and the surrounding area and heard how he had transformed it into a centre for all (black and white) audiences, defying apartheid and the struggles that this had entailed.

As before, we were going to visit with a company of directors, actors, stage management, designers, teachers and administrative staff at a very exciting moment in South African history. Nelson Mandela had just become president.

There was a frenzy of preparation and a great deal to organise. We were only going for a short trip, but there was still so much to get together. I always marvelled at the efficiency of the NT stage management team. My table was packed and transported without damage. Anything else that I needed to go with it was treated in the same way, with the greatest care.

We were told to have vaccinations against everything. The malaria injection was a bit of a disaster because we didn't really need it and I was one of the ones who seemed to suffer most, feeling sick and dizzy for the first few days.

On our first evening in South Africa, there was a big reception for us and Lady Mary Soames, the chairman of the National Theatre, attended. I had several interesting talks with members of the British Council, who had sponsored our visit, and who wanted to know about Alexander and what it entailed.

We had also been sponsored by the Oppenheimers, one of the richest families in South Africa, and were staying in a five-star hotel in the centre of Johannesburg. We all had our own en-suite rooms, which were lovely, and the breakfast was delicious – and enough to get one through to supper. Our security was top priority and Antony Sher, who was with us, insisted that we obey all the rules, which to begin with I found a bit extreme. We were not allowed to even walk across the road to a shop alone, if at all, and the pavements in the daytime were lined with Africans plying their goods in a desperate effort to get money to survive. In the morning, we piled into a VW combie van just a few feet from the front door and were ordered to close all of the windows immediately even though it was very hot. We were warned that watches on wrists would be snatched off – or anything else that could be grabbed through the window.

I realised just how necessary this all was when one day there was a great commotion outside the hotel. A great many taxis had gathered with ambulances and police cars. One taxi driver had killed his brother in a fight over who was to take the first fare paying passenger. It was very disturbing but after that, we all did as we were told.

The Market Theatre was about twenty minutes from the hotel. It was amidst a small complex of three theatres, shops, restaurants and the internationally known Kippie's Jazz Club. I was a great jazz lover and had sat with Ronnie Scott at lunch one day as he was visiting. I knew him and some of the band through my ex-husband, also a jazz musician.

Our schedules were put up on a board each day. I had been given a small room with a mirror and a couple of chairs, which is always what I had asked for. Helen Chadwick and I would go into the first session each day to meet all the actors we were going to be teaching.

Getting their names right I found so difficult and for me, the pronunciation was sometimes almost impossible. Helen was much better than me as she had travelled a great deal and spoke several languages. Some names had to be said with a click in the middle, which for me was hopeless. Even rolling my R's has always been an impossibility as it involves using my tongue in ways that I have never been able to get a handle on.

The work followed the same format as with the groups that we had taught before, but with the Africans I certainly found it much more difficult. They were so filled with energy, seemed to take every opportunity to sing and dance and found it very difficult to be still, so waiting before you reacted was not in their remit.

However, learning the whispered ahs and then using their voices, did make an impression on all of them – and what wonderful voices they had. I would then persuade them to take individual lessons and I remember being rather surprised that the actors doing the courses were mostly white, or mixed race, but at least there was no language problem as we had had in Lithuania, or later in Japan.

Barney Simon had many sessions and was such an interesting man. I found listening to his experiences really fascinating. Once I had explained the principles and Alexander's journey, he understood immediately and I gave him my work tape so that he could carry on working without a teacher. I felt very privileged to have known him because, to everyone's great sadness, he died only a short time after our visit.

Johannesburg was alive with joy and excitement at the election of Mandela as president. Although we were not allowed on the street near the hotel, there were many areas where it was considerably safer, as long as we went around in small groups.

The big event was the Gay Pride march and, as we had Sir Ian McKellen with us, his photograph was all over the local papers. There were huge crowds following the march through the streets.

A trip to Soweto was organised for us. Although I had seen endless photographs of the families living in extreme poverty, I was not prepared for the reality of the squalor and the indignity of the living conditions of thousands of Africans. I was struck by the cheerfulness and welcoming smiles that we received and, like Pied Pipers, we were followed by a little line of children while we handed out sweets and biscuits as we went along.

One tiny shack had a small patch of earth with a fence outside the door. Here there was a gorgeous sunflower standing up alone, boldly, as if to say, 'in spite of everything we're alright here'.

As we drove off in the combies, we saw many townships, which apparently just appear overnight, as the people grab anything they can find just to put a roof over their heads. Sheets, planks of wood and up it goes – until the police come and order them to demolish everything.

I found it difficult to sleep that night as it had been so disturbing. The feeling of helplessness was with me throughout the trip because there was nothing that one could do. As is my wont, I felt both guilty and grateful for my life and privileges that I have.

Just outside the Market complex every Saturday, a particularly good flea market was held. I felt that one way of giving was to buy as much as I could, mainly as presents for my children and grandchildren, so I went and spend I did – in fact I had to buy an extra suitcase to get it all back home.

The Africans I met had music and dancing coming out of every pore, it seemed to be their way of coping with the hardships of life. The original idea was for us to go to the townships to watch their shows, but in the end we had several nights of them bringing their shows to us.

The plays had been devised and written by them. They made their own costumes and scenery and the subject matter was always about coping with poverty, AIDS, illness, birth and death. They usually had positive endings though, showing how they could get through with love, faith and the help of God.

At the end, we provided them with refreshments, drinks and biscuits – and always they would ask if they could take more back to their impoverished families.

One evening we went to a Shabeen, which was a regular occurrence in bars all over town usually on a Friday night. A jazz band would play and everyone just got up and danced, usually on their own, mothers, fathers, children and especially the grannies. Everyone dressed for the occasion and much beer was consumed, but the feeling of joy and excitement was paramount. We all forgot our troubles and had a great evening.

Then we had a day of complete luxury given us by the Oppenheimers, our patrons. We went to their large house out in the country. There was a pool, endless drinks and the most wonderful lunch served to us by very cheerful servants, our every whim was catered for. The weather was lovely and warm, luckily, because it hadn't always been so – in fact one day we even had a flurry of snow.

Another treat was a day trip to a game park ending up with dinner at Sun City. I was with Ian McKellen, Sean Mathias, Antony Sher, Greg Doran, Patsy Rodenburg and Selina Cadell, all of whom I knew very well. The game park was quite a small one in that it was mostly zebra, deer and warthogs, with no sign of lion or elephant, but many very beautiful birds.

The best part was the dinner. Sun City was an amazing place, just like a film set. The outside looked like a collection of castles with turrets all floodlit and rather forbidding. At either side of the entrance there were two, at least seven feet tall, black doormen who looked us up and down rather dismissively. We were all in shorts, pretty scruffy and dirty.

Tony Sher took control of the situation saying that he was from The Times newspaper in London, England. He said that he had been asked to write an article about Sun City and we were coming to dine in the restaurant. They stopped Ian and me as we were the last of the party and Ian was looking particularly shabby with muddy trainers.

I said rather feebly, as Ian did not seem to be putting up much of a fight, that he was a knight of the realm and they just had to let us in – and so in we went.

We were all starving hungry, so the next step was to get into the restaurant, which looked to me worryingly expensive. There were women in evening dress, men in suits and low lights with soft music playing. The headwaiter came up to us and started to remonstrate saying that we were not welcome, looking as we were like a party of ne'er-do-wells. Tony said his piece again about The Times newspaper. Reluctantly, we were ushered into a table right at the back of the restaurant. That way, we would not be noticed by other guests and possibly put them off their food. Tony was asked whether he would mind putting a rather large table napkin over his hairy, bare knees – so as not to offend the waiter I suppose.

We all found it very difficult to control our laughter but with the arrival of food and drink, we felt much calmer. Eventually several members of the party disappeared to the gaming tables. Luckily, not for long as exhaustion had set in and I was longing for my bed. So ended another day to remember.

Towards the end of the trip I was invited to have dinner with a friend of mine, who happened to be staying in Johannesburg at the same time. It was late, and after dark, so I took a taxi. This I found rather nerve wracking. It was meant to be safe if one ordered through the hotel, but I was still very nervous. Arriving at the large house, which was in darkness, I rang my friend. As I paid the taxi driver, the huge iron gates swung open and in I went. I noted that the driver waited to see that I was safely inside and the same thing happened on my return, so all was well.

We were also taken to a wonderful exhibition displaying pictures taken by a war photographer, then to a show at their equivalent of the National Theatre, which was a musical with, as always, plenty of singing and dancing. I remember one dance vividly as they were all dancing in wellington boots and singing at the same time. As always full of joy.

On our last night a sing song, conducted by Helen, had been arranged. It was unaccompanied and everyone sang their hearts out, ending as always with the national anthem.

For another memorable trip, thank you National Theatre and Sue Higginson for arranging it all.

Ireland

The Studio, with our workshop of teachers, directors, actors and designers, visited Belfast just after the Good Friday agreement in 1998. As in South Africa there were country-wide celebrations going on. It was a very short, unstructured trip so we just tried to fit in with everything else that was going on.

We were staying in one of the best hotels, which was absolute bliss as I had my own bedroom, bathroom en-suite and a lovely view out over the city. We all met up at breakfast and once again Helen and I were working together, although this time it did not seem to be so organised. We taught small groups of actors and I gave hardly any individual lessons.

We went to talks from writers and then watched Irish theatre every evening. I found the northern Irish accent phenomenally difficult to understand, a bit like strong Glaswegian, so I am afraid a lot of it passed me by. Another time I think I would need an interpreter. I find the northern Irish accent so much more difficult than the southern Irish as when I visited Dublin, I had no problem at all.

The trip was not as full of impressions as the other trips I had made. But, as my return plane ticket was not until the Monday, I hired a car for the last weekend and decided to go north to the Giant's Causeway. The weather was perfect and the roads practically empty. The little villages where I stopped for lunch and tea were very friendly. I do love the Irish, they are so warm and hospitable and I did have a wonderful day.

Scotland

This was a similar experience to the Irish trip where the Studio took us up to the Edinburgh Festival for, in my case, four days.

I found I was in the situation of not really being able to plan the day very well as it was interspersed with short performances all over the place. Then there was adapting to small rooms for teaching and often the actors could not make the lesson as they were wanted elsewhere.

I was also having difficulty in understanding the strong Scottish accent, so communication was often unsatisfactory. Altogether I did not enjoy the experience. Everything was rushed and I didn't feel that there was enough time to help the actors with the use of the technique.

Helen and I had many laughs over our rooms, which were very similar to the ones in Lithuania. They seemed to be rather dark, the beds extremely uncomfortable and the water was either very cold or piping hot and, to begin with, came out dark, peaty brown.

I was not feeling at all well, so came back early. I was very sorry that I had not enjoyed my first and only time so far at the famous Festival.

Japan

My visit to Japan all stemmed from my Alexander work tape, which I had converted to a CD and is described earlier in the book.

One day I received a phone call from a Japanese girl, Megumi Kawaminari inviting me to go to teach in Osaka. She had listened to the tape. She told me that there was a great need for voice and Alexander lessons for the actors in Japan. There were no drama schools and the actors were thirsting for more knowledge to help with their work. There were, of course, the traditional theatre groups, the Noh and the Kabuki, but they were exclusive and you had to be born into them. Apart from that, there seemed to be no tuition available.

I was very reluctant at first, as I wondered if I would be able to do it, but Megumi was very insistent. Almost before I knew it, I was booked onto a flight, arrangements were made and I was off into the unknown, feeling very nervous and excited.

I was met by Megumi who spoke perfect English, but no one else seemed to. All communication from then on was through interpreters.

I was booked into a large hotel in the middle of Osaka. It had been arranged that I should rest up for the weekend so the first day we walked around Osaka. I became used to the hotel, which had delicious restaurants in the basement as well as a shopping arcade. Finally, there were the hot springs (women only), to which I went every day after teaching.

Megumi suggested that I have a massage after my journey and she left me in the hands of four powerful looking Japanese men. They set upon me until I had to cry out for help to get them to stop – it was agony. I felt I was going to disintegrate. It was then that I discovered that the Japanese understanding of the word NO seemed to be very different from ours, which was going to prove tricky for teaching the Alexander Technique.

Megumi came to my rescue and we ended the day by going to the sushi bar where I identified my favourite dishes. Megumi translated them for me so that I was able to go down on my own to eat. I was always greeted with much merriment by the rather handsome, tall waiters, who would know exactly what to serve me. 'The Engrish lady, here she comes', I imagined they were saying, full of smiles and little bows, always very courteous. Everyone was rather amazingly polite and solicitous. I don't know what I had expected – certainly not that sort of cultural behaviour – but it made me feel very good.

Osaka was a very busy bustling city, but during my whole time there I only saw half a dozen English faces. Then on the Sunday, off we went to Kyoto, which was about half an hour away. I don't know how I would have coped on my own as there were no signs in English and no one spoke anything other than Japanese. There seemed to be no one from any other country, nothing but Japanese faces, no tourists at all, which was very surprising, but it may have been because it wasn't the holiday season. There was one occasion when I was walking down the street and a small child pointed at me before rushing under his mother's skirt, screaming. It made me feel that he had never seen a European person before.

Megumi was very thoughtful and took me to see some of the sights for which Kyoto is so well known. The temples and gardens were very beautiful and immaculately cared for. I learned that Kyoto had been the capital of Japan for more than a thousand years before Tokyo.

Sue at the Kiyomizu-dera Temple in Kyoto

We went to a restaurant where to start with you were seated on the floor on a cushion. There were no chairs in sight but in the middle of the floor was a short legged table. Their tea cups had no handles and there were chopsticks to eat with. All the Japanese people, waiters and waitresses were extremely courteous and unhurried.

On arrival in Japan I had been given my per diems, which were very generous, so I felt confident that I would be able to pay for myself although I had brought some Yen with me. If possible, I wanted to take back Christmas presents for the grandchildren and friends. Megumi said that the place to do it was Kyoto.

I was still jet lagged, so we didn't do much shopping that day, but went back at the end of my visit to Japan. Then I bought kimonos for the whole family, really lovely ones for the boys with little loose trousers, fans, combs for the girls' hair and little tiny bits of pottery. The fans were really exquisite. I bought some for girl-friends and a very special one for Judi Dench as a thank you.

On the Monday reality struck. Megumi arrived to take me to the theatre where we were going to work. I was extremely nervous. In fact, I can say that never before had I felt so inadequate. I had managed to get the little introductory notes, poems that I give pupils at the beginning of their lessons, translated by Megumi and photocopied for all the students. They really looked extraordinary written in Japanese. I went through everything very carefully with Megumi to make sure that we had the translation clear.

We walked to the theatre where the workshops were going to take place. In the following days, I was going to have to find my own way, so that was an added worry. Luckily, it was a short enough walk and there were some identifiable landmarks, which helped a great deal the following day. There was a field of 'lice' (they pronounce their Rs the same way as their Ls) and an intriguing little house that had an amazing collection of bonsai trees, which made me want to take one home for my botanist daughter Sophie.

When we arrived at the theatre, there were a great many introductions. It was here I met Emiko, my Japanese interpreter, a really sweet girl whose English was fluent. She had been to a few Alexander group sessions, so was not entirely ignorant of what I would be trying to get across to the actors.

The teaching room was one of the rehearsal rooms, quite large for the twelve actors, light and airy with chairs and walls that could be used for both wall and monkey. At my request, they also had mats to lie on. I had planned an introductory talk before we went onto actual chair work or lying down with directions.

Megumi joined in with the class some of the time. Otherwise she sat and watched. The major problem was that there appeared to be no Japanese for the concept of the Alexander NO, but the rest of the directions were fairly easy to explain. I sometimes used Emiko as a pupil to demonstrate my meaning, so it was very helpful that she had had previous Alexander experience. On the other hand, I sometimes demonstrated myself with her invaluable interpretation.

It was fascinating observing the difference between the cultures. Africans, for instance, who understood English, were so much the opposite from the Japanese. Africans are full of energy and enthusiasm, but the Japanese actors found it almost impossible to take on board what I was trying to explain about inhibiting as they are very disciplined and DO what they are told. The teacher, the 'Master', is to be obeyed and revered, so I had a bit of a problem explaining the basics of the technique.

I found that the Japanese appeared to be over inhibited due to their education and strict upbringing. Letting go of the habitual was something they had never experienced. I found that the way around this problem was to make them laugh, as hidden behind their serious and anxious expressions lurked a great sense of humour. They had been brought up to get it RIGHT, whatever happened, even more so than us Westerners and this was what I had to break through in the short time that I had.

What I was not used to was the politeness, almost reverence, with which I was treated. They listened intently to everything that I was saying and, when asked if they understood, they had indeed remembered all that we had discussed. Most days, there were a variety of people, actors or directors from the theatre who would come and watch and listen. I was always asked beforehand if this was alright. I realised that to them I was the 'Master', not a role I was accustomed to.

I very much wanted to see an example of the Kabuki or Noh theatre companies work, but this did not seem to be possible. During the time I was there, Tokyo was the only option and I did not have the time.

Later, the Kabuki theatre and the Noh theatre company came to the National. The Noh gave a succession of workshops, which were fascinating, and the Kabuki theatre presented a week of different plays on each night. Traditional Japanese theatre has no women performers, there is an all male cast with the men dressed as women. When a boy is born to the Kabuki or Noh family his future is mapped out for him, he will be an actor. The training is a strict regime that has to be adhered to for life.

One thing I saw when I went to one of the Noh company talks, with an interpreter, was how they stood in a perfectly poised way. Their heads were balanced, going forward and up and their backs were lengthened. Their knees were softened, legs firmly planted and their weight was evenly distributed between their two feet. When they bent over, they were in a perfect monkey.

There were questions afterwards and one person asked why they always seemed to stand with their knees slightly bent. The actor looked surprised. He said that if they stood with the knees tightened, it would throw the whole body out of balance. I was thrilled and wished that I could have had a conversation with them, but the language barriers made it impossible.

Since that trip I remember one evening I was watching TV listening to Timothy West talking to Piers Morgan. This reminded me of an incident with Pru Scales at the Studio.

It took me back to the Noh theatre company visit to the National. Whilst of great interest everything was being relayed to us through an interpreter. Part way through the show Prunella and Timothy, sitting in front of me, were getting slightly bored. Pru suddenly leapt to her feet and said, in her unmistakable Prunella Scales voice, 'Come on, Timmy, we must go – it's time for supper'. They walked out causing quite a disturbance, but I thought it was rather delightful.

Then one day when Pru came for her lesson on my birthday she brought me a little present of a tiny, dried plant covered by a glass case. I was very touched by her thoughtfulness.

When my ten days in Japan were up, I was given a wonderful, joyous leaving party in a restaurant with all my pupils. I was given bottles of sake and a pure white umbrella, which could be used as a sunshade. It did the trick for rain or shine and it was treasured along with all my other goodies from Kyoto.

My time in Japan was a truly unique experience. I was invited to return, but so far have not found the time as life is very full at the RSC and The National.

17. Working with Challenging Conditions

I have taught some pupils with Parkinson's disease and I felt that I wanted to mention two of them because these were such interesting and humbling experiences. The first was the brother of a friend of mine, a very eminent plastic surgeon who performed operations whilst being filmed for television. His work depended on the stillness and precision of his hands whilst working on the patient, but fate cruelly brought him this incurable illness. This meant that he had to give up the career he loved, for which he was very well known and respected.

The surgeon was a delightful man whose condition had deteriorated considerably. His inability to continue working was of course a great sadness to him. He was taking several drugs, particularly L-DOPA, a drug which the body converts to dopamine. The Alexander Technique helped him a great deal, especially as he was writing. He found that using the technique sharpened his focus and, when using the computer, he was able to steady his hand and continue typing for quite some time without shaking.

I found this very interesting and it reminded me of the story of a watch and clock repairer who also suffered from Parkinson's. The condition was very advanced and his hands and arms would shake all the time until you handed him the watch that needed attention. Immediately he took hold of it, the shaking ceased, he opened the back, saw what the problem was and the watch would be mended perfectly.

Another pupil, who also had early stages of Parkinson's disease, was a writer. He came to me once a week for several months to take lessons. Teaching him was a quite unique experience and I learnt a great deal, as did he, about using the technique with his very particular problem. He was very young, in his late thirties, to have been afflicted and he had the characteristic walk of many Parkinson's sufferers. It is a sort of shuffle, with the weight positioned almost entirely over the toes, which means that the soles of the feet and the heels hardly touch the ground. His speech was also very soft and it was sometimes difficult to hear clearly what he was saying. When I explained the principle of the technique, he understood it intellectually and accepted the challenge of using it with sitting, writing, walking and also with speech.

Sue Higginson, when she saw how much the lessons were helping him, generously changed the 'only six lessons' rule so that it did not apply to him. It was a joy to be able to work with him once or twice a week as he learnt to use the inhibiting to great effect. He would, with my guidance, inhibit and use the directions, for instance, when walking. He then began to walk normally putting his heel to the ground first and walking through the foot. He was filling his body with directions having inhibited his habitual way of walking. Natural dopamine, which is linked to our internal reward system, acts as a messenger in the brain and is not present in adequate voume in the Parkinson's patient. It seemed to me that by consciously inhibiting poor habits with the technique, the patient is 'rewarded' when, in this case walking, is successful.

Obviously I could not be with him all the time, but at least he knew that the technique could work. In addition, the change in him was noticed by others, in particular his mother and relatives whom he did not see too often. This further 'reward' gave him a much needed boost in confidence.

One day he came to me looking very pleased and happy. He reported that he had attended a routine visit with his consultant and at the end of the examination, he had been told that he could cut down on his drugs. This said a great deal for the work he had been doing on himself using Alexander.

Unfortunately, after teaching him for many months he disappeared off the radar, so I don't know how he is progressing. Although I do know that he is now married and I am trying get in touch to find out how he is doing.

What I found fascinating about teaching both those pupils with Parkinson's was the way they were able to use the technique in the way that I felt FM Alexander intended. For

FM teaching the pupil to work on themselves was the main purpose of the teacher. In both of these Parkinson's sufferers' cases, they had a very definite situation, which could be life threatening or at least curtail their working life for several years. The desire to change was very strong and this encouraged them to work hard on themselves.

The results of a randomised, controlled trial researching the merits of the Alexander Technique with Parkinson's patients were published in 2002. The results were very encouraging. During the trial, patients were also given massage therapy and, although this was beneficial, Alexander was found to be the more helpful of the two interventions. In the words of the report, 'The study showed that Alexander lessons led to a significantly increased ability to carry out everyday activities'.

The Alexander Technique is most frequently publicised as a therapy that helps back pain, which it certainly does. But that is only one of the many problems that learning the technique can help with.

Phantom pain is one such example. A great friend and earlier neighbour of mine was the late Admiral Sir Caspar John, who, when he retired from his prestigious career, worked for several charities. Amongst them was The Back Pain Association, of which he was Chairman, where he frequently promoted the use of the technique.

Tragically, when he was in his seventies, he developed a rare illness known as Buerger's disease, a condition that causes inflammation of the small and medium sized blood vessels in the legs and arms. It is also described as vasculitis, where blood clots can form and so lead to a complete blockage of the blood vessels.

The disease, which is progressive, currently has no cure. First the blood flow in one of his legs ceased, requiring his leg to be amputated just below the knee. Then the same thing happened to the other one, so the poor man was then a double amputee.

He became a regular visitor to the Douglas Bader

Rehabilitation Centre at Queen Mary's Hospital, Roehampton, where they fitted him with prosthetic limbs. He would stay with his friends, John Bury and his wife Liz, who also were neighbours of mine. I went to visit him to find out how he was coping. He was suffering acute back pain from having to manipulate the wheelchair and also had excruciating pains in his non-existent legs. Could I give him some lessons?

Liz had a very long dining room table, so I brought a sheet of foam and several soft cushions. Between us, we put Caspar onto the table.

I went through the basics of the technique and FM Alexander's journey. Then on the table, his back got a great deal of relief by being gently lengthened out. His shoulders were also very tense and painful through getting himself in and out of the wheelchair.

The next thing to deal with were the phantom pains – the pains coming from his non-existent legs. Caspar found these very often excruciating, stopping him from sleeping or even relaxing. In those days, there was no treatment for the condition.

Caspar quickly grasped inhibition and direction. I encouraged him to direct to his legs as if they were there, working through the pain so that he was almost believing that his legs were still part of him.

I gave him lessons every day for about a week, not nearly long enough, then he had to go home to Cornwall. He promised that we would meet up every time he visited Roehampton. On the last day, when I went in he was sitting up and looking really cheerful. He said, 'Sue darling, it works, when I use the No, and those thoughts, the pains GO'. It was as thrilling for me as for him to see the results of a pupil really working and being determined not to give in. He had not been the First Sea Lord for nothing.

I saw Caspar once more when he had gone back up to his other cottage in North Wales. Once again I was amazed at his courage in mastering the artificial limbs. The ground around the cottage was extremely uneven and stony, but he had his garden to tend and the greenhouse to water. That is where he ended his days – in his beloved Welsh cottage. It was a privilege to have been able to help him. He was a great man.

Osteoporosis is a condition that affects all the bones in the body. The bones become weak and fragile, lose density and become much more likely to fracture. This seems to become most obvious with people over sixty. I have worked with some who were beginning to stoop and were very often in a great deal of pain.

One lady had been sent by her doctor for lessons, which I found very interesting as I had not thought that a GP would have imagined Alexander could help her.

Providing the lessons was very encouraging because, although she must have been in her eighties, once she understood the principle, there was a great improvement in her poise.

I would work with her against the wall and taught her to do the exercise daily. When she came for a lesson, I would measure her both before and after the lesson and she gradually began to grow upwards out of the stoop. In the end, she grew about two and half inches so she went back to her doctor and told him what had been happening. To my real disappointment, he told her that now she had had enough of that and she should stop the lessons.

Another pupil, who was in his late sixties, came to me with a very curved spine. In fact, he had shrunk by about four or five inches. He was a painter who had refused to acknowledge that there was a problem, even though he was in quite severe discomfort. However, after a great deal of encouragement from friends and his wife, he came for lessons. It was extremely difficult to work with him on the table because of the spine curvature. Eventually, however, with the help of many soft cushions, I managed. This helped me to realise that he was finding it increasingly difficult to breathe because of the sinking of the chest and the diaphragm becoming squeezed, as the back curved forward. So we started by using the whispered ahs.

The effect was miraculous. His back began to open out onto

the table and his voice changed as he began to lose the fear of letting go.

Normally, I always left the breathing, using whispered ahs, till the pupil had had several sessions. I generally felt it would be a matter of too much too soon. But it was appropriate in this case, because he immediately saw that if he worked in this way the benefits were noticeable. Alexander began to make sense and here was something that he could do to help himself.

Over the years, I have taught many people with osteoporosis and nearly always with great benefits. Scoliosis is another condition that is very common with all ages. It usually begins to cause problems in adulthood, but there are cases of children suffering and sometimes action is taken, very often involving surgery.

I was brought one such young girl who was growing very fast and had a severe curve in her back. As well as being painful, it was making her increasingly self-conscious about her appearance. An operation was being planned, but her parents were still hoping that it could be avoided.

So we began the work. The most important thing was for her to work each day with wall, breathing, walking and sitting, all the while using inhibiting and directing. Her parents became thoroughly involved in the lessons so that they could help her keep up daily work. Things began to improve. Unfortunately, the family needed to go back home to Germany, so I found a teacher there for her to continue her lessons. A few months later, I had a message from the parents. They were absolutely delighted as after continuing with lessons the operation had been avoided, and they were of course hoping that she would never have to have one in the future.

For fifteen years, I regularly gave lessons to a very courageous multiple sclerosis sufferer called Chrissy. When she was first diagnosed with the disease, Chrissy determined to do everything she possibly could to prevent the illness from getting worse. She investigated anything alternative that she thought might be useful, diet, homeopathy etc. and eventually found great benefit in Applied Kinesiology. This is a whole body diagnosis and treatment method which includes, amongst other tools, testing of the muscles for their strength or weakness.

To begin with, I found it very difficult to help Chrissy use Alexander. She had become so dependent on being told what she needed to do – for example, what food she should eat, pills she should take, practically what side of the bed she should get out of in the morning, that to persuade her she needed to take responsibility for herself was very difficult.

I learnt so much from working with her. I am certain that when we did eventually get onto the same wavelength, the combination of Alexander with her incredible determination was the reason she lived a much longer and more fulfilled life.

I was very sad to learn of her death, after a spell of not seeing her for some time. She had had problems with her skin, a form of cancer and had gone to the Charing Cross Hospital frequently for treatment. Chrissy is often in my thoughts. She is a reminder of someone who fought with great courage throughout her illness to remain positive and never once lost her great sense of humour.

Very often when teaching, there were embarrassing moments. I had to judge whether one could get the pupil to have a laugh, or whether it was too insensitive to say anything at all and just work on.

One day, a rather beautiful woman came in dressed completely in black which suited her as she had black, black hair. She said she really only wanted table work. I never really like that diktat, but carried on with my explanations before she lay on the table. When it came to lifting her legs up, the left leg was fine, but when I came to lift up the right leg, to my complete surprise, it was a prosthetic made of iron bands, quite light and bent at the knee. I had to pull myself together and ask how she had lost her leg.

Apparently she had had a car accident many years ago but, luckily, after she was fully grown. She apologised saying she was so used to it that she had forgotten to say anything to me at the beginning.

Another girl had also had a car accident and both her legs were severely scarred. They had not been very well stitched and had mended badly. Very bravely, whatever the weather, she always wore very short shorts. I sensed, however, that it might be a form of attention seeking – she wanted me to sympathise and ask her all about the accident. I did, but that didn't stop her wearing the shorts.

During lessons, if I had shown that I minded the look of her legs, I felt she would think that she had won by making me suffer, a little bit as she had suffered. I found her a strange girl, but we carried on and she changed remarkably. Later she seemed to be an altogether happier human being.

I had a very unusual pupil from the IT department at the National. He came through the door announcing that he was bipolar. He was also getting a very bad back caused by working on computers all day long.

It was my counselling skills that helped me deal with the situation, otherwise I think I would have had to say that I could not teach this very disturbed man.

I asked a little about his life, what medication he was on and importantly, if he was taking it. I do know that someone with this condition will sometimes think that they are perfectly alright and doesn't need further support. Then there is a relapse.

I learnt to ask him what sort of mood he was in each time he came and work with him accordingly. Sometimes he needed to be really relaxed and quiet, other times the reverse. We would do chair and computer work, walking and wall. We always did breathing work as there was too much tightness in his chest area. He was very sharp and I had difficulty sometimes, when he was 'high', in stemming the flow.

One day, it became really quite frightening. He entered in a rage, throwing his arms about and mouthing off about the head of his department. I thought he might hit me if he mistook me for her. I gently put my hands on his head and made him look at me, lay him down and asked him to talk through what had happened between him and the other person.

I thought that maybe I should go to the nurse or the company manager to report this episode, but decided to wait until the next lesson and see how he was.

I was glad that I did. His mood had completely changed and apparently he'd had a very reasonable exchange with his supervisor. He had sorted out several issues and was momentarily in a much calmer mood – until the next time when he was thrown off balance or had forgotten to take his medicine.

As mentioned earlier, there had been a great many problems in those close to me with addiction to drink and drugs. At the time, I became very involved with Al-Anon and Families Anonymous, support groups that help the relatives and friends of addicts. I had become very interested in the processes these organisations used and took several counselling courses.

I met up with Tristan Millington-Drake, who was initially responsible for starting Thurston House in Clapham, a halfway house and also the Chemical Dependency Unit, a rehab centre in Earls Court at the time.

Tristan had Alexander lessons with me regularly and felt that it would be extremely useful to give lessons to the addicts in recovery at the halfway house in Clapham.

Mixed in with my teaching I did a year of evening classes on counselling supported by the Institute of Psychology from St Thomas' Hospital. The course took place at Sudeley Castle, which was the most beautiful setting. I studied four modules – working with addiction, addicts in recovery, families of addicts and alcoholics and drug addicts. This was using the 'Minnesota Model' with trainers from the Hazelden Betty Ford Foundation in the USA.

The 'Minnesota Model' is an abstinence model for treatment of drug and alcohol addiction which regards addiction as a disease. Through counselling and continued support, the addicted person can recover as long as he or she maintains lifelong abstinence from drugs and alcohol.

By attending this training and going to many meetings of Al-Anon and Families Anonymous over a period of more than fifteen years, I had gained an insight into what the addicted person has to go through during recovery. I felt I could see how Alexander could help them.

When the addict first comes into treatment, it is much too soon for them to be able to take on board anything that might seem completely irrelevant.

The drug, or whatever will do the trick, will have been taken to cover up or obliterate the painful feelings, whether they be emotional, mental or physical. When the drug is denied the pain reappears in full force and the desire to use again is very, very powerful. Without help, all those temptations to go back to the old ways seem almost impossible to reject.

I was told in my counselling course that to plead with the addict to stop using, was like asking someone to give up the only thing in the world that made them feel better.

However, when the addict starts at the halfway house, they have been 'clean' for at least six months and, more often than not, have a part time job. They are beginning to return to the real world.

Individual lessons would not have been possible unless there was some knowledge of what using Alexander was about, so group lessons were arranged at the beginning to explain how the changes could be made.

The Al-Anon program is based on using the AA 'Twelve Steps', during which the individual gradually becomes aware of the habits that have been ruling their existence. By working through these steps, whilst being given support, they learn to let go of the old habits. They realise that they can change these habits, that they have a choice, which before, when filled with 'mind altering substances', was not possible.

This is similar to what happens with Alexander lessons. The

situation with these pupils is not as extreme as in the case of an addict, but the basics are the same. The pupil is being taught, through inhibiting their thoughts and reactions, thinking NO at the point of stimulus, to wait for a moment.

In this space, this magic moment I call it, because unless we make it we do not have it, the addict can become aware of those feelings. The habitual temptation may be to rush to a drug or drink when the pain they feel is so strong that they feel they need to quell it, to block it out in the only way they know how.

Instead, by using this new awareness, a new thought process can begin. This is, of course, to think of freeing the neck muscles and of the back opening out, lengthening and widening, the tummy softening, releasing the knees, noticing the weight and shifting it from being all on the front of the foot to underneath the ankles. By following this new routine, the body gradually releases the tension brought about by the stressful thoughts and achieves a new freedom, a lightness of being that has it has not experienced before.

The only way to give lessons at the start was by a series of weekly group sessions, so this is what I did. There was a very busy schedule at the centre and unfortunately my visits did not continue for as long as I would have liked. However, the time that I did spend at Thurston House was very useful. I would have persisted, but due to my heavy commitments with the RSC and the NT, my time was rationed.

I taught the psychiatrist Dr Desmond Kelly, who was Medical Director of the Priory Hospital at Roehampton for some time. There were many patients with addiction problems at the Priory and this led to us to having many fruitful discussions about the Minnesota Model. Shortly after that, a new re-hab centre attached to the Priory, Galsworthy Lodge, was opened.

Dr Kelly, and other consultants who worked there, often sent me individuals with addiction problems or families who needed help coping. I did give some group sessions at

Galsworthy Lodge, but not with a great deal of success, as it was too early in the recovery process.

I have found that the situations I have illustrated above recur over the years. Teaching the patients has made me grateful for what I learnt from past experiences and it gives me much pleasure to see how Alexander and counselling combined can give so much help for these people.

18. In their Own Words…

Here is a selection of the feedback that I have received from my Alexander Technique pupils.

Anita Bennett

Anita was a pupil of mine from way back in the days when I had just started teaching. I was working at Albert Court, along with several other freshly trained young teachers who were being fed pupils by Bill Barlow.

Along came Anita with several issues which we gradually began to sort out.

I saw her through upset love affairs, a pregnancy and the difficulties of being a single mother. Anita eventually trained to become an Alexander teacher, which was a very satisfying outcome for both of us, and has resulted in a long-term friendship.

This is what she reported about her experience of lessons:

> 'Alexander was recommended for my bad back, caused by severe depression, growing too tall too early and playing the flute with my head tilted sideways…It was with some effort I dragged myself to the Barlows in Albert Court where Dr Barlow listened to my problems and said they could be fixed.
>
> He offered me Sue Laurie to sort out my slumping, aching back and my workaholic habit pattern. At that time, I was an investigative reporter on the Sunday Times Insight team, under the heroic Harold Evans.
>
> Sue was literally just what the doctor ordered. No nonsense, she insisted. So I came in for early morning 30 minute sessions three times a week. Very early I was taught to do monkey and work against the wall, with so many instructions to stop, inhibit and give myself directions, I felt I was in an English boot camp.
>
> Words cannot describe that first sense of peace and

security, when her amazingly wide directed hands encouraged me to release onto the table and let go of all those unnecessary tensions. It was then so difficult to sit up, race to the station, jump onto the tube and face the nearly all male, sixth floor, editorial hub.'

Helen Chadwick

'We began teaching Voice and Alexander workshops together after I had been having one-to-one sessions with Sue for some time. I had been trained as a voice coach and was doing some one to one sessions with actors, as well as my weekly NT Studio warm-up classes, which included voice and singing, so I had a great interest in the application of Alexander to both singing and speaking.

I was already incorporating my awareness of Alexander into my own singing and teaching practice, though of course not trying to teach the technique myself. I found it brilliant in dealing with the moment to moment tensions that arise when performing and how these can affect my singing, and it enhanced my ability to be relaxed on stage and to stay present in each moment.

Thanks to Sue Higginson's encouragement, we would book a series of six afternoon sessions over three weeks with the same group, with up to twelve people at each session. In our workshops we began with some Alexander exercises and then moved into some voice work, and ended with one on one coaching on speeches.

The focus of our workshops was mainly on the speaking voice though we sometimes included some singing. What was really powerful was not what came out of the exercises that either of us led. The thing that was transformational was what happened to the actor's voice when Sue used her hands to help free their neck and body. Suddenly there came a truer, richer, easier, more powerful voice, with great authenticity to boot. It was often very powerful and moving. I have always wished that her hands could be secretly present with me when I perform or record or run workshops, to stop me doing all my usual habits of throwing my head forward or twisting my body, or rushing forwards in time and space. It was all about Sue's hands and the way our bodies responded to them and it seemed quite magical.'

Edward Bennett-Coles – Actor/Director

'My experience of working with Sue Laurie has been a very rewarding one. She has been working with me on Alexander Technique, having just completed a rehearsal of *Afterbirth* at the NT Studio.

I arrived for my first class feeling what I thought was relatively relaxed. Historically I tend to hold most tension in my jaw, neck, chest and shoulders. It was very interesting to learn how the tension will always start with the neck and work its way down the body.

I have always thought that I have chosen Acting as a profession and for the first part of my life, made a conscious decision not to let people affect me. 'I will never be hurt like that again' and, 'Yeah, I'm fine', and 'No, nothing is wrong', became my internal mantras.

What a joy it was to get to drama school and decide to just 'let go'.

For quite a few years now, I fully realise that my greatest gift that I have to offer is honesty and the greatest gift I could receive is to let people in. Hence the gift of acting – you cannot hide from yourself or the audience without both of you being aware of it.

I grew an inch in my first class, which goes to show how much emotion and life I must have been compressing. All trapped energy.

Alexander with Sue has given me permission to keep growing (in many ways). And the fact that it helps my acting is really of secondary importance. I have often believed in the quote, 'You cannot be a better actor than a person'.

I spent weeks, months and years at drama school. What good the voice exercises were actually doing for me, I'm not sure. I know deep down that in some ways the voice had to be connected to a feeling of empowerment and ownership of space and oneself. And that those feelings, and indeed good speech, were available at the point of committing to oneself.

Alexander has deepened my understanding of body, mind and spirit once again and, as I mentioned before to Sue, those are the greatest gifts that I could have been given.

There are times that I have wanted to just cry, not from sadness, but from just extreme joy and the realisation of what a self-imposed prison I had put myself in.

It confirms my belief that my mind is the greatest weapon against myself and also the greatest gift, if you can only get it to work for you and not against you.'

Brian Cox

'I started to use the Alexander Technique in the 1970s. I was performing Brutus in *Julius Caesar* at the NT. My first teacher was the remarkable Peggy Williams who had been an original student of Mr Alexander. Peggy was, through the technique, an incredibly settling force on the young and somewhat volatile Brian Cox, who was not having a particularly rewarding time at the NT.

But my sessions with Peggy instilled in me an everlasting sense of purpose in the work of the actor. But also a quality of physical life that sustained me beyond my working life but into my day to day civilian life as a functioning human being. Through Peggy I worked with Walter Carrington and the vivacious Glynn MacDonald who perfected the group sessions at

LAMDA where I was on the board.

Then there was a gap of about 8 years in my Alexander life until I worked at the RSC in the late eighties.

Which was when I worked with the effervescent Sue Laurie. Sue's commitment to both the technique and its place in a working theatre is total. She completely understood the practice and integration of the work as a reflection of the actor's rehearsal process. The actor in the course of one performance can put him or herself through the most physically and vocally taxing work imaginable. But Sue's Alexander work with each performer during the course of, and in conjunction with, the play's rehearsal, mitigates a controlled and balanced sensibility of form and movement, which resulted in a dramatic cohesiveness for the individual performer. This care and technique is in turn reflected through the whole ensemble. Resulting quite often in an extraordinarily high standard of playing throughout.

Sue's commitment to the work in relation to the dramatic is quite nonpareil.

To my mind, the Alexander Technique is as vital and necessary an addition to the performing ensemble as the very breath of such a body.'

Benedict Cumberbatch

'Sue is a wonderful teacher. She has expert experience from her years at The National Theatre and insight into how the Alexander Technique can affect the human form in all scales of performance space. Not only is the technique helpful in healing, and a brilliant diagnostic for improved stage craft, but, practised properly, the unconscious and subtle adjustments it encourages can have a profound impact on your general posture and health.'

Janie Dee

I must talk about the wonderful actress Janie Dee, whom I taught on and off for many years.

As I've said, I think I must have first met Janie during the 1993 production of *Carousel* where she played Carrie Pipperidge. Alan Ayckbourn was a great fan of Janie and nearly always asked her to be in his plays wherever they were being produced.

I would see Janie even when she was in any play outside the National. I also taught her when she was pregnant with both babies. It was the first one, which gave me quite a fright. I was working with her against the wall and breathing (as she was very near her due date, she was using whispered ahs). Suddenly she got a sharp pain and cried out. 'Right, my girl', I said, 'I am taking you home NOW'.

However, Janie wouldn't hear of it and wanted to finish the exercise – and then she would get the bus. Don't mess with Janie. She did exactly that and, as far as I can remember, gave birth either that evening or the following day.

I also particularly remember working with her during *Shadowlands* in the West End where Charles Dance was CS Lewis and she was Joy Gresham, his wife.

Janie was finding it very difficult as it is a tragic play and gradually dying of cancer was emotionally challenging for her. She needed to talk it through with me and relate her emotional reactions to her physical body, which was becoming very tense and painful.

I went to see the play twice, once in preview and later when it was more established. I could not stop the tears even though I had seen it once before with Jane Lapotaire and Nigel Hawthorne and cried buckets then. However, I felt that this time Janie was a better Joy and Alexander helped along the way.

I think that Janie must be very difficult to cast as she is not only a superb actress, she is also such a talented dancer, singer and beautiful to boot. I feel that she needs a part written for her in which she can use all these talents in equal measure.

In Janie's words…

> 'My time with Sue Laurie has been one of the most precious experiences. Always helpful, always nurturing, both physically and mentally. Alexander has helped me, through Sue Laurie's teaching, with my work as an actor and also as a human being in tricky situations and relationships. Both pregnancies were natural, home births using the Alexander Technique.'

Sir Lenny Henry

> 'Meeting Sue Laurie at the National theatre when I was performing at the Olivier theatre in a Dominic Cook production of *The Comedy of Errors* was a boon. With just a few words of encouragement and some very careful manipulations, she had my voice booming and my body and mind relaxed. I will never forget her gentle words and intelligent way of working; never too forceful, always respectful and incredibly smart about the actor's 'Inner Critic' and the whys and wherefores of performance anxiety. Sue's a one off … Big love and respect.'

Jeremy Herrin

> 'I think the provision of Alexander Lessons at the NT is one of the many factors that make it the best place to make theatre. Sue's lessons help the actors conserve energy and use their voices to their maximum emotional capacity. And as a director, I've benefitted enormously from the centring and alignment that Sue's teaching gives me. It's the perfect tonic over busy and stressful rehearsal and production periods and I know that my regular sessions have helped me deliver my best work.'

Rory Kinnear

> 'First encountering Alexander Technique at drama

school, and having hurdled the initial scepticism of youth, I now know of no other system that helps reorder and re-energize body and mind quite so effectively – and painlessly. From easing niggling back pain to increasing physical and vocal freedom on stage, its disarmingly subtle practice continues to help me, and performers of all ages and experience, maximize our physical and psychological potential like nothing else.'

Paul Miller

Paul Miller was the Artistic Director of the Orange Tree Theatre Richmond, Surrey.

'Over many years, I have found that the Alexander Technique helps actors to be open, free and strong in their work. And certainly Sue's teaching has helped me personally too.'

Joe Mydell

While Joe Mydell was playing in *Evening at the Talk House,* he shared an interesting experience. He related that he had a fall in the Dorfman and was not badly hurt in spite of it being quite a heavy one. He said he was convinced that it was due to Alexander that there was so little damage, apart from bruising, as when he fell it was in a balanced way. Others watching said it was like watching him in slow motion. He said Alexander took over.

Paul Ready

'The Alexander Technique formed part of the basis of my drama school training. Being led through this subtle work on the body, I was able to discover many things essential to acting in the theatre. But it was really when I started working with Sue at the National Theatre that it became clear how essential the technique was to me. The stages of the National have very different demands but, with the help of the technique, I was able to learn how to inhabit my full height and connect to my body in a way that is needed to play those spaces. Through repeatedly working with Sue, I was reminded to return to a place of stillness and simplicity from which to start discovering a character's physicality, rather than relying on my already formed habits. Finally, the Alexander Technique enabled me to find a freedom of movement, breath, and physical receptiveness in performance, giving me essential help to meet the challenges of very different roles and styles of theatre.'

Alan Rickman

I first met and taught Alan Rickman at Stratford in the early eighties. For me it was a very exciting time as I had just started at the RSC. I did not realise at the time that, amongst my first pupils, there were what turned out to be an extremely talented group of actors. They had all come from RADA and were involved in many productions throughout my years at the RSC.

In Stratford that group of actors became Alan's friends for life (I taught practically all of them) and he then went on to work with many of them in other productions – especially Juliet Stevenson in the Anthony Minghella film *Truly Madly Deeply*.

Over the years I worked on and off with Alan, we always kept in touch. Several times he came and saw me at my home for private lessons. Then I remember sitting in the Gate Cinema in Notting Hill when suddenly, from behind me, this unmistakeable rich, silky voice boomed out, 'Just my luck to be sitting behind Sue Laurie, I can't see a thing'. Referring to my sitting up with a lengthening back I trust.

I often bumped into him during the intervals at the NT when he would always greet me with a hug and would generously buy a bottle of wine for us all to share. I know I am not the only one to say what an incredibly generous man Alan was.

We met once just after he had been in *Sweeney Todd.* He said, 'I nearly got you to come and straighten me out during the shooting. It was very tiring – and you could have got your hands on Mr Depp'. Rima Horton, his wife, was with him and she scolded him for not asking me. She, like me, was a Johnny Depp fan.

Alan asked me to give him lessons during the making of *Robin Hood* at Shepperton, which sadly I could not fit in with all my other work. He made me laugh as he recalled one day when he and Harold Innocent, playing as the Bishop of Hereford, were flailing around almost waist high in a pool of mud and he said to Harold, 'Whatever are we doing?', to which Harold said, 'God knows, but the money's good.'

In *Private Lives,* where he played Elyot with Lindsay Duncan as Amanda, they asked me to go up once a week to give them sessions in their dressing rooms before the show. Quite how I managed it, I don't know. However, I was quite young and strong, I suppose, and used to haul my table up to St Martins Lane, heave it up to the stage door and into their rooms.

Afterwards I would treat myself to an Italian meal at a lovely little restaurant hidden away down a passage behind the main road.

Another example of Alan's generosity was when he arranged for me to take my eight-year-old grandson onto the site of the filming of the Harry Potter films. We were taken around to all the different sets in a little buggy. We met the animals, the owls and the rats. We went into the prosthetics studios and ended up actually where they were filming in the Great Hall at Hogwarts and sat up behind watching it all taking place.

At lunchtime, we met up with Alan in the canteen where we were joined by Juliet Stevenson with her two children and were then introduced to many of the cast.

Samuel, my grandson, had read all the books and chatted away very knowledgeably to whomsoever we were with. It was a day neither of us will ever forget, thank you Alan.

The totally unexpected news of his death was shocking and filled me with a great sadness. It was especially poignant as only a few weeks previously, I had been in touch with Alan to ask him if he would be kind enough to write me a few lines about his lessons. I had asked him to say whether he had found them helpful as I was doing a chapter on feedback from pupils, performers whom I had taught over the years.

He must have been ill at the time but nevertheless, always kind and thoughtful, he came straight back to me with not only a few paragraphs but with two photos that I had taken of him in 1985. One was of him before the lesson and the other, showing a marked difference, afterwards.

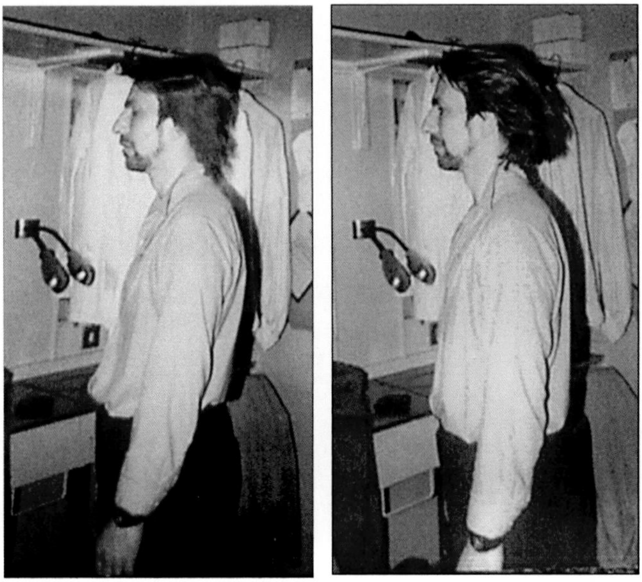

Alan Rickman, Before and After Alexander

In Alan's words…

> 'Stratford season, 1985.
>
> An exciting time.
>
> I was playing Jaques in *As You Like It*, Achilles in *Troilus and Cressida* and Valmont in *Les Liaisons Dangereuses.* Three dark and complex forces. I hadn't initially spotted that they were also all on one train or another to Self-Destruct. As the season wore on, living with them, so was I. Working with Sue Laurie and the Alexander Technique was a lifesaver.

> A space in the day where mind and body could have a quiet but solid conversation.
>
> Never hearing, "Just relax". "Release", is a far more rigorous word.'

These photos and words will be treasured and will be in my book for all to see, so thank you dear Alan for being there over the years. You will never be forgotten by me or by many, many other grateful people to whom you gave so much.

Lesley Sharp

I met up with Lesley first of all in *Uncle Vanya* whilst we were rehearsing in the NT Studio. Then working with Lesley individually came much later in *Harper Regan* in 2008. I have talked about that in an earlier chapter, but in Lesley's words...

> 'Alexander technique and Sue Laurie have saved me from acting with a permanently nodding head and from my self.
>
> *Uncle Vanya* in 1992 was the first project we worked on together. There was an investment in that production from all the actors and the creative team that was aptly mirrored by the work we did with Sue. The notion of physical and mental agility, flexibility and freedom. A Jungian touch for the body which released minute beads of response and understanding.
>
> Its not always that one works in such a way in the rehearsal room itself, but I have found since that time that there is something missing in my preparation if I do not practice Alexander during the rehearsal period and through the performance schedule and try to let go all the time of the enemies of creative freedom…ego, fear, presumption, any enemy of acceptance and being open to possibility.
>
> Alexander at its best and with the best teachers allows the body to mimic the mental creative process and in so doing enables strength and discipline to support and

hold the stress of live performance.

I have been enabled and held in my working life by Sue Laurie and her understanding and gift for Alexander.

And thank goodness that it is available for ALL of us actors at the National Theatre. It is fantastic to be in an environment, working but still training to get better, to be better at our job.

I would suggest that it is as vital to an actor's performing life as a daily physical warm-up is to a dancer.'

Simon Shepherd

Feedback from Simon Shepherd, who had never had Alexander before, was extraordinary. He listened very carefully to the initial explanation and after only the second lesson, he remarked that he felt that I was supporting his knees but then realised suddenly that I wasn't there. My hands had been on his knees, but now they were somewhere else. The next thing he noticed was that at the end of the lesson, he felt as if he was glowing inside and that the base of his spine felt hot.

I explained that I used to have a similar experience when I first started lessons. It was the circulation being now free to flow as his back released and spread onto the table, that he was feeling.

Geoffrey Streatfeild

Geoff trained at RADA and was was a strong believer in Alexander work, which he described as the bedrock of his training. He is such a versatile actor, comedy, tragedy, and, of course, a Shakespearean actor at the RSC. I remember talking about Geoff to the Head of Casting at the NT, Wendy Spon. She said, 'We must get him away from the RSC'. And she did.

In Geoffrey's words…

'Sessions with Sue have been nothing short of a life saver on every show I've done at the National. In the hectic build-up of rehearsals through to previews and press night, her ministrations have never failed to calm my nerves and soothe tensions. Alexander work is a vital component of theatre acting and always succeeds in readying the body and restoring energy, both physically and vocally. Sue's experience and understanding have also always been much appreciated for maintaining a sense of perspective and humour, even in moments of great pressure.

Working on big stages takes its toll and Sue's support for the work and the care for those of us lucky enough to be doing it, is immense. Both she and the Alexander lessons are one of the real unseen jewels of the National and a vital part of keeping the show on the road. Long may it and she continue.'

Michelle Terry

'Alexander has been hugely important to me from the first time I was introduced to it at drama school. Learning that a series of seemingly simple instructions can have such a profound effect on the mind and body continues to be a revelation to me, and a lesson that I repeatedly forget. It is hard to explain why something so simple can be so essential, but it is amazing that theatres like the National recognise the importance of Alexander. For everyone.'

Frances de la Tour

'I have known Sue Laurie for over 20 years, throughout my career as an actor, both at the RSC and the National Theatre. And as actors we sometimes do untold damage to our bodies in the quest for perfection on un-perfect stages. It is in that regard that Sue came to my rescue. I would have been quite at a loss without her support and her amazing gift to both heal and aid one's body into the state it should be, but which we all too often ignore.

Sue is the "maestro" of the Alexander Technique, which in itself seems simple, and without her long-lived knowledge and guiding hands our loss of self would be far greater than we ever feared. It is an extraordinary technique, invented by one who knew what actors in particular require. Not all Alexander teachers have the gift that Sue possesses. I know she is anxious to "pass it on". Long may she prevail.'

19. Conclusion but not an Ending

What we call the beginning is often the end
And to make an end is to make a beginning.
The end is where we start from…
…And every phrase and every sentence is an end and a beginning.
'Little Gidding', TS Eliot

I always remember Peter Gellhorn fondly. He was a pupil of mine for many years and had lessons once a fortnight right up until he died aged 92. Peter believed in going on learning – he said that the minute he stopped, it would be time to leave the planet.

He was a well known conductor and pianist, who had been a répétiteur at Covent Garden and also ran a choir, in which I was a member for a short time. With the baton in his hand, he was a fairly fearsome man and would stop everything in its tracks if anyone sang a wrong note. He would bang his baton on the music stand shouting, 'It's F sharp not flat'. Once when he was giving a concert, he discovered that the last F sharp in the bass was not working properly and we all had to wait until the piano tuner came and adjusted it.

Writing these memories has been sometimes painful as I have taken myself back to the age of forty when my life was in a state of turmoil. My mother had just died, my husband had left me and others close to me were suffering from heroin addiction and alcoholism. On top of that, I had just finished my Alexander training, was having the menopause and had to sell up the wonderful house that we had lived in for seventeen years where my children had spent a blissful childhood.

A very dear friend of mine said, 'Darling what you need is a really good NB' (meaning 'nervous breakdown') 'But knowing you, you won't.'

He was right, as without my invaluable training in Alexander, I think I would have collapsed with the stress of the situations that followed.

Thankfully I was working at the Barlows in Kensington nearly every day of the week and being provided with pupils by Dr Barlow. Without that support, I don't know what I would have done. I had very little money and needed to earn enough to keep everyone afloat with two of my children still at school.

This is not going to continue as a great sob story. I am just saying how things were. In fact, for at least twenty years of my teaching career, there were many ups and downs that had to be sorted and were very stressful.

I became passionate about my teaching at the RSC and at the National Theatre. It has been exciting being able to help so many people – seeing the changes that they have made in their lives.

The more I go on teaching, the more I realise what an extraordinary technique it was that FM Alexander discovered, simply by working on himself with no one to guide him. Teaching the technique to another human being is a communication between two beings that is almost impossible to explain.

Some might think that it would be an invasion of a body to move them around even in this gentle way. Or that it could promote excited feelings in a sexual or emotional sense, but the very fact that the teacher is getting the pupil to think in a way that conforms with what the teacher is doing prohibits this interpretation. The mind is diverted into more productive channels and other avenues of awareness are opened up.

I find that if I am working on myself whilst I am working with the pupil, my hands seem to have minds of their own and they tell me where to go, what to say.

If I am tired, which I very often am, it is usually because I am DOING too much. I am trying to achieve some change in the pupil that they aren't ready for. I am projecting, trying to control all the things that I abhor. IF I can manage to work on myself, take my time and never take my hands off too suddenly, we both benefit. The pupil has time to digest, to feel what is happening and will realise what they have just noticed. Then they too will have time, which is what we all need so desperately in these stressful times.

I will sometimes say to pupils: *'Life is Short, So Go Slowly'*

What we are really learning through using the technique is how to stop. Without that moment of inhibition, we are always anticipating, projecting the next moment, day, week or the rest of our lives.

We are fearful of what may happen IF we stop. Even for a moment. So influenced are we by what is going on around us, that we must make a conscious decision to think NO. And to wait, so there is time to make a decision about whether we change or bash on in the same old way.

FM's way of teaching, first himself and then others, the value of inhibition, of thinking NO, of consciously changing the thought pattern, which changed the reaction from habitual to conscious, was indeed a stroke of brilliance. During my first twenty years of teaching, I practised Buddism, but eventually left the lay organisation because I found it was too controlling. There was too much of being told what to do, which didn't suit me at all. I still use the chanting and the principles, as they are very in tune with Alexander. I have found that transcendental meditation gives me the peace of mind and quietness I need, essential if I am teaching others. It also prevents me from taking their troubles home with me, which would not be at all helpful to me, or to friends, or to other pupils with whom I come into contact.

The year I spent on counselling training has been invaluable in my work. I sometimes wish I could have afforded to go to the Hazelden centre and taken the whole course.

The twelve step programme of Al-Anon / AA became part of my life and fitted perfectly with Alexander teaching. It is essentially about letting go of the old ingrained habits of behaviour. I would often illustrate the importance of letting go of the controls with stories from meetings (not mentioning names, of course).

The process of letting go always comes back to inhibition and presentness. We learnt not to project or anticipate what the addict would do next, not to try to control and in this way giving not only ourselves freedom, but others as well.

One story I treasure, and have told to several pupils over the years, was when the chair at a meeting was held by a very jovial Irish woman. She told a horrendous story of her large family, eight or ten children, all of whom seemed to have been multi-addicted to various drugs. Suicide and death had come into this terrible story but Kathleen, as she was called, appeared to be extraordinarily calm and serene.

When someone afterwards asked Kathleen how this could be, how did she look so cheerful and happy in spite of all that had happened in her life?

In the AA fellowship, the Higher Power, or God as we understand Him, is referred to as HP. Kathleen said in reply,

> 'Well you see, it's like this – I have this pot in the middle of the kitchen table and whenever there is a problem, I write it on a bit of paper, fold it up, pop it in the pot and say, "There you are, I can't cope with that, HP, you take care of it."'

When you let go, wonderful things happen, by thinking NO you make room for things you would never imagine to take place, things for you to see and understand about yourself and others.

Pupils often question the thinking No, saying that it is negative, but of course it is positive. It is No to the old way, the habitual response, it is just a waiting before you go on to letting go, freedom.

I often say this to pupils when I am talking about the importance of inhibition, of being in the moment, present:

> 'The moment alone is decisive; fixes the life of man, from that instant your destiny changes, your life develops, history begins.'
>
> Adapted from Johann W von Goethe

At times pupils come in and complain about someone else, that if only he or she would change, everything would be better, easier. In these circumstances I will say that there is no way we can change others directly. Only by changing our reactions can we have an effect on others.

People are plumbed into how we react. If suddenly we don't follow the expected pattern, they have to react differently, to wonder what's going on and have to 'think', albeit unconsciously, before they go on behaving in the same old way. It's miraculous and can be great fun if we consciously practise it.

The psychological and emotional effects of the technique have always fascinated me and I found that my training in counselling married so well with teaching Alexander. Pupils that I am working with have sometimes had a complete change in attitude to their problems, which have very often been hidden for years.

As I discussed earlier, one case was that of Mary, whom I had met when I was a trainee teacher. Her mother had died when she was very young. Eventually she let go of her need to control and changed into a much more sensitive and caring human being – and a happier one too.

Another case, also when I was a trainee teacher, was that of Shirley and her two adopted children. When she finally 'let go' her physical ailments melted away.

It is so important to listen to the pupil, encourage them to tell me their troubles, trust me and trust what I am trying to teach them. I always say that, 'anything you say stays within these walls'. (These stories all have fictitious names)

There are many, many stories about similar instances over the forty or so years that I have been teaching. I've repeatedly mentioned these particular experiences as they so well illustrate the importance of not treating the technique as just a purely physical teaching. Neither is it philosophical or religious in any way. However, if the pupil really works on the technique, preferably with a teacher, it can open the doors to so much more to discover within themselves. It can give them a choice as to how to live their lives rather than just blindly lurching from one situation to the next.

Looking back over my life, and especially the time that I have been teaching, I am amazed that I have ended up teaching this extraordinarily, unique technique. When I think of all the careers I wanted to have, dress designer, sculptor, singer, writer, psychotherapist, I would never have dreamed that this is how my life would have panned out.

Working in the theatre for all these years has been a thrilling, stimulating time. I have been privileged to meet so many fascinating people, the famous and the not so famous. I've heard their stories, cared for them, loved them for their courage and tenacity, and seen how they never give up their dreams, however difficult life has been.

Nevertheless, I have often found that I am lonely. My pupils all pass through my life so quickly, often coming back and then leaving again, as is the way of the theatre. The community is a transient one, constantly changing, always on the move.

I stay still, I am there, but I am working alone and sometimes, as I am prone to depression, I can get very low.

FM Alexander is reputed to have said, 'I never stop working on myself, I dare not'.

I know I sometimes do and remembering that, I will pull myself up again. I have learnt to do that through using the technique, meditation and changing the negative messages that can often get out of hand. I can then find a different energy and carry on with the day, not projecting an image of what the future holds as I don't know what it holds. All things are always changing, but I can make those changes constructive ones, by staying in the present and so giving myself a choice as to how I live the day.

A phrase that you hear nowadays on everyone's lips is 'Mindfulness' and suggestions that one take up the practice.

I know I have at various points suggested to my pupils that they have NO moments and have indeed suggested how to work on themselves. Lying down and letting go of all the stressful thoughts and achieving a state of peace, quiet and awareness by using the Technique. Is this Mindfulness with the Alexander Technique?

With the addition of learning to inhibit and give the directions I feel, I know, it gives the ability to create these moments in daily life when something radical changes, whatever one comes up against, transforming our reactions and giving one the freedom of choice in how we live our lives.

I really love these words from George Bernard Shaw and remind myself to read them whenever I am feeling negative:

> 'This is the true joy of life, the being used for a purpose recognised by yourself as a mighty one.
>
> The being a force of nature instead of a feverish, selfish little clod of ailments and grievances, complaining that the world will not devote itself to making me happy.
>
> I am of the opinion that my life belongs to the whole community and as long as I live it is my privilege to do for it whatever I can. I want to be thoroughly used up when I die, for the harder I work the more I live.
>
> I rejoice in life for its own sake. Life is no brief candle to me. It is a sort of splendid torch, which I have to hold up for the moment. I want to make it burn as brightly as possible before I hand it on to future generations.'

My time at the NT, which started in 1989, is continuing. Eventually I shall have to hand over, to let go, which is going to be a very difficult process. I think that I wish, as Churchill wished, to die on the job. Hardly fair on the poor pupils or the NT though. I shall, instead, try to retire gracefully from my job as Alexander teacher, a job that has given me such pleasure and fulfilment in my life.

So, to end and to begin, I always remind myself of how fortunate I am to have touched all these lives, however fleetingly. How lucky I have been to have fulfilled my dream of working at the RSC and the National Theatre – the greatest theatre companies in the world – for all these years, passing on Alexander's invaluable discoveries to so many people.

20. Index